VIN SCULLY

D1172861

I Saw It On the Radio

By
RICH WOLFE

A Tribute Book

Published by Rich Wolfe and Lone Wolfe Press, a division of Richcraft. Distribution, marketing, publicity, interviews, and book signings handled by Wolfegang Marketing Systems Ltd.—But Not Very.

The author, Rich Wolfe, can be reached at 602-738-5889.

International Standard Book Number: 978-0-9800978-5-6

Printed in the United States of America

10 9 8 7 6 5 4 3 2 1

Photos provided by, and used with permission of Rich Wolfe, Getty Images, NewsCom, the Associated Press, UCLA Special Collections, Barney Epstein and the individuals whose stories appear in this book.

Cover design: Dick Fox
Cover photo: George Rose
Interior design: The Printed Page, Phoenix AZ.
Author's Agent: T. Roy Gaul

Page Two. In 1941, the news director at a small radio station in Kalamazoo, Michigan hired Harry Caray who had been employed at a station in Joliet, Illinois. The news director's name was Paul Harvey. Yes, that PAUL HARVEY! "And now, you have the rest of the story...... ➡

Dedication

To:

Denis Ducey, Harvey Pearlstein and Nick Rizza—
my ecumenical Dodger friends

Acknowledgments

Compiling the material for *Vin Scully—I Saw It On the Radio* was a wonderful experience. I am grateful for the hundreds of people who cooperated so willingly to make this book special.

The author is personally responsible for all errors, misstatements, inaccuracies, omissions, commissions, fallacies...if it's wrong and it's in this book, it's my fault.

Sincere thanks to Bob Ahrens, Lou Wasson and Syd Steinhardt from Fordham University. They were great.

A special tip of the hat to Ellen Brewer from Edmond, Oklahoma and Lisa Liddy at The Printed Page in Phoenix.

Thanks must also go to Jim Hill, Curt Smith, Gary Owens, Dick Enberg, Roger Kahn, Ralph Branca, Carl Erskine, Steve Hartman and John Wooden.

We wish to thank NPR and WFUV Radio at Fordham University. Also Jerry Derloshon at Pepperdine University and the whole crew at UCLA Special Collections—Simon Elliott, Angela Riggio, Genie Guerard and Mauricio Hermosillo.

The book would not be possible without tremendous efforts by Larry Bortstein and Lloyd Flodin.

A special thanks to Clay Luraschi of the Topps Company, Inc. for use of their wonderful cards...and the biggest bow of all to Linda Murray, a neat lady, and Tommy Hawkins, a fine Notre Dame man!

PREFACE

You are about to be swept into the brilliant minds of Vin Scully fans, awe-struck by their far-sighted scheming, stricken dumb by their wonderful stories as they lay bare their sordid love affair with the greatest announcer in baseball. Until now, there has never been a book like this, mainly because there's never been any book done on Vin Scully in his almost-sixty years of broadcasting for the Dodgers. This book has become a vehicle for Scully fans to share their funniest stories, happiest times and craziest moments. Every story is a reflection of their personal Vin Scully memory bank.

It's amazing the pull that baseball announcers have on their fans, probably because fans spend more time listening to the announcer of their favorite team than they do listening to their spouse every summer.

For many of us, baseball and Vin Scully and Jack Buck and Harry Caray and their kind defined our youth. Baseball is a game of memories, baseball is a game of sounds...the crack of the bat, the thud of a ball hitting a mitt, the roar of the crowd, the vendors hawking, the infielders chattering. But the sound the Dodger fans came to cherish the most was the melodic voice of Vin Scully.

No matter where we're raised, each baseball fan has their initial memories of the first announcer they ever heard. For me, those announcers were Harry Caray and Jack Buck. We go back a long time. We met over a half-century ago, when Vin Scully was just starting with the Brooklyn Dodgers...and I was finishing my first decade on this planet. An intermediary named Philco introduced Harry Caray and Jack Buck to me one night in a granary on a farm in Iowa as I was practicing

> ...each baseball fan has their initial memories of the first announcer they ever heard.

basketball. Once the chores were done, it was the same ritual every night: start way on the left side of the radio dial. There was Earl Gillespie on WTMJ in Milwaukee covering the Braves action for the team that had moved from Boston the year before....A little further south on the dial was WIND, which carried the Cub games until **WGN*** took over the next year. Almost nightly, when the Cubs were on the road you could listen to Jack Quinlan, the Cubs talented, new young play-by-play man....A little bit to the right was Detroit's WJR where Van Patrick, and later Ernie Harwell, sang the praises of Goebel's Beer and Harwell would tell stories about being baptized in the Jordan River or being Margaret Mitchell's paperboy in his Georgia youth....Slight twist of the dial towards the right was WLW-700 AM—The Big One in Cincinnati where the Reds' Waite Hoyt talked about the taste of Hudepohl Beer and the exploits of Klu.... Skip past the middle of the dial where the White Sox announcers were excruciatingly boring.... A quarter-twist more and you could listen to the Davenport Tigers in the Class B Three-I League. They were not as exciting as they had been in other years because their best player, Harvey Kuenn, and their announcer Milo Hamilton, had gone to the big leagues the previous year.... Just a smidgen further on the dial, towards town and there it was.... Magic flowing through the air from St. Louis, Missouri. From the flagship station, KXOK (KMOX did not become the flagship station until the following year) excitement and enthusiasm from Harry Caray and this new guy Jack Buck.... Yup, that was the game to listen to tonight. It was going to be fun. It always was.

In those days when Elvis was the King, Little Richard was the Queen, and Springsteen wasn't even in middle management,

> Once the chores were done, it was the same ritual every night: start way on the left side of the radio dial.

---

*WGN is an acronym for "World's Greatest Newspaper." For years the Chicago Tribune Company owned WGN and later, the Chicago Cubs.

---

there were slide rules, but no Major-League team west of St. Louis, a Rapid Robert Feller but no batting helmets, a bazillion Wayne Terwilliger and Tommy Glaviano baseball cards but no Frank Lejas or **MICKEY MANTLES***, the Cubs were in the forty-sixth season of their first five-year plan, there were bomb shelters but no A-Rods, and there was the Cardinal announcing team and no one else. They brought their friends with them. They had neat names like Jabbo and Rip and Slats and Country, Vinegar Bend and the Kitten, but it was clear their best friend was Stan the Man.

It was a great era in America. The people of my generation grew up during the very best time to be a sports fan: baseball cards were collected not for investments, but for the pure joy. You raced for the baseball diamond every free moment to play until you were called home for supper—without an adult being anywhere in sight. A trip to a Major-League baseball park, if it happened,

> Doubleheaders were plentiful. There were only eight teams in each baseball major league.

was magical. Doubleheaders were plentiful. There were only eight teams in each baseball major league. A trade was a major deal. There were no free agents—there were no agents. There was no **ASTROTURF***. There was no designated hitter. It was speed and control, not velocity and location. There were no World Series night games. You waited impatiently each fall for the *Converse Basketball Yearbook* and every spring for the *Louisville Slugger Yearbook*. It was a great time to grow up in the Midwest and the Cardinals and Jack Buck and Harry Caray were a vital part of millions of childhoods.

> *Jason and Jeremy Giambi's dad loved **MICKEY MANTLE**. His sons' uniform numbers were either "7" or added up to "7." The Giambis grew up in West Covina where their father was a banker.

> *An announcer once asked Tug McGraw about the difference between **ASTROTURF** and grass. Tug replied, "I don't know. I have never smoked Astroturf."

To all Dodger fans, Vin Scully has magic. And while Vin may be getting up there in years, he still has a lot on his fastball, much more than Harry had near the end of his magnificent career.

The biggest problem, by far, in doing a Vin Scully book is everyone—there were no exceptions—went off on long tangents about Vin Scully's kindness, his generosity, his quick wit, his helpful nature and on and on, with great testimonials about the type of person Vin Scully is.

Sometimes repetition is good. For instance, in a book I did on Mike **DITKA***, seven people described the run Ditka made in Pittsburgh the weekend of JFK's assassination as the greatest run they had ever seen. Yet, only one of those descriptions made the book. The editor didn't understand that when the reader was through with the book, few would remember the importance or singularity of that catch and run; whereas if all seven had remained intact, everyone would have realized that one play summarized Ditka's persona and career.

So, too, the repetition with Scully...except many times greater. It was overwhelming. More than two hundred pages were deleted from this book because there were constant, similar and duplicate testimonials. Even so, many remain.

Since the age of 10, I've been a serious collector of sports books. During that time—for the sake of argument, let's call it 30 years—my favorite book style is the eavesdropping type where the subject talks in his own words. In his own words, without the "then he said" or "the air was so thick you could cut it with a butter knife" waste of verbiage that makes it so hard to get to the meat of the matter....Books such as Lawrence Ritter's *Glory of Their Times* and Donald Honig's *Baseball When the Grass Was Real,* or any of my friend Peter Golenbock's books like *The Bronx Zoo.*

*When Joe Girardi played for the Cubs, he caught a ceremonial first pitch from Mike **DITKA**. Girardi had a football curled behind his back. After catching Ditka's pitch, Girardi fired the football at Ditka which Iron Mike caught easily.

Thus, I adopted that style when I started compiling oral histories of the Mike Ditkas and Harry Carays of the world. I'm a sports fan first and foremost—I don't even pretend to be an author. This book is designed solely for other sports fans. I really don't care what the publisher, editors or critics think. I'm only interested in Dodger fans having an enjoyable read and getting their money's worth. Sometimes a person being interviewed will drift off the subject but if the feeling is that Dodger fans would enjoy their digression, it stays in the book. If you feel there is too much extraneous Dodger material, just jot your thoughts down on the back of a $20 bill and send it directly to me. Constructive criticism can be good for one's soul, as well as for the pizza man.

> ...how some people will view the same happening in completely different terms.

In an effort to get more material into the book, the editor decided to merge some of the paragraphs and omit some of the commas which will allow for the reader to receive an additional 20,000 words, the equivalent of 50 pages. More bang for the buck...more fodder for English teachers...fewer dead trees.

I'm the least likely person in the country to write a book. I can't type. I've never turned on a computer, and I've never seen the Internet. I refuse to sit in press boxes and corporate suites. I have a belief that the cheaper the seat, the better the fan. No matter where you sit, you have to sit back and admire Vin Scully as you reflect on his incredible career. The Jesuits educated him well. He's the definition of a true professional, and we could all learn from his humility.

Vin Scully may be nearing the end of an illustrious career...but, one thing is sure: Vin Scully memories—like Dodger heroes—never grow old!

Rich Wolfe
Celebration, Florida

Chat Rooms

Prologue

LOU WASSON

Lou Wasson, 23, is a newsman and sportscaster at KGET in Bakersfield. The Southern California native was a sophomore in 2005 at Fordham University in the Bronx, N. Y., when he put together a one-hour tribute to one of Fordham's most illustrious graduates, Vin Scully.

About the middle of my sophomore year in college, 2005, I had been discussing with my boss at WFUV, Bob Ahrens, the idea of working on some sort of a tribute to Vin Scully. Vin was my hero growing up.

I always turned on the television and there is that nice "old" man who talked to me about the baseball game—about the Dodgers. I loved listening to Vin Scully. When you're growing up in Southern California, and you're growing up as a Dodger fan, he is the Dodgers. I know there are a lot of people who say, "There's Sandy Koufax, or **DRYSDALE***, or Tommy Lasorda...." I will tell you he is the Dodgers. Without him, I may not even be a fan today. I could very easily be an Angels fan because of how that organization has absolutely dragged me all over the place, but Vin keeps the fan going.

He keeps you watching the game. Vin Scully was one of the many reasons why I wanted to get into broadcasting. You listen to him do the game and, first of all, he makes it look so easy, but then again, after I got into Fordham and started working on my play-

---

*The late Buzzy Bavasi, when G.M. of the Dodgers, once offered his pitchers $25 if they would run a mile. Don **DRYSDALE** said he would do it right after Jesse Owens won twenty games. . . . Drysdale once said that his most important pitch was his second knockdown pitch. "That way the batter knew the first one wasn't an accident."

by-play skills, I realized it's a lot harder than it looks. He influenced me to want to get into broadcasting. When I got to Fordham, it was funny because I didn't know Vinnie had gone to Fordham. I did not know that. You'd think being a big Dodger fan and a big Scully fan, I would have known that, but I didn't. Further, I didn't know that Vin actually worked at WFUV, the Fordham student station, and that he had helped pretty much start the station. That's where he got his start. For me, being one of the few people at Fordham, from Los Angeles, it felt like fate in some ways that I would be there.

> I didn't know Vinnie had gone to Fordham...I didn't know that Vin actually worked at WFUV...

I was a fan of the Dodgers. I knew they had come from Brooklyn, but I didn't realize the extent to which Vin had been part of the team. I didn't know he had started off in Brooklyn, being mentored by Red Barber. Those things didn't come to fruition in my mind until I got to college and started appreciating his being the influence he really has over me.

Because I was from L.A., WFUV felt I should work on the Vin Scully project on my own. That was easy on them to not have to spend the money to send me out to L.A. It took me roughly four months to put the program together in the summer of 2005. I needed to line up so many interviews. I literally interviewed 40 different people—didn't use all the interviews. They were from all walks of life...all different aspects of Vin's life. For example, there were some of Vin's **FORDHAM*** baseball teammates. The Larry Miggins story was a great one. When he told me the story over the phone, it was unbelievable to hear it straight from his mouth. And when Vin spoke to the Fordham graduates, he cited that story about Larry Miggins and himself at Fordham Prep, talking about what they wanted to be when they grew up.

> *The St. Louis Rams, once the Los Angeles Rams, and prior to that the Cleveland Rams got the nickname from the FORDHAM Rams.... The L.A. Rams were the first pro team to have a logo on their helmet.

Miggins was a childhood friend whose first Major-League home run was broadcast by Vin Scully. That story brought tears to his eyes when he thought of it. It meant so much to him knowing that two young kids from Fordham, who knew nothing—didn't know anything at the time—wanted to follow their dreams and live their dreams and made it happen. If you were to ask Vin to rank his one or two or three most important calls of his life.... It didn't have anything to do with baseball. It had to do with life. I think that is why Vin is such a great broadcaster because he takes you to that next level. When you hear Vin talk, he's not just telling you a story about a baseball game, he's walking you through the next three hours of your day. Baseball just happens to be why he's on television or on the radio.

We get the games on radio here in Bakersfield, which is terrific because I prefer listening to them on the radio. I started at KGET in Bakersfield in February, 2008. I was lucky to get to come here because it is so close to my home, and yet it's still a big enough market to get really good news work.

Bob Ahrens—my boss at WFUV—and I had some contacts with the Dodgers. We put in formal requests to the organization that we wanted to talk to Vin. We also had a home phone number for Vin. We called him, and he told us he would be glad to do it, but we had to clear it with the Dodgers first. They cleared it. After that it was a matter of making it work timewise. The thing that made it really special is that Vin doesn't do many interviews, especially on radio or on television. He never has done that. People are always wanting to talk to him. I'm not saying he's tired of it, but he doesn't do many. He said one of the reasons why he accepted the interview with WFUV was of the influence Fordham and WFUV had on him. He said that if it hadn't been for WFUV, he wouldn't be where he is today. That got him his start. He felt like he owed Fordham and WFUV.

When I got to Dodger Stadium to interview him, I was more nervous than I'd ever been for any other interview in my life. Keep in mind, I had been a beat reporter for the New York Mets and had

> I was more nervous than I'd ever been for any other interview in my life.

gone into the clubhouses of the Mets and the Yankees in the past. WFUV had credentials to cover those games. It was a great experience for a kid in college. If the game was on Saturday, we would do live reports from the stadium reporting what was going on in the game. If we weren't going live at the time, I'd get post-game sound bites and bring them back to the station for the drive-time sportscast.

Since Vin never travels back east, I'd not had a chance to meet him out here. I had the opportunity to see Alex Rodriguez and **DEREK JETER*** and Joe Torre and other guys so I'd never really thought about it. "Aw, these are just baseball players." I would be a little nervous being in their clubhouse.

But on Friday night, June 23, 2005, when I got to Dodger Stadium to talk to Vin, I found I was more nervous than I'd ever been for any other moment in my life up to that point, even though I had been in the presence of so many great athletes. All of a sudden, it just shocked me for a moment. It stunned me that, "Wow, I am terribly nervous for this interview. I don't want to screw this up." Then, of course, there's also the possibility that Vin might not be a nice person. All of that started to sink in...when you're a kid and have never met your hero...you're hoping for so much. You're hoping he is nice. You're hoping that he's everything he's supposed to be. You're also hoping that you do a good job in representing your station and in impressing him.

I was told that I should get there three hours before game time, "Don't worry, if you get there three hours before game time, you're not going to be the only one in the press box...Vin will be there, too."

I walked into the broadcast booth where Vin was preparing for that night's game against the Angels. He turned around and had

*DEREK JETER was named after Derek Sanderson, former National Hockey League star with the Boston Bruins. Jeter's middle name is Sanderson.

these huge "Coke bottle" glasses on, which you don't see on the air. Then there was his voice—"Hello, Lou. Come on down. It's nice to meet you." He shook my hand. Within 10 seconds flat, all nervousness had washed away. He made me feel so at ease.

When I sat down with Vin to do the interview, it was terrific. I said, "How long do you want to do this?" Vin said, "About 10 minutes would be fine." I said, "Great." I was trying to be accommodating to him. We do this for about 10 minutes, almost on the dot. We chatted for a few moments afterward about the team and about me. He wanted to know who I was. We were talking and chatting it up. At the time, I was thinking, *"I'm B.S.-ing with Vin Scully!"* Things couldn't get any better. Shooting the breeze with Vin Scully. Unbeknownst to me, I unfortunately found a way to erase the interview that I had done with him because I removed the battery pack. I had lost the interview. It erased from the hard drive. I had not plugged it into an outlet. When I unplugged the battery pack, everything got erased. I was told the day I started working at WFUV, "Never unplug that unless you have saved everything." I had not done that. But I was not thinking properly. I was there with Vin Scully.

> My face goes white. I realize I've lost the interview.

About ten minutes later, when I'm sitting down to do another interview with Rick Monday, I realized what I had done. I looked down at my player and I could see that no time has elapsed because it says "000" which *can't be right* 'cause I just did ten minutes.

My face goes white. I realize I've lost the interview. Rick Monday looks over at me and says, "Lou, are you okay?" I said, "Oh yeah, I think I'm all right." He said, "You don't look so well. Are you sure you're okay?" "Don't worry about it. I think I just might have messed something up—no big deal." He said, "Are you sure?" I said, "Yeah, it's fine." I did the interview with Rick. Meanwhile, my heart is in my throat. I'm ready to kill myself. I had screwed up the biggest interview of my life. I do the interview with Rick, and he's terrific. We're done. He walks off to do his thing. He's having dinner in the dining room with Vin and **CHARLEY STEINER***. I'm out in the press box now, and I'm looking out over the stadium and talking to another WFUV alum who I ran into at the stadium who was working for ESPN. He and I were shooting the breeze and having a good time. I told him I had just screwed up my interview with Vin and I have to figure out a way to talk to him again. I've got to get this interview. This is the crux of my story. He said, "Man, I don't know what to tell you. He's always so busy."

> ...a big burly hand slapped me on the shoulder...It's Rick Monday.

The next day's game, Saturday, was going to be on national TV on FOX, which meant Vin wasn't going to come down to do the game. The next day, Sunday, was an ESPN game so he wasn't going to be there either. This was the only chance I had...and I had messed it up.

A few moments later, a big burly hand slapped me on the shoulder and I turn around. It's Rick Monday. He said, "Lou, I just want you to know I talked to Vin at dinner. I told him what happened. Don't worry about it. He'll talk to you after dinner." I said, "Are you sure? Is this okay?" He said, "Absolutely. It happens all the time. It happens to the best of us. We all make mistakes. Don't worry about it. He'll see you after dinner." I could have hugged him in front of the entire press corps. It meant so much to me that Rick went out of his way to do that for me.

I did the second interview with Vin. We sat down in Tommy Hawkins' booth about half-an-hour before game-time. This is when Vin is supposed to be in his crucial prep mode. Half-an-hour before the game, we go into a press box and we do the interview again. I come up with all new questions because I don't want him to repeat answers or search for the ones he had used before. We did the interview. He was once again terrific. We

*__CHARLEY STEINER__ got his big break with ESPN on the recommendation of his pharmacist.

chatted for another moment. I remembered to save it this time. He walked off to his booth and did the game.

I got my interview...and it was all because of Rick Monday. The show aired in July, 2005. I was back in New York, hosting our weekly sports show *One on One*, New York's longest-running sports call-in show.

I was broadcasting from **SHEA STADIUM*** that day for a Mets-Dodgers game. Vin was not there, but Rick and Charley were so I said hello to them and told them that this was the day the show was airing. They were happy about that. We aired it in the final hour of the show. It's a three-hour show. We spent the first two hours talking to Gary Cohen, the voice of the Mets, about how the Mets were doing. We also talked to him about Vinnie a little bit.

We got near the end of the first two hours and turned it over to the 56-minute broadcast, "Vin Scully, Voice of Heaven." I was actually afraid to listen to it. I listened to bits and pieces of it. I was so nervous. You work on something for so long, and I had put blood, sweat and tears into this project—everything from my writing, my transitional writing from sound-bite to sound-bite to the music to everything. I was so nervous that people might not like it because it wasn't meant to be an hour long initially.

It was meant to be 20 minutes. There were so many stories, so many things happening that I realized it couldn't be 20 minutes—it just couldn't. Bob realized that as well. We had to make it an hour because it was literally becoming a life-time story from his days at Fordham—to where he is today. At the time, he was 56-years strong with the Dodgers. It aired that one time. If you go to WFUV.org and go to the one-on-one sports page, scroll down on the right-hand side, there should be a link to the piece.

I was not that surprised that no one had approached Vin about doing an interview. No one else had come from Southern

*During a 1979 Patriots game against the New York Jets at SHEA STADIUM, a remote control model airplane crashed into the stands at halftime, hit a Patriots fan, and killed him.

California to Fordham to work at WFUV Sports. That was the issue. When Bob Ahrens found out I was from Los Angeles, that's when he said, "Okay. I've got someone here who understands what I'm talking about with Vin Scully—who knows how good this guy is. I don't have to school this kid because he already knows. I don't have to beat it into his head that Vin Scully is the greatest broadcaster of all time. He already knows it." So I was not that surprised when Bob told me that no one had ever done a story on Vin Scully at Fordham. It was a little surprising and, even in some ways, disturbing to see how some people didn't quite understand how good he is. They look at John Sterling, "Oh, Yankees Win! Yankees Win!" thinking that's baseball poetry. You put Vin's voice next to his and you realize there's no comparison. Vin has never said, "Dodgers Win! Dodgers Win!" He doesn't need to. He lets the story play out for itself.

A terrific Vin call, which is underrated, occurred about two years ago. The Dodgers hit four home runs in a row against the San Diego Padres in the bottom of the ninth to tie the game and go to extra innings. Nomar hits one. Then there's a terrific call where he says, "And the Dodgers win. There's **NOMAR*** rounding the bases and Dodger Stadium is in euphoria." I'm in New York watching the game on TV on the MLB package. I'm jumping up and down in my Bronx apartment living room. I'm screaming and going absolutely bananas. It all topped off at the very end when Vin comes and says, "Oh, and I forgot to tell you, 'the Dodgers are in first place.'" Are you kidding? Who does that? Who thinks of that?

When I told that to my friends...when I showed them that, they were like, "Man, that's a great call." It was a great call. It's the icing on the cake. The game had gone into extra innings in L.A. so it was probably about 1:45 in the morning in New York when the game ended. My friends and I were watching it. We were going to go to bed but, of course being college students, we don't go to

*NOMAR's full name is Anthony Nomar Garciaparra. Nomar is his father's name spelled backwards.

bed at ten o'clock at night. We were about ready to call it "lights out" when the Dodgers hit the four home runs. We decided to stay up and watch then. The game ended an inning later in the bottom of the 10th. It was such a great thing to watch. I showed it to my roommate who also works at WFUV. He said, "Now I see why you guys love him so much."

Being in that press box for the first time was so intimidating on so many levels. I had sat in seemingly every single seat in Dodger Stadium up until that point in my life, except the press box. That really changes your perspective. It gives you a different view of the stadium. It's the most beautiful view I've ever had. When I was there, I first said to myself, "Man, I could live with being in the press box forever." Being a part of this business—whether it be sports or news—I wanted to be a part of this business. Right then and there I said to myself, "This is why I'm here. Who gets this kind of access—this unfettered access to not just people like Vin Scully, but to all the behind-the-scenes action that the world doesn't know is going on?" I didn't go into his broadcast booth while he was doing the game. I didn't want to get in the way of anything.

> Being in that press box for the first time was so intimidating...

Vin gave me 10 minutes again. I didn't deserve another 10 minutes but he gave it to me because he knew that I was a young kid, 19 years old, and I had obviously made a dumb mistake, and it was the first of many mistakes I've made since then.

If we had not been able to do the interview again, I never would have had as good of a documentary. I could have probably still done it, but without him answering the questions I needed to have answered, it would not have made the documentary as good as it was. The only line I used of Vin, when he talks about what people will remember most about him, not being a broadcaster, but being a good father and grandfather and husband—that line came because he gave me my extra 10 minutes. If I hadn't had the extra 10 minutes, I could not have opened up with that line. I also closed with him telling me that line. I felt that was the most poignant line of the entire interview—him telling me, "Listen, it's not about me being a baseball broadcaster. It's about me being a good person. I'm hoping that people see me as a good human being." I said, "Man, that's the line. That's it right there." I'm a lucky kid. I tell you. I was the luckiest 19-year-old kid in America that day.

> I was the luckiest 19-year-old kid in America that day.

I didn't ask Vin any questions about what I needed to do to be a successful broadcaster. What I was able to figure out from him and from his life was that good things are going to happen to good people—but sometimes even bad things will happen to good people. Vin had some good things happen to him as far as the fact that when he was a year out of college after working at WTOP in Washington, he was all of a sudden being mentored by Red Barber at Ebbets Field in Brooklyn. He was given his dream job at a very young age. I still don't have my dream job. I'm young—23 years old, but I don't have my dream job yet. It may not come for another 20 years. It may never come. For Vin, working at WTOP was the jumping-off point for him.

I had read in a book by Curt Smith that Vin was a terrific lip-reader. I didn't realize that—that Vin could figure out what word may or may not be said. Sometimes Vin could look down onto the field or the television monitor showing close-ups of guys talking and read their lips pretty well. I asked him about that. I said, "Tell me about your lip-reading ability. I've heard a little bit about this." He started to chuckle a little bit. I said, "Why are you laughing?" He goes, "Well, you have to remember Tommy Lasorda managed the Dodgers for all those years, and it's fun lip-reading Tommy from time to time." We both laughed about that.

It was a little bit tougher to interview Tommy Lasorda. I almost felt bad for him. It must have felt like, from his perspective, that I was attacking him. His right-hand man didn't prepare him for me. We had the interview set up but a lot of things went wrong at the last minute. We did find Tommy eventually and I did get to do the interview with him, but we ended up having to do it in the middle of the dining room and in front of a lot of people. It was noisy. It wasn't a good interview. I didn't use a lot of lines from Tommy.

One person I interviewed, who I never used, was Mike Scioscia. I wanted to. He was the manager of the Angels and now he's won a World Series title. He was with the Dodgers for so many years. There was Kirk Gibson's home run. He must have a Vin Scully anecdote. I'm interviewing him over the phone, and—nothing. I was like, "Are you sure? You can't think of anything?" He said, "It's not that I don't want to...I was on the field."

People like Kirk Gibson who was part of that memorable call—he doesn't know anything about it. He got the great call, "the impossible has happened," but he was rounding the bases when Vin said that. It's played over and over, and he's aware of it, but at the time he was there celebrating the moment...and Vin was calling the moment. And calling it so perfectly. I wasn't old enough to appreciate it when it happened.

I've watched that happen over and over again, and when I talked with Bob Costas about it, he was the one who said, "Listen, Jack Buck's call may go down in history as the better call, with the "I don't believe what I just saw." And rightfully so. It was a great call. Vin's overall presentation of the bottom of the ninth inning was special. It was better because he can take it and bring it to a new level.

> He makes you think about other things... about the human emotions...

What I mean by that—and I always feel bad for this—it's not just about baseball. It really isn't. He makes you think about other things... about the human emotions...what's going on in Kirk Gibson's mind right now...how nervous is he...how nervous is Tommy Lasorda watching...how nervous is Tony LaRussa, over in the opposing dugout there thinking, "Man, all I need is one more strike, and I'm up one game to none." All these things are flying around, and Vin is able to grab them and bring them down to earth and show it to you...paint it for you. If you're watching it on TV—he can make you think of things that aren't necessarily right in front of you to watch. If you're listening on radio, not only can you see it in your head, but you can feel that emotion as well. Vin can do that. I don't just say that as a Dodger fan. When I get other people who are not Dodger fans, when I get Yankee fans, when I get Padre fans, when I get Red Sox fans to listen to Vin, they take a step back and go, "Man, he is good—really good."

Vin has such objectivity...not taking sides during a game...saying, "if the Dodgers are playing well, they're playing well. They're 10 out of their last 11 games so I say they're playing pretty well right now." If they've lost eight in a row, he'll say, "Yeah, they've lost eight in a row, and they're playing bad."

Anyway, thanks to WFUV, the following is an excerpt from our Vin Scully Fordham program:

Voice of Heaven

Fifty-six years...56 million memories in the making. Vin Scully is, and always will be, the "voice of heaven." From Brooklyn to Los Angeles, father-to-son, grandparent-to-grandchild, Vin Scully has established himself as one of the most important figures in baseball history. He's been considered the Babe Ruth of broadcasting—not too shabby. Remember...there was only one **BABE RUTH***.

But if you were to ask Vin what he wants his legacy to be, "I'd hope they would think of me as a good human being, more than anything else. If anybody wanted to dig into my life, I'd like them to appreciate that I was a good husband and a good father and

> *****BABE RUTH** was the first player ever to hit 30 home runs in one season, the first to hit 40 in one season and the first to hit 50 in one season . . . and he accomplished those feats in the same season.

grandfather—the last thing of all would be the fact that I was a pretty good broadcaster." That's Vin Scully...husband, father, grandfather, graduate of Fordham University and voice of the Dodgers for 56 years.

He's done it all and called it all. From Hank Aaron's 715th home run to Kirk Gibson's fairytale ending. But to understand Vin Scully, we have to go back in time to the Bronx, New York, where all the magic began.

> He's been considered the Babe Ruth of broadcasting...

At Fordham, Vin played for the Rams baseball team. One of Vin's teammates, Nick Baldino, remembers Vin the ballplayer, "He was our centerfielder. He was a very good fielder. Our trainer used to call him 'the phantom.' He was very good on fly balls. Vin was a better fielder than a hitter. That's what led him to the broadcast booth. We used to tell him his form was okay...but you still have to hit the ball."

But don't sell him short. Even Vin had his one shining moment as a baseball star. "I hit a home run here at Jack Coffey Field against CCNY." So how many home runs did that give Vin for his career? "The only one I ever hit." Vin couldn't hit a baseball so he decided to shelve his dreams of being the next Stan Musial and chose a different vocation. Scully recalled the time in his life when he knew exactly what he wanted to be.

"You know, it is written that somewhere in every childhood a door will open, and there's a quick glimpse of the future. When my door opened, I saw a large radio on four legs in the living room of my parents home. When I was eight-years old, which was shortly after the discovery of fire, I used to crawl underneath the radio—the loudspeaker was directly over my head—and I would listen to college football games. The roar of the crowd would come out of that speaker, and it would wash over me like water out of a showerhead, and I'd get goose bumps, and I would dream that I would be there someday and I would hope that I might become the broadcaster."

Baseball teammate Johnny Bach recalls Vin's different lifestyle.

"Vin, at that time, was studying broadcasting. One of the earliest people in Fordham's program. He was carrying around a recorder that weighed about 30 pounds, doing his work, both at school and playing around, I'm sure, imitating the great announcers of the day, Red Barber and Mel Allen."

Nick Baldino remembers Vinnie the broadcaster.

> ...Vin had his one shining moment as a baseball star.

"We couldn't understand his love for the broadcasting. I guess he must have known what he was going to become.

When Vin was playing in games, or even broadcasting them, most of his time was spent at WFUV.

It was a great training ground. We also had a lot of fun. I remember we did a Saturday night disk jockey show. We decided to be funny—we thought it was funny anyway—we had the **QUEEN MARY*** docking on Fordham Road. It shocked everybody."

Did this red-haired kid really have a chance to become as good as Red Barber or Mel Allen? The inevitable answer to that question was not far down the road. Vincent Edward Scully graduated from Fordham University in 1949 with a degree in communications, one of the first to ever hold such a degree. Vin wasted no time applying for jobs at some of the larger radio stations. In the words of Scully, "What did I have to lose but the three cents for the stamp?"

He applied for a position at WTOP Radio in Washington, D. C. What do you know—he got the job.

Mack McGary worked with Vin at WFUV. He'll never forget how Vin helped him jump-start his career. "I heard Vin Scully directly over the air on WTOP out of Washington. I was surprised and

---

*While playing golf in 1567, **MARY, QUEEN** of Scots, was informed that her husband, Lord Darnley, had been murdered. She finished the round.

---

said, 'My gosh, he only graduated a little while ago, and he's already got a big-time, 50,000-watt station job, and here I am up in Pittsfield on a 250-watter.'" I called Vin up and said, "How did you work that so fast?" Vin said he had gotten six letters of introduction from one of our professors at Fordham. A man named Bill Coleman advised me to do the same. I did exactly the same. I got the six letters. Called the same six people that Vin called, only about a year later, and I hit. I became the summer-relief announcer for WTOP in Washington in 1950. I owe Vin Scully an awful lot.

It didn't take long for Vin to get the coveted break that all young broadcasters dream of. Only a year after joining WTOP, Scully would embark on a journey that would last a lifetime.

> ... "What did I have to lose but the three cents for the stamp?"

So how did Vin Scully land in Brooklyn? In 1990, an NPR audience heard exactly how from Red Barber.

"If a lot of things hadn't happened, Scully might not have ever gotten to a microphone. At the end of the season in 1949, we were doing football. I was then Director of Sports at CBS, and we had a show called *The Football Roundup*. It was a tremendous show. We really covered football then like it had never been covered before. We had a game late in the season coming up in Boston. We couldn't find an announcer up there to do it. I remembered that Vin Scully had come to CBS looking for work. He had graduated from Fordham and he had worked as a summer replacement down in our CBS station in Washington. He came into the studio in New York, and he talked to me. We didn't carry a sports man in New York then. I had nothing for him so I didn't even take his name. I didn't know his name or his phone number. This thing at Boston came along, and we needed somebody to do a little spot up there. I remembered this young redheaded man. I went to the news director, who had brought Scully into my office. I asked him, "Who was that young man you brought around?" He said he didn't take his name down. Then I remembered he had said he had gone to Fordham. Jack Coffey, the Director of Athletics at Fordham, had a fabulous memory. He even remembered birthdays. I told my associate at CBS, "Call Coffey at Fordham and find out who the redhead was who graduated from there." He came back with "Scully" and his phone number. We called him. He came in.

> ... "Call Coffey at Fordham and find out who the redhead was who graduated from there."

We sent him to Boston, and he did an excellent job. They put him on the roof in the wind and the rain. He had to throw his papers away...but he didn't complain over the air, which impressed me very favorably. I detested then, and I detest even more now, announcers who complain about their lack of physical comfort or the difficulties of their physical situation. They're there to broadcast to the people. People care about the event. They don't care whether the announcer is comfortable or not.

A month or so later, I'm sitting out at Stanford during a football game, the last football game of the season that fall. I get word at half-time that Ernie Harwell had elected to go over to the **POLO GROUNDS*** and broadcast with Russ Hodges. Now we've got to have a man in Brooklyn, and we don't need a real full-time announcer. We just needed to have somebody to come on and do an inning here and there. I'd always had an idea in the back of mind that it would be interesting to take a young man and train him right on the air. I thought it would add to the broadcast. You'd say to the audience, "Here's this neophyte. Connie Desmond and I are going to take care of him." So I got back and talked to Mr. Rickey about that principle and he told me that would be fine if I found the right young man. I sent for Scully and asked him if he would be interested. Oh, my goodness. His eyes got big as teacups. I told him to go over and talk to Mr. Rickey. In about an hour, Mr. Rickey called back and said, "Walter,"—that's

*The lights from the **POLO GROUNDS** are used today at Phoenix Municipal Stadium, the spring training home of the Oakland A's.

what he always called me—"you found the right man." So Scully joined Connie and me. I will say this, for the years that Scully was with us, through '53, that's the best three-man baseball team in history—Connie Desmond, Vin Scully and the old redhead. What we did was anytime he made a mistake on the air, we corrected it. The audience loved it. He didn't like it so much at times, but he was a very quick learner...and he never made the same mistake twice.

Scully is my boy. I'm very proud of him. I guess you might say that he's my legacy."

In 1950, only a year after graduating from Fordham, Vin joined the Brooklyn Dodgers broadcast team, anchored by Red Barber and Connie Desmond. What kind of impression did the rookie announcer make on the players? Hall-of-Famer Duke Snider, "Vin informed us immediately that he had played college baseball. We chuckled at that."

Vin's famed career as a college baseball player had reached its peak. From here, Vin would have to find other ways of making casual conversation with the players, and he had no problem doing that.

"He knew the game well, and it came across that way. He just fit right in. He blended right in and knew the right things to ask and the right things to say, and we became very good friends."

Hall-of-Fame broadcaster Ernie Harwell, a young broadcaster himself in those days, would help Vin get acclimated to calling professional games. "He had sort of a quiet confidence about him. He had a wonderful personality. We got to be friends because when he first began to work, he would come in and we would talk over the situation about breaking into the Major Leagues. He always seemed to be very alert, very willing to listen."

Brooklyn Dodgers pitcher Carl Erskine was instantly able to recognize something familiar about the young man. "My first reaction was—Red Barber was our senior announcer, a redhead, and I said real fast, 'This is a pup out of Red Barber,'" That was prophetic.

Indeed it was. Author and broadcasting historian Curt Smith recalls Vin's days in Brooklyn under Red Barber. "There's a great deal of Red Barber in Vin Scully's DNA. Barber taught him so much...taught him not to listen to other announcers because it dilutes the wine. He taught him to be prepared. He was a taskmaster. Barber could be severe, but Scully learned so much. He really learned the poetry, the reporting, the accuracy, the honesty, the fidelity to truth, the ability to tell a story. I think he had these inherently in any event, but Barber certainly embraced and caressed them as well."

> "There's a great deal of Red Barber in Vin Scully's DNA...."

From the tutelage he was receiving from Red, the "father," and Connie, the "uncle," Vin was finding that he provided some players with a little bit of luck—something Carl Erskine knows all too well. "Vin came down to the dugout just before a game against the Cubs. I had about five minutes before I was to warm up. I'm sitting in the dugout just waiting for the time to go out. Vinnie came walking over and sat down by me. It was not unusual for a broadcaster or newspaper guy to come over and talk a little bit before the game. We chatted for a minute. I tossed the ball up and down, and I said, 'I wonder what this little ball has in store for me today,' and that was it. Vin went up to the booth to broadcast, and I pitched a no-hitter against the Cubs."

It didn't take long for people to realize that Vin had a special talent. By 1957, Vin had gone from the rookie with potential to a veteran who knew all the tricks.

Since he had joined the Dodgers in 1950, Vin Scully has had the privilege of calling some of baseball's most memorable games and moments. One game, however, that does not stick out in the minds of many fans took place on May 14, 1952—a typical game between the St. Louis Cardinals and Brooklyn Dodgers at Ebbets Field. This game was just a little bit different because it involved a couple of guys with a couple of crazy dreams.

Vin Scully: "I'm on this campus at Fordham Prep. I'm talking to the best athlete in school. His name is Larry Miggins. We were talking about what we wanted to be when we eventually got out of school. Larry said, 'I want to be a Major League baseball player.' Wow, I wonder what the odds against that would be. I said, 'I'd like to be a Major League broadcaster.' Oh, I wonder what the odds of that would be. Then I said to Larry, 'I wonder what the odds are if we both make it. And how about this one? I wonder what the odds would be if I were broadcasting a game in which you played.' A few years later, I was broadcasting at Ebbets Field in Brooklyn. The Dodgers were playing the St. Louis Cardinals and Larry Miggins was playing for St. Louis. I did two innings in those days, the third and the seventh. Larry Miggins' turn at bat came up in the third inning. Suddenly I am sitting there overwhelmed that it has happened. I'm broadcasting a game, and he's playing the game...and he hit a home run. As I described him going around the bases, I was as close to breaking down while doing a baseball game or any other sporting event I have ever experienced." Larry Miggins also remembers that afternoon. "Sure enough, he threw me a cantaloupe—as big as a cantaloupe. I hit it off of the man who had been nearly unbeatable for us, Preacher Roe. Scully was on the microphone. I'll never forget it."

Speaking of long shots, that home run was one of only two Miggins hit in his whole career. "It's just amazing...absolutely amazing."

... the first voice I heard on the radio in my mom's kitchen— a Zenith radio about the size of a microwave today...

But it wasn't just Vin and Larry who had their dreams come true. Little did he know, but Vin's voice is having an early impact on a young lad in Brooklyn named Charley Steiner.

"The first time I went to a baseball game—my father took me to Ebbets Field. The first time I heard a game on the radio, probably in '55 or '56, the first voice I heard on the radio in my mom's kitchen—a Zenith radio about the size of a microwave today—was Vin."

It didn't take long for some of the Dodger players to realize that Vin was more than just a broadcaster. He traveled with the team and was always willing to help out. Players would often ask Vin to recommend a book for them.

Scully had successfully integrated himself into the Brooklyn Dodger family. After Red Barber's final season with the club in 1953, Vin was named the "Voice of the Brooklyn Dodgers," a title that would last at least 56 years.

He was the perfect guy for the situation. His voice was terrific. His descriptions were great and his knowledge of the team, combined with his youth and enthusiasm, made for an ideal broadcaster.

A year later, the Dodgers finally defeated the Yankees in the **'55 WORLD SERIES***, giving Brooklyn their one and only World Championship. Less than a year later, Dodgers owner Walter O'Malley envisioned a baseball team in Southern California. The word spread throughout the borough that O'Malley was considering heading West. Despite heavy complaining and desperate pleas to keep "dem bums" in their birthplace, the Brooklyn Dodgers played their final game at Ebbets Field on September 24, 1957. The team's departure broke the hearts of millions who had come to know the fabled *boys of summer*—Duke, Pee Wee, Campy, Jack. It marked the end of the golden era of New York City baseball...and started a new era of transcontinental baseball.

But what about the broadcaster? What about the man who painted the picture? Walter O'Malley may have deserted Brooklyn, but he wasn't about to desert Vin Scully. And Vin made the long arduous journey from Flatbush to the beaches of Los Angeles.

*In 1955, *Sports Illustrated* selected horse owner William Woodward as their Sportsman of the Year. Woodward's wife shot and killed the unfaithful Woodward before the issue went to press. S.I. then selected WORLD SERIES hero, Johnny Podres.

"Personally, it was difficult. After all, my family, my friends, my roots, my school—everything was in New York. However, I had just married and at least I had a job. That's the biggest thing of all. I was saddened to leave, but thrilled that I was still working. Mr. O'Malley was a man who really appreciated loyalty, and I guess he felt that Jerry Doggett and I provided that, and he brought us out here."

It doesn't take a rocket scientist to realize that Brooklyn and Los Angeles are two very different cities. In the late 1950s, Brooklyn was bursting with energy at every subway stop. Los Angeles, meanwhile, was still searching for an identity. And it was Vin Scully who would give them one. As the Dodgers arrived in Southern California, they were greeted by a city of fans who had never experienced Major League baseball.

> It doesn't take a rocket scientist to realize that Brooklyn and Los Angeles are two very different cities.

Carl Erskine: "The Dodger fans in Los Angeles were curious when I pitched the opening game in 1958. For the team's historic first game, 80,000 came to the Coliseum. Vinnie is the one who sold the team to Southern California and beyond."

Vin Scully: "Representing the new team arriving in town, it was my good fortune to have the birth of the transistor radio. The transistor became a necessary thing for the fans. They knew about Mays. They knew about Musial. But they didn't know the rank- and-file player. If you're sitting 70 rows away, and you have a guy telling you about some of the other players, that helps."

It was Vin's job to educate Southern California about baseball and to be baseball's ambassador. And what an ambassador he was. He became the "transistor kid." It's been said, I think not apocryphally, but quite correctly no one was more responsible for the explosion of transistor radio sales in the late 1950s and early '60s than Vin Scully.

With Vin Scully dominating the Southern California airways, it did not take long for him to become a fixture in the hearts and minds of Dodger fans. Just ask Jaime Jarrin, Hall of Fame broadcaster and voice of the Dodgers on Spanish radio since 1959, and Ross Porter, who worked with Vin for 28 years. "Vin took the city by storm. He became the king of Los Angeles. It was a situation where everybody brought their transistor radios to the games to listen to Vin. As a result, he was an immediate hit out here. To this day, I would say he's the most popular man in Southern California."

> ... "Vin took the city by storm. He became the king of Los Angeles."

Vin even used his creative side relaying information to the players on the field via the transistor radio.

Duke Snider said, "He would always give the Giant scores when we were in a heated race with them. From the playing field, we could hear the transistor radios that were in the stands."

At other times, Vin used the transistor radio to give the crowd a little comic relief.

An anecdote that is often told...the Pirates are playing the Dodgers at the Coliseum. Scully starts leafing through the National League media guide. He comes upon the fact that Frank Secory, that day's home plate umpire, was having a birthday. He says over the radio, assuming and knowing that there are thousands of transistors at the Coliseum, "This is Frank Secory's birthday. I'm going to count, on the radio, 1-2-3, and when I do, would you please say, 'Happy birthday, Frank.'" He does this, and after "3," there is this explosion of noise all over the Coliseum, "Happy birthday, Frank." Secory looks as if he has just stepped from another planet, looking at the crowd, and then looking at the booth because he knew it was Scully's doing. It was a *transistor revolution.* No one ever could have anticipated that the transistor radio would become a necessary every-day appliance. Many people believe that the popularity of transistor radios only lasted until 1962 when the Dodgers left the Coliseum and moved to a real baseball park. Curt Smith tells people to think again. "When the Dodgers moved in 1962 to their Taj Mahal, Dodger Stadium, where from any seat you could see the game, the habit endured to today. Even now, tens of thousands of people bring transistor radios out of habit to Dodger Stadium. It all began with Scully now more than 50 years ago."

Growing up in Santa Monica, former Dodger player and current radio announcer Rick Monday got to know Vin at a very young age. "Vin Scully and Jerry Doggett were friends of ours and friends of our families way before we ever met them. When the Dodgers played, we turned on the television or we turned on the radio and invited them into our homes and into our cars. When we made a trip on a Saturday or Sunday, Vin Scully went with us because we listened to Dodger games."

"He was one of the reasons I rooted for the Dodgers. I grew up listening to his voice on the transistor radio. I thought the world of him. I learned so much about baseball. I got a baseball education listening to his broadcasts of every game. Vin even got the players' wives to listen to the broadcast. My wife heard him a lot, and when I came home one night she said, 'Do you choke up at bat?' I said, 'What do you mean by that?' She said, 'Well, Vin Scully said you choked up at bat?' I said, 'Well, I choke up on the bat about ¾ of an inch from the bottom of the **BAT***—I choke up on it. I guess that was what he was talking about.'" People listened and he was able to describe and paint a picture for people that not many people could do.

In a few short years, Vin Scully had transformed Los Angeles into a true baseball city. O'Malley is a name commonly cursed in Brooklyn, but one of the smartest decisions he ever made was bringing Scully to Los Angeles to help make baseball work in Southern California. Not only did it work...it made Vin a household name across the entire city.

> *Orlando Cepeda used more BATS than any player in history. He felt each bat had exactly one hit in it. When Cepeda hit safely, he would discard the bat. He had 2,364 hits in his career.

"I don't think there's any question that anybody who was around in those years or the years since could take exception to the fact that the one thing that stood out for the Dodger acceptance in Southern California was the voice of Vin Scully."

Fast forward to 2005 and, as Charley Steiner notes, Vin still knows how to tell a great story. "It was the second or third week into spring training, and I'm trying to get my sea legs, and Rick Monday and I are working together for the first time. We're doing pretty well, and getting it all figured out. Then Vin does the first three innings of this game. It doesn't even matter who it was against—I don't remember. There were those terrible hurricanes, and Holman Stadium was badly damaged. A lot of the big palm trees were broken. Vin is doing this incredible rhapsody about the palm trees, about how the old palm trees were able to withstand it. Some of the newer ones were damaged, but they're still here. And a bunch of brand new ones. He said, 'Isn't that what spring training is all about?' I was spellbound! That's why he's Vin Scully, and that's why I'm sitting there listening. He's talking about palm trees for 3-4-5 minutes and all of a sudden, there was this beautiful conclusion and a wrap-up. I just had to walk out of the booth for a while. Wow! If I had tried to say something like that, I would have fallen all over myself."

Tommy Hawkins: "Clearly to me Vin is the poet laureate of broadcasting. Above all, I think he has something that was learned at Fordham—and that is an appreciation of the English language. No one caresses and manipulates the English language better than Vin Scully. He can say things seamlessly. How do you improve upon a guy who once said of a day in St. Louis, 'It was so hot today, the moon got sunburned.' That's Vin Scully."

> Clearly to me Vin is the poet laureate of broadcasting.

Rick Monday still finds himself amazed at Vin's ability to demand attention through words. "You talk about pinching yourself because when you sit with Vinnie for any period of time, whether it's in a car or in your home, and especially when you're in a broadcast booth, you really have to ask yourself, 'Is English your second language,' because he is very poetic about even saying hello. I think you could pipe in his voice reading the phone book to a kindergarten class at recess, and I think they would stop playing in the sandbox...I think they would stop playing on the merry-go-round because Vinnie has that type of presence. When he speaks, time stands still."

But if you ask Vin about his mastery of the English language, "I have never considered myself a master of anything. I just hang on with both hands and do the best I can."

Vin may not consider himself to be a master of anything...but certainly there is something about the man that mystifies everyone from co-workers to other broadcasters. WFUV alum and voice of the Washington Nationals, Charlie Slowes, is even going to admit that Vin is just a little different from all the rest.

"We were in Los Angeles earlier this year. I was in the hotel the second day of the series, and I was doing some prep for our game and went to Fox Sports and watched the replay of the Dodgers telecast of the game with the Nationals the night before. I thought, 'Wow, what a treat. I get to watch and listen to Vin for nine innings.' I saw him that night, and we were talking. I said, 'Vin, I spent a lot of time today listening to your broadcast from last night on the TV replay. I learned a lot about our team.' He laughed. That was my compliment to him."

"The strangest thing to me was to call his house and actually hear his voice on the answering machine."

Some people are so mystified by Vin they don't think he's a real person. Just ask Dodgers radio producer, Tom Bowman.

"The strangest thing to me was to call his house and actually hear his voice on the answering machine. That freaked me out because you don't picture Vin as being a normal person. I picture Vin as when it's game time, he appears out of some mist. He walks in and does his little pre-game stuff, calls the game, and disappears out into the mist again.. To hear his voice and actually have him on the answering machine—like the rest of us—that was one of the oddest moments I've ever had."

Yes, Vin is an actual human being. When you're as famous a guy as Vin, it's not surprising that people from all over the country recognize him wherever he travels.

Ross Porter: "Everybody knows what a talented broadcaster he is. He's the best sportscaster of the 20th century. That says it all right there. But what people don't understand is, and they have no reason to 'cause they're not around him like I was, but, in all those years with him, I never saw him, once, be rude to a fan. He was hounded for autographs and pictures and by people who wanted to stop and reminisce with him and tell him how they were at Ebbets Field when he did this. And they were at the Coliseum....He would be very patient and smile."

Tom Bowman: "One time, we were in Chicago to play an afternoon game. After the game, we went to dinner. We were walking down Michigan Avenue after dinner. It was a beautiful evening, and people were coming up to Vinnie and saying, 'Oh, hi Mr. Scully.' He would say hello and they asked to take pictures with him, which he did. They asked him for autographs, which he did. One fan came up and said, 'I've been listening to you for years, and I just love you.' He said, 'Oh, you ought to get a medal.' It was a precious moment."

As Bob Costas knows, there was no bigger fan of Vin Scully than the late, great Ray Charles:

"About 10 years ago, I had occasion to interview Ray and, as we talked before the cameras rolled, it became clear to me that he was a very knowledgeable sports fan, especially a baseball fan. He said to me at one point, 'You know who I'd really like to meet.' This was in all the world—not just baseball—all the prominent and interesting people he might have named—and I said, 'Who?' He said, 'Vin Scully.' I was a little bit surprised and asked him why. He said, 'You've got to remember—to me—the picture doesn't mean anything. It's all about the sound. To my ear, Vin Scully's sound is almost musical. No one is quite like him. I would love to meet him. Could you introduce me to him?' A few years later, that opportunity arose, and we took Ray to Dodger Stadium. Vin was, of course, very gracious to him. He certainly had an appreciation of who Ray Charles was and what his historical standing was. But Ray was like a little kid taken to see Santa Claus. He was just beside himself. The man was beaming... clapping his hands...just throwing his head back in delight."

Rick Monday: "It's no secret that Vin has touched the hearts of baseball fans all across the United States. He even has an impact on the players and the people he works with. When the Dodgers played, we turned on the television or we turned on the radio and invited Vin into our homes and into our cars."

> "To my ear, Vin Scully's sound is almost musical."

Charlie Slowes: "He's a living legend. There is no better broadcaster than Vin Scully. When you first have that chance to go in the booth and introduce yourself to him, you're very, very nervous. He really puts you at ease. The thing I noticed and that people who have come in and worked with me—new people over the last few years—the first thing they noticed about Vin is that he makes them feel very comfortable. In fact, he always remembers their name. If he sees them in the hallway, he'll call out to them, 'Hey Josh, Hey Joe.' What I get from people who work for me is 'I can't believe he remembers me.'"

Tommy Lasorda says Vin is the greatest Dodger of them all:

"I've got to call him Mr. Dodger. He's got a heart as big as his body." As Mr. Dodger, Vin Scully won the hearts of Dodger fans all over the world. When it came time for the fans to reward Vin, they came through. He was voted, as most people know, the most popular personality in Los Angeles Dodger history. For a broadcaster to get that type of an award, when you have pitchers like

SANDY KOUFAX* and Don Drysdale and all these great players who have played for the Dodgers through the years, for a broadcaster to get that honor is really something special. It says so much about the man and what he's all about.

They see a pitcher like Koufax, and he certainly had an impact, but Vinnie lived with the fans. He was with them when they were at work, on vacation, or at home ironing a shirt. Wherever they were...Vinnie was a part of people's lives.

So, Vin, do you ever think about the impact you've had on Dodger fans? "No, not really. I honestly don't. First of all, we've had so many great players. But their impact is only for a short period of time. With me, it has been day after day, night after night, for 56 years. I guess the fact that God allowed me to do it for so long, was really the thing that won the vote. But to think about it—no. I'm just very, very thankful that the Good Lord gave me this job at a very early age, and then allowed me to have enough health to continue to do it for all these years."

Vin may not think about his impact but the rest of the country does. In 1982, Vin Scully was inducted into the Baseball Hall of Fame as the recipient of the Ford C. Frick Award for Broadcasting. In typical Vin fashion, he wasn't about to gloat over this prestigious award. "Why me? Why, with the millions and millions of more deserving people, would a red-haired kid with a hole in his pants and his shirt tail hanging out, playing stick ball in the streets of New York, wind up in Cooperstown. I think, when I'm on the air and the crowd roars and the adrenalin that seems to suddenly go through my body, the goosebumps that jump up after a great play—those are all parts of the job that I love very much."

Don't fool yourself. Vin knows how good he is. How can he not? The entire world has told him time and again. Even Bud Selig can't help but rave about Vin. As Washington Post columnist Dave Sheinin knows all too well.

---

*The late actor, Richard Widmark, was **SANDY KOUFAX**'s father-in-law.

"To have the commissioner of baseball on the verge of tears talking about Vin Scully was a pretty neat experience."

But the *voice of heaven* continues to brush it off as meaningless. He's just thankful...thankful for the gift he has...thankful for the life he's led and the people he's met along the way. He's thankful he can still do it. Thankful for his family. Thankful for his co-workers. For everything that Vin has given to every person who has ever tuned in to that harmonic voice, he still wants to give a little more. He reminds us all to be thankful for what we have in life, whether it is great or small.

There is a legend in the West of an Indian chief who was wont to test the manhood of his young braves by making them climb up the side of a mountain as far as they could in a single day. At daybreak, on the appointed day, four braves left the village. The first one came back in the late afternoon with a sprig of spruce to show how high he had climbed.

> For 56 years, Vin has climbed the mountain and looked at the sea.

Later that afternoon, another came with a branch of pine, and much later in the day, the third came with an alpine shrub. But it wasn't until late that night, by a full moon, with the stars dancing in the heavens, that the fourth brave arrived. "What did you bring back? How high did you climb?" asked the chief. The brave said, "Where I was, there was no spruce nor pine to shield me from the sun. There was no flower to cheer my path. There was only snow and ice and barren rocks and cold, hard ground. My feet are torn and bloodied. I'm worn out and exhausted. I'm bare-handed, and I have come home late." And then a wondrous look came into his eye, and he said, "I saw the sea."

For 56 years, Vin has climbed the mountain and looked at the sea.

In Case You're Ever on Sports Jeopardy!

Tom Hanks sold Cokes, Mrs. Fields was a ball girl and M.C. Hammer was a bat boy for the A's in the 1970s.

Tommy John surgery was first done in 1974. From '95-'98 Dr. James Andrews operated on nine high school pitchers. Now he averages over 50 per year.

Dusty Baker's dad was Bobby Bonds' Little League coach in Riverside, CA.

Ron Fairly is the only major-leaguer with over 200 home runs while never hitting 20 in any season.

The Florida Marlins have won the World Series twice but have never won their division—the NL East. The Marlins are the only team that travels north for spring training.

A recent Houghton-Mifflin fifth grade history text devoted more space to Cal Ripken than to the Great Depression.

Bud Selig's annual salary is $14.5 million. David Stern makes nine million.

The teams with the most losses in the four major sports: The Phillies (over 10,000 losses), The Warriors (NBA), Blackhawks (NHL), and Arizona Cardinals (NFL).

Nolan Ryan, president of the Texas Rangers, is the first Hall-of-Famer to be a club president since Christy Mathewson in 1925.

The head football coach at Army makes three times as much as the President of the United States.

Chapter 1

Hear Me Now, Listen To Me Later

Fellow Broadcasters Pay Tribute

THE GOLDEN THROAT
IN THE GOLDEN WEST

DICK ENBERG

Dick Enberg was born in Mount Clemens, Michigan and went to Central Michigan University. He received his masters and doctorate degrees at **INDIANA UNIVERSITY****. While at IU, he did play-by-play for the football and basketball teams in 1961. He was an assistant professor and baseball coach at Cal State Northridge—then known as San FernandoValley State College. In the late 60s, Enberg began a full-time sportscasting career. He called California Angels baseball, Los Angeles Rams football and UCLA basketball. He did boxing matches at the Los Angeles Auditorium. In the early 70s, Enberg hosted the game show* Sports Challenge *and co-produced the sports history series* The Way it Was *for PBS. Enberg is now doing NFL football ,NCAA basketball and Grand Slam tennis. He resides in Rancho Santa Fe, CA.*

Vin Scully is the poet laureate of our business. He was always the best at calling baseball play-by-play. He still is. He still has his fast ball. I think all of us who have had the privilege to call a Major League baseball game, in the back of our minds, hope someday we can be almost as good as Vin. He's the best at painting the picture, being sharp in those few moments. Baseball is the most difficult game of all to broadcast, especially on radio. You have to describe three hours of activity when maybe there are only 10 outstanding plays. To me, the real test of a terrific baseball announcer is what does he do between the action plays...and there are only a few of them...and how does he keep your interest, paint the entire canvas until that moment

*By winning percentage, __INDIANA__ ranks 12th in all-time Big Ten football standings behind the University of Chicago.

comes where there might be a bases-loaded double or a superb double play or a potential shut-out or no-hitter. That's the challenge. I feel very fortunate to have been in Los Angeles, and working in sports in the mid-sixties, being able to listen to **CHICK HEARN*** do basketball, Vin Scully work baseball, and for 25 cents read Jim Murray every day. That was pretty good stuff. I'm not sure there's another Vin Scully out there.

I moved out to California to coach baseball at Cal State Northridge in 1961. I'd heard sprinkles of Vin Scully's work back in the Midwest. He brought baseball to the West Coast like Bob Kelly brought in football as the Rams' announcer.

> I moved out to California to coach baseball at Cal State Northridge in 1961.

The only other personal thing is Vin unknowingly motivated a change in the whole broadcast technology for the Angels when I became their announcer replacing Buddy Blattner in '69. My first thought was there's no way we can compete with Scully. One—he's the best... and two—he's describing a team that owns Los Angeles. The Dodgers were the better team, and they were well entrenched as the southern California favorite. The Angels were the Johnnie-come-lately and "how can we at least be competitive?" Compete— those were my first thoughts when I started in '69, first with Don Wells and then with Don Drysdale.

There had been, traditionally, in baseball broadcasting one guy gets six innings and the other announcer gets three. In Scully's case, he did seven and two. My feeling was there was nothing sacred about my six innings...that my fellow announcer should be able to come in anytime he has something interesting to say or I could even bring him in with a question and have a discussion

---

*In late 1953 the Cardinals chose Jack Buck for play-by-play over **CHICK HEARN** from Peoria, Illinois. Buck got the job because he had done excellent Budweiser commercials that summer while broadcasting the Rochester Red Wings, the Cardinals' AAA team in New York. The Cardinals had just been purchased by Anheuser-Busch.

---

with him, especially in games that become "not" interesting. When it's 9-1, you don't have to "ball and strike" it quite so carefully. Especially when Don Drysdale came aboard, in '71. I asked Dick Nelson, our KNBC engineer on the Angel Network, "How can we have a system where, at any time, I can join Don's three innings and, more importantly, any time in my six innings, Drysdale can enter with a conversation or a comment or reflection or some humor." In some of those Angel seasons, we certainly needed that latter quality, especially when they had this penchant to languish in last place in August and seem relatively happy about staying there. We had fun in bad games, and that was the only way we could even come close to competing with the Dodgers. We had to go two-on-one against Vin. I mean that in the most respectful way. We wanted to make our broadcast the highest of quality. We knew that Scully and the Dodgers had a tremendous edge on us, but hopefully we could find a way to be not only accurate in our call but entertaining. Drysdale, with his infectious laugh, his tremendous background and his storytelling talent, was good and entertaining.

> It was because of Scully that we developed the two-man broadcast style...

There were a few seasons where the Angels actually made a decent run and had a chance going into September. We started to get mail, "You guys aren't nearly as much fun as you were in the past." I'd go, "The game now is the thing. We've got to be more serious." Don brought such an important element to our two-man team. And that's really what it was. It wasn't, "I do mine...you do yours." It was that we were a team, and there was never a time where he would look at me and say, "Wait a minute, this is my inning. Stay out of the way."

It was because of Scully that we developed the two-man broadcast style and not a one-man-per-inning approach. Dick Nelson created these little boxes that had a toggle switch on them. When we wanted to join the other man's broadcast, the engineer didn't have to open up a pot so that we could get on. He had those all pre-set so that if I wanted to come in, all I had to do was flip the toggle switch and say, "Hey, Don, interesting thing down right field in the bull pen I just noticed." Obviously we had eye contact and body contact and didn't cut into the middle of a sentence, but it was a flow—I think a really good flow—between two announcers that love the game and really loved each other. Don Drysdale was such a wonderful guy to be around. I can honestly say that in all the years I worked with him, there were a lot of bad games, and perhaps some broadcasts we weren't totally pleased with, but I never, ever had a bad day working with Don. It was always a happy day.

It's natural to compete. The media was more Dodger-oriented and justifiably. They were winning games…the Angels, many times, were not. Not only did Vin have the more popular team, but he, being an established announcer and one of incredible Hall-of-Fame talent, was the one we measured ourselves against. You sometimes said, "Gee, I wish they'd write a good review about us." His work is nonpareil and you had to face up to that and do the best you could.

> The media was more Dodger-oriented and justifiably.

As a kid, we all dreamed about being an athlete, but sooner or later, the legs and arms or something is going to fall apart and you find your career is over. The beauty of being a broadcaster, as my friends have often said to me, "Enberg, you always thought you were a good athlete, but you only talked a good game." Fortunately talking a good game doesn't carry the stress on the key elements—your brain and your voice! Look at **CURT GOWDY***— he was great to the very end. We picked good parents, and for that I'm forever grateful. My father had a wonderful voice and I'm sure that Vin's did as well.

***CURT GOWDY** was a young announcer for the Yankees when Vin Scully "broke in" with the Brooklyn Dodgers. Gowdy was an All-American basketball player at the University of Wyoming.

Whenever I have a cold, or my voice is thin, or I'm not 100 percent, I have to take care. Ernie Harwell used to drink hot lemon tea. I have a lozenge that I buy in England that has saved me. I've never, in 52 years, missed a game due to illness, and I'll bet Scully's record is just as solid. You learn to take care of yourself. It's easy to abuse your voice, and part of that is knowing how to use your voice. If you're a screamer and pressing, it takes its toll. Scully, when he's on the air with that mellifluous approach, that's about what you get if you were talking to him on the phone, or if you were having a conversation over dinner. He's not pushing. That's his voice, and he's using it intelligently...as well as his mind.

I'm from a small town in Michigan, Armada. I went to Central Michigan in Mount Pleasant. It was there that I applied for a $1 an hour custodial job at the only radio station in town and wound up as a weekend disk jockey at $1 an hour. Later, I became the sports director, as a 20-year old, also at $1 an hour. But...when you did a game on the road, they bought a steak for you. As a farm kid, I'd never had that luxury so that was the bonus.

> There is no more exciting opportunity for a play-by-play announcer in any sport than calling a no-hitter.

Baseball is the best announcer-game. It allows you, because of the pace, and the cerebral Shakespearean nature of the game, to constantly analyze and project possibility and bring in outside elements. So the challenge of calling 200 games a year, counting pre-season, is the ultimate test of a professional announcer. I've often said that if you wanted to have a little game with me and give me only one day and you've got 100 young guys, all of whom have some talent, but in that 100 you hide one, unbeknownst to me, that is obviously the best—the best of those 100, give me one day what I would do, I'd have each of them call one inning of baseball, and I'd find him.

Baseball ultimately will reveal. You can hide in basketball and hockey because of the pace of the game. In football you can hide, especially on TV because you have a color analyst. Football on radio is a little different—that's a good test. But baseball really separates the great from the good.

A 0-0 game in the ninth inning still has its wonderful character. Somebody is likely to pitch a shutout and the drama that builds within a game where there is no scoring is also exciting. The beauty of the game is that the clock isn't going to run out and everyone is going home after watching a 0-0 game...somebody is going to win it.

There is no more exciting opportunity for a play-by-play announcer in any sport than calling a no-hitter. When you get through that sixth inning, and you see those zeroes up there...now every pitch, every subtlety, every movement by an infielder becomes significant. You build to the seventh...and eighth...and ninth. To sink your teeth into a no-hitter is the ultimate joy of a play-by-play announcer. There's nothing quite like it.

I've been asked what was the most exciting game I ever called. There are a lot of exciting moments and somewhat momentous games. The most exciting is when you've sunk your teeth into a no-hit, no-run game and you're into the seventh inning.

Vin's call after Koufax's perfect game is just part of his genius. With the risk of exaggerating, Vin is as close to a baseball play-by-play genius as anyone we've ever had.

Now and then, Vin and I see each other. Or he'll send a note, or I'll send a note. It's typical of us to be usually going in opposite directions. There are very few times when we intersect and have a chance to sit down. Maybe before it's all over, I would love to be able to open a nice bottle of Claret and talk baseball with Vin for an extended period of time.

During the World Series games we both did, we'd speak as we'd meet, but there was nothing where we sat down to talk. In the press club, you might have dinner with him. There's never been a time for us to have a social relationship. If anything, that's my loss.

Vin, when he was doing football, was the #1 or #2 announcer at CBS. He did golf. He's shown that his talent isn't limited to baseball. He'd have to be the one to say why he didn't pursue being a full-time network announcer. Obviously he settled in to a situation where not only did the fans love him, the players love and respect him and maybe, most importantly, the Dodger management does. They've done him right. They've rewarded him, as they should have, with an open-ended contract.

Somebody who is so highly qualified and brilliant and as talented as Scully, the truth of the matter is he probably should do all nine innings—he now does. The virtuoso performer doesn't need to only play two or three movements of a symphony. He should play all four.

THE CHOICE VOICE

CURT SMITH

A 1973 graduate of SUNY at Geneseo—Curt Smith is the author of eleven books, including Voices of Summer. *He has been a speechwriter for Presidents George H. W. Bush and Ronald Reagan. Of Curt Smith, Bob Costas says, "Curt stands up for the beauty of words."* USA Today *says, "He shows that broadcasting can be art." Currently, Smith hosts the weekly perspectives series on Rochester, New York's NPR affiliate, WXXI. He is a senior lecturer at the University of Rochester. He has appeared on numerous local and network radio/TV programs, including "Nightline" and ESPN's "Sportscenter."*

L anguage has been my career, not simply writing books on baseball broadcasting including *Voices of the Game* and *The Storytellers*, but also as a former presidential speech writer to former President Bush and also some speeches for Ronald Reagan. Winston Churchill once said that "words are bullets—ammunition you can use against the enemy." Churchill used words against Nazi Germany.

Vin Scully has used words against boredom and ignorance. He is an extraordinary practitioner of the English language. The ability to utilize language is exceedingly important in a game like baseball. Let's say the game lasts three hours. A ball may be in play for eight to ten minutes. So the broadcaster, by definition, must fill empty air. He must describe plays as they occur, but he must tie those to anecdotes and stories and reminiscences—he must compare yesterday to today. In a 10-1 game, the broadcaster becomes the stage. If he fills that stage, the listeners don't turn the dials. If he doesn't fill the stage, listeners do

> He is an extraordinary practitioner of the English language.

turn the dials. So the ability to utilize language matters far more in baseball than in any other sport.

I think Vin understood what Winston Churchill meant. If you look at some of the anecdotes Vin has used over the years...for example, at a game in St. Louis, he said, "it is so hot today, the moon got sunburned." He will talk about a very poorly hit ground ball, and he will quote Eugene O'Neill, "a humble thing, but thine own." For example, when a ball eludes the catcher, Vin will evoke *The Ancient Mariner*. Vin understands how to surpass the actual game on the field.

When I think of Vin over the years, he's done virtually everything you can in broadcasting. In baseball, he's covered everything there is to cover—2009 is his 60th straight year of play-by-play... every year with the same team. He's aired **NBC*** Television's Game of the Week more superbly than anyone ever has or is ever likely to. He has aired 12 network All-Star Games, a record 18 no-hitters, a record 25 World Series. He has done network football, golf and tennis. He's made virtually every major radio-television Hall-of-Fame. He's won a lifetime Emmy and a lifetime Achievement. He has a star on the Hollywood Walk of Fame. He's been named the "most memorable Los Angeles Dodgers franchise personality."

Vin is the total package. Vin has set a standard. He's the blue-chip consortium for broadcasting today.

Vin is unique. People use that term...but Scully is unique. He is the only broadcaster today to address the audience, not a broadcast partner. He does all nine innings of every Dodgers home game, three on radio and all on television, and some road games as well. He never works with a partner. Every one but Vin has a

******NBC*** **Sports President Dick Ebersol, recently paid $50,000 at a charity auction to have Carly Simon tell him the name of the subject person in her song, "You're So Vain." Only Simon, Ebersol and that person know the identity, rumored to be Warren Beatty, James Taylor or Mick Jagger.*

partner. Partners kibitz. Partners exchange *happy talk.* If two broadcasters in the booth like one another, the empathy is real. If not, it's feigned. Vin talks to the listener. He learned this from Red Barber, of course, Barber being his mentor. Red taught him to simply address the audience, to establish an intimacy between himself and the listener or viewer at home. The umbilical cord between the public and its game. This was standard procedure when Vin began in 1950.

James Fennimore Cooper wrote *The Last of the Mohicans.* Vin is the last of the "one-man, one-booth practitioners." This has accounted for a great deal of his popularity. Other aspects that Vin brings to the booth—a very lovely Irish tenor, an encyclopedic knowledge of the game derived in part from his playing baseball at Fordham, and an ability, which is unsurpassed, to tell stories.

I wrote a book, *The Storytellers*, and baseball is a story-telling medium. No one tells stories as often, as well, and as germanely as Vin. He can segue from Duke Snider in 1955 to **MANNY RAMIREZ*** in 2008. He does so, not awkwardly…but seamlessly. He invites the audience in. It's no coincidence that his trademark phrase is "pull up a chair." He invites every listener to pull up a chair, beginning every broadcast that he does with, "A very pleas-ant good afternoon," or "A very pleasant good evening." And it is pleasant because Vin makes broadcasting pleasant in the best sense of that term.

Something that matters enormously to me, being the father of two young children, is that we have evolved into a "cesspool sewer kind of culture," with profanity everywhere, people trying to deviance or dumb down. You find none of that with Scully. Scully, and I say this unstintingly and accurately, has never once sworn on the air. How many broadcasters is that true of? Not many. Talent will *out*…and it certainly has with Vin.

***MANNY RAMIREZ** grew up in the Washington Heights area of New York. His two sons are both named Manny Ramirez, Jr. Vin Scully also grew up in Washington Heights.

Another marvelous quality of Scully is his wearability. I segue back to my background in politics. The president of the United States, especially in our 24-7 "cable age," is seen by Americans every day. He'd better be wearable. He'd better be the kind of person you'd like to invite into your living room, or you will boot him from 1600 Pennsylvania Avenue. A baseball broadcaster is exactly the same. He comes at you every day. Broadcasting, as Vin once did, all 162 games...add pre-season...add perhaps post-season, and it is not inconceivable that you could do 200 baseball games a year.

> Another marvelous quality of Scully is his wearability.

Every game now seems to approach or surpass three hours. Add pre-game...add post-game... you're talking about a broadcaster who may, in fact, ask you to spend nearly 1,000 hours of your life with him every year. Think about that. If he doesn't have wearability, he won't be spending much time at all with you because you will turn him off.

If he does have wearability, he becomes, what I call, an extended member of the family...and Vin certainly is. He certainly was in doing Game of the Week. Today, he most surely is in Southern California. That's an enormous asset.

Baseball is not football. Football comes at you once a week. Howard Cosell could do football...he could *never* do baseball. He would wear out his welcome by about the third inning of the first game. Baseball is daily. In the end, you feel you know as much about your favorite announcer as you do about your Uncle Fred or Aunt Ethel.

Add Vin Scully's other manifold assets and you can see why he is so beloved by, not simply Dodger fans, but baseball fans everywhere.

Regarding the flap going on now on sports talk radio, my first question to Jeff Kent would be, "How does he know Vin Scully talks too much?" Is he in the living room listening to Scully? I thought he was in the dugout trying to play ball. Of course, we live in a free country and everyone is free to utter any view they would like. I don't think that Kent's views were well-founded.

Being a casual Dodger fan as I am, it's obvious Kent has benefited from having Ramirez. He might not like to admit that, but that's the "elephant" in the room. And of course, Vin would be remiss not to recognize and report that.

> Howard Cosell could do football...he could *never* do baseball.

Not only has Vin stayed ahead of the curve, but he retained an enthusiasm, which I find amazing, given that even those of us who love the game would find it difficult to stay alert and enthused for every inning of every game. He somehow does. It's amazing to me. I speak as someone who has loved baseball since I was seven years old and for whom, outside of my family, baseball has given me more joy than any enterprise I can think of.

I maintain that baseball has never been as wonderfully broadcast on network television as it was in the 1980s. On NBC Television, Vin became the embodiment of the game. On CBS Radio, Jack Buck broadcast baseball as well as that network has ever aired it. They both called Kirk Gibson's home run in 1988. Both of those calls belong in the Hall of Fame in Cooperstown.

What I think of Vin, I expressed in *Voices of Summer*, in which I rated the 101 best baseball broadcasters of all time. I rated Vin #1...but not simply #1 on a point scale of 1 to 100, I gave him 100. That means, to me, Vin is the perfect baseball voice.

Jerry Doggett said he worked with the best broadcaster to come down the road, and they were great friends. Vin once said, regarding Jerry, "We haven't got married yet. We've got to pick out silver and get ready." Then Jerry also said, "I was an average announcer whose greatest break was to work with Vin. Also to be second banana to the biggest banana on the tree."

VIN SCULLY
YESSSSS!

MARV ALBERT

Marv Albert attended Syracuse University before graduating from NYU in 1965. He was the voice of the New York Knicks for 30 years on radio and television. In addition to the Knicks, Albert had a lengthy tenure as the voice of hockey's New York Rangers. Many consider him one of the greatest basketball play-by-play announcers ever.

Albert has also called Monday Night Football on radio for Westwood One. Albert's son, Kenny, is the current voice of the Rangers. His daughter, Denise, is also in the business as a reporter for NBA-TV. Albert has two younger brothers—Steve and Al, who have been successful sports announcers.

I grew up in Brooklyn in the late 40s and early 50s—the greatest town in the world to grow up in. Listening to Dodger games was a key part of my childhood with Al Helfer, Red Barber and then Vin Scully.

Scully was really young when he started with the Dodgers, maybe 10 years older than I was at the time. I was a sportswriter for my junior high newspaper. I was at Ebbets Field one day trying to interview a player when a new guy in radio came over to me and said, "Hey kid, would you like to be on a weekly radio show?" That guy was Howard Cosell, who was just giving up his full-time law practice and trying to break into radio. He had a show called "All-League," a weekly show out of New York City. It was done every Saturday morning and was syndicated nationally.

Each show they would have a pretty well-known celebrity on there, and they would give us puff questions to ask these celebrities. For a 13-year-old kid to be able to meet a lot of famous sports stars was very exciting.

One of the people being interviewed one Saturday was Fresco Thompson. He wasn't the general manager of the Dodgers, but he was the closest thing to it. After the show was over, he said, "Hey kid, how'd you like an office-boy job with the Dodgers?" Of course I accepted. I couldn't believe it was even being offered to me.

So there I was at the age of 13-14 working at 215 Montague Street, which was Ebbets Field. I was a go-fer—I'd go get coffee; I'd go get newspapers; I'd do whatever odd jobs the Dodgers needed done. For that, I got two tickets to every game, which I thought was an incredible amount of pay.

> We would pretend to broadcast the games...which drove the people sitting around us crazy...

When the games would come around, my buddy and I would sit in my seats, which were on the overhead right behind home plate. We would pretend to broadcast the games...which drove the people sitting around us crazy—they thought we were nuts. Long after the game was over, we'd sneak into the broadcast booth and would get Vin Scully's notes and commercial copy and promo copy and use them in our broadcast for the next game. My buddy and I would be sitting there broadcasting the Dodger game at the ripe old age of 15. We'd look to our right, and there'd be Al Helfer and Vin Scully broadcasting in their booth.

The final year the Dodgers were in Brooklyn, 1957, they played some of their games at Roosevelt Stadium in Jersey City, New Jersey. A lot of people forget that the Dodgers weren't drawing that well at Ebbets Field and they actually played some of the regular season games in Jersey City. They only sold tickets for those Jersey City games at Ebbets Field until the morning of the game. So, every afternoon of a game in Jersey City, they would hand me thousands of dollars worth of tickets, and I'd take the subway and a bus to Jersey City to the ticket office there. Then I'd stay around for the game, and I got to ride back on the team bus because the players would park their cars at Ebbets Field and take a bus over to Jersey City to play the game that night.

Because I wanted to be an announcer, I would try to grab a seat somewhere near Vin Scully. It might sound like I had terrible parents to allow me to run around like that, but the reality of the day was that there were not the heinous crimes we have in this day and age. Kids my age were taking the subway all over New York City, going to see ball games or to play in pick-up basketball games or whatever.

> ...they actually played some of the regular season games in Jersey City.

When I was doing the office-boy job, Vin Scully didn't come into the office very often. Sometimes you'd see him at a promotional event. Years later, I asked Vin if he remembered me as an office boy for the Dodgers. He laughed and said, "No," but we did have a great time reminiscing about those long-ago days in Brooklyn.

To a young boy in Brooklyn, who wanted to grow up to be an announcer, Vin Scully had a voice from God. Ironically, the two biggest announcers in New York at that time—Mel Allen with the Yankees and Red Barber with the Dodgers—were both Southern gentlemen who basically had lost their accent.

Another guy from the same era is Ernie Harwell. He was with the Tigers forever. When he was a youth, he was Margaret Mitchell's paper boy in Atlanta. Margaret Mitchell was the woman who wrote "Gone with the Wind." Ernie Harwell was baptized in the Jordan River and has written songs that have been recorded by Kenny Rogers and Willie Nelson. When you talk about longevity in the game, you need to add Ernie Harwell to that list along with Vin Scully.

Vin is 81. I'd love to be able to be announcing when I'm 81, but the odds aren't good for anyone to do that.

When the Dodgers moved to L.A., it caught everyone by surprise, although it really shouldn't have, given the games in Jersey City and the **LOW ATTENDANCE*** at Ebbets Field. We found out about it in the newspaper. It was hard to envision a life without the Dodgers. After the Dodgers office boy job, I became a ball boy with the New York Knicks in the late 50s and early 60s. That was right at the time the Minneapolis Lakers moved to Los Angeles so we're starting to think that every sports team in America pretty soon is going to move to California.

When the Dodgers moved to California, I got a letter one day from Walter O'Malley. It was a form letter inquiring whether I wanted to move to Los Angeles with the team. Of course I got all excited about this, but my parents didn't think it was very funny. Of course, it was just a form letter they sent to every Dodger employee. I guess they didn't realize how young I was.

The problem with Vin Scully when he was with the Dodgers is, to a young guy like me trying to be an announcer, the tendency at the time was to copy other announcers, but it was impossible to imitate Vin Scully's voice because it was so distinctive and so fluid—it was too hard to copy.

Later I had the pleasure of working with Vin on the NBC Game of the Week. Vin would do the play-by-play, and I did the studio pre-game and post-game wrap-up shows. Sometimes we wouldn't even be in the same city when we were working together on that job. Later we both sat at the Emmy's, each expecting maybe we were going to win an Emmy, but we didn't...it was still a great thrill.

The things I remember about Vin Scully from his days in Brooklyn were that he was always professional...he was always prepared...he was always nice. I love listening to Vin on the Dodger broadcasts, but I usually don't call him when we're in Southern California because I know how busy it gets during the season.

Vin Scully is a real pro.

***ONLY 6,700 FANS** attended the Dodgers' finale at Ebbets Field in 1957. The park—built 44 years earlier—had a capacity of 32,000 with only 700 parking spaces. An apartment building now sits on that site.

FOLKS, YOU'RE LOOKING LIVE AT A VIN SCULLY STORY

BRENT MUSBURGER

Brent Musburger was born in Portland, Oregon, raised near Billings, Montana, and graduated from Northwestern University. He began his career as a sportswriter for the now-defunct Chicago Herald-American *newspaper. He started in television at the local level in Chicago and Los Angeles. He worked alongside Connie Chung during his time in Los Angeles in the early 70s. By late 1973, Musburger was doing play-by-play for CBS Sports. In 1975, he rose to prominence as the host of the network's studio show,* NFL Today. *He has covered college football and basketball, the NBA, the US Open tennis, The Masters golf, and Major League baseball.*

Nobody is better than Vin Scully. When I worked with him in the CBS Radio booth, I was—and I use the term carefully—an analyst. What I noticed when listening and working alongside Vin, was that no broadcaster ever came into the booth better prepared than he was. Being in that particular role, I made sure that I listened carefully because he covered it so very well that there would not be a lot left for me to say about a play...or a player, and I was very mindful of that. I didn't want to be redundant in the booth.

At one All-Star game, Steve Carlton was pitching for the National League. There was a runner on first base. I seized the opportunity to squeeze in a quick fact and an observation about how good Carlton's pick-off move had been during that season for the **PHILLIES***. About that time, Carlton snapped one over to first

*P. K. Wrigley and Milton Hershey were bitter business rivals. When Wrigley bought the Chicago Cubs, Hershey tried to buy the Philadelphia PHILLIES...and sell chocolate gum. Hershey failed in both efforts.

base, and the tag was made for the out. While I was calling it, I of course called the out. Then I realized that I had done the impossible...I had stolen an out from my friend, Vin. I felt terrible. I was trying to be so, so careful and give him the space that he needs because along with being as prepared as he was, he's so eloquent. I've always wondered if I was the only broadcaster who ever stole an out from him in the radio booth.

I wouldn't say Vin and I are close friends. We are certainly friends and *friendly*. I, through the years, have had the utmost respect for Vin. Beyond a shadow of a doubt, he's the finest all-around baseball play-by-play man that I've ever heard...and that goes *way back* to a lot of great radio voices.

> **Nobody is better than Vin Scully.**

If you listen carefully, there seems to be a theme behind his preparation. Maybe something that is not known about someone's personality, Vin will go back and dig it up. I know that the last time I listened to him, he told a couple of things about a player I didn't know. I was unaware of that part of the player's history.

Vin is very interested in people when he presents a broadcast. He weaves throughout, certainly the first three innings. Then in the last three innings, he's pretty much into the game of the night. He stays very up-to-date on pennant races. He's very good about keeping up with other teams who are close, now the Diamondbacks and the Dodgers are neck and neck. Back in the early days, it was always the Giants that he was very mindful of.

Along with a specific view about the players in the game, Vin brings a broad view of what's going on, particularly in the National League...and certainly he knows what's going on in the American League too.

Vin has got the best eye of anyone I ever sat with in a baseball booth. He sees what's going on out on the field. When he takes off and reads a note or looks up a stat or a player, there's nothing going on out on the field. He does not miss important action.

All of us, as we go along—we make certain mistakes as we get older. It's still amazing to listen to him. You don't hear the first name incorrectly. If there are a couple of Crawfords out there, he'll get the first name right. He's very, very well prepared for what's about to unfold on the field.

> Vin has got the best eye of anyone I ever sat with in a baseball booth.

A lot of us get close to the players, but I don't think Vin wants to get close. This is just my feeling, but if he has to say a player makes a mistake, he doesn't harp on it.

The only player I ever remember who he had a little bit of a public spat with was a relief pitcher by the name of Mike Marshall. I don't remember the details of it. Vinnie just kind of shook his head. Recently, Vinnie was very complimentary of Lopes, Garvey, Cey and Russell. Vinnie bragged on that quartet.

He was equally as well prepared when he did the golf broadcasts. Golf is a lot like baseball in that the person who is at the center of the activity is a solo figure on the television screen. Therefore, Vinnie knows better than most that the public, especially the female part of that audience, wants to know something about the person they are watching—not just whether or not it's going to be a hit or an error, double play, or six feet from the cup, off in the rough—things like that. There is great similarity in the presentation—certainly no similarity in the two sports—one ball moves and the other is stationary, but there is a lot of similarity in the presentation. They both fit the Scully style perfectly. If there was ever another sport that I would say Vin is great at, besides baseball, it would be golf.

The one that's a little trickier for that style, because of the way we present it, is football. There you bring an analyst in after every play. You get analysis...paralysis. That doesn't fit Vinnie's style of presentation. It has nothing to do with ego or anything else...it's just that they're very different styles. There are only a handful of guys I can think of who would ever be able to do a baseball game alone like Vinnie does...and do it well. There are a lot of announcers who get up there and babble on and on and on. They can't do the kind of job Vinnie does. In a golf tournament, if you gave Vinnie the only tower seat, and let's say three roving reporters out on the course, he would do it well. It just fits his style with how he weaves in the great stories with the action.

For what Vinnie does and what he has done, nobody has ever done it better. That's for sure.

> Back in 1970, ABC immediately thought of Vinnie to do Monday Night Football...

Back in 1970, ABC immediately thought of Vinnie to do Monday Night Football broadcasts. Vinnie could not see himself working alongside Howard. That was just not something Vinnie felt would work, and he was right about it. That would not have worked...good move by Vinnie. Roone Arledge himself told me about trying to hire Vinnie.

A few years later, Roone tried to hire me to do **MONDAY NIGHT FOOTBALL***. I was just fascinated talking to him and hearing all those stories about the past, and I remember he told me that Scully was his first choice as an announcer. And, of course, they always wanted Howard in there to stir things up. I said that I didn't think our two styles meshed and Roone agreed. It took a different kind of a cat to work with Howard, let me tell you. That's a whole different story.

Howard and I were pretty good friends. I got to know him very well, and we would talk. I didn't agree with him on some things. Howard was an announcer who grew very, very bitter. If he was on the same side of an issue as you were, a lot of us would just as

*John Lennon's death was first reported to the nation by Howard Cosell on MONDAY NIGHT FOOTBALL...In 1999, Monday Night Football became the longest-running prime-time entertainment series ever, breaking a tie with Walt Disney at 29 years...Even when Monday Night Football ratings hit an all-time low, it still ranks in the top five during prime time for the entire year.

soon duck over to the other side so we didn't have to listen to him go on and on.

> We all know that there was nothing as big as the Dodgers...

Somebody in the Dodger organization wrote that Vin Scully was the most important Dodger of all time. I would concur. When baseball first came out there, Vinnie helped market that product in Southern California and made it what it is today. We all know that there was nothing as big as the Dodgers—the Rams were up and down—Raiders were up and down—Lakers probably came the closest when they had the big runs with Magic and Showtime and things like that. And USC football is big again in L.A. Because of Vin, the Dodgers are #1.

Vin Scully is somebody I admire and respect as much as anybody I've ever been around in the industry.

TAKE THIS JOB AND LOVE IT

AL MICHAELS

Al Michaels was born in Brooklyn where he grew up a Dodger fan. His family moved to L.A. the same year the Dodgers moved from Brooklyn-1958. He attended Hamilton High School in L.A. and then went to Arizona State. He began his broadcasting career in Hawaii. He was named Hawaii's sportscaster of the year in 1969. In 1971 he joined the Cincinnati Reds and in1974 moved on to the San Francisco Giants. During this time he called the 1980 Olympic Hockey games. After 30 years with ABC, he now calls Sunday Night Football for NBC.

I was 13 years old when the Dodgers left Brooklyn. Then...of all the crazy things...my father got transferred in his job to Los Angeles in 1958...so I never missed a beat. The Dodgers are going to move...and I'm heartbroken. They're moving out of Brooklyn. By that time, we were living on Long Island—I lived on Long Island for a year when I was 12. Two months after that, my father comes home and says, "Guess what? We're moving to Los Angeles."

At the time, my father was an agent working for a company called General Artists Corporation, which would now be ICN. He represented show business people, and then he wound up going to work for MCA and ran their sports division. One of the things he did was he negotiated the original American Football League television contract. To this day, I see **BUD ADAMS*** and Ralph Wilson, and I knew these guys when I was a kid.

> *When the Houston Astrodome opened in 1965, it was hailed as "The Eighth Wonder of the World." <u>BUD ADAMS</u>, the owner of the AFL's Houston Oilers (now the Tennessee Titans) agreed but said the rent was the "ninth wonder of the world."

In 1955, I was a kid living there in Brooklyn and could keep up with the World Series. They didn't play night games so we knew at four o'clock in the afternoon we were the world champions. It was phenomenal.

> They didn't play night games so we knew at four o'clock in the afternoon...

After Bobby Thompson hit the home run in '51, you know how he got home? He took a cab or a bus down to the terminal in Lower Manhattan...and went home on the Staten Island Ferry. He had just hit the most fabled home run, maybe in the history of the team, and you're going home with all the commuters on the Staten Island Ferry. Phenomenal.

Vinnie and Chick Hearn are two superhuman guys. How either of them have been able to do this is astonishing to me. I watched Chick through all the years and simultaneously with Vinnie. I listened to Vinnie when I was a kid growing up in Brooklyn.

The fact they've been able to do it and the longevity to me is astonishing. It probably speaks to a few things, one of which they both loved what they do. In Vinnie's case, I think it's probably kept Vinnie younger. He's been around the players and while he's gotten older, they've pretty much remained basically of the same age. Maybe it's like being a **HORSE TRAINER***—horse trainers live long lives as well. I think a lot of it had to do with the trainers loving what they do. They're out there with the animals in the morning, living their dreams.

I think it's the fact that Vinnie can go to a baseball game every night...yet he still has that sense of wonder where he never knows if he's going to see a perfect game or a triple play. Baseball enables you to do so many things that you don't have the opportunity to

---

*In what sport was Chris Evert the leading money winner in 1974? The answer: HORSE RACING. The owner, Carl Rosen, named his horses after tennis players. The horse named Chris Evert won $551,063 with five wins in eight starts.

---

do otherwise. The pace of the game and the way the game is played and all of the inaction between pitches enables you to do a lot of things you can't do in any other sport.

Vinnie truly has taken it to an art form and continues to do it. You can look back to 35-40 years ago and he pretty much sounded the same. He's got that style and that lilt, and the way he puts words together. It's the enthusiasm more than anything else. Vinnie *wants* to be there. He enjoys being there. He's having fun. He's having a good time. He's not bored. Obviously if he's doing a game that's 10-1, you're going to be a little bored, but Vinnie would never let that show through. There's always something. He'll find something in every interchange, to get himself more interested in the game, and by extension you become more interested in the game.

Thank God I feel pretty good right now so I try not to think of how old I am. It's a fun thing to do. Vinnie and I have had a couple of discussions through the years about what it is that we don't like. What we don't like is the traveling. He's cut back on that. I'm not doing all that much. I'm doing football on an every-week basis. I'm putting a lot of mileage on. The fact that you can spend more time doing what it is you love to do and less time in a tube flying around the country—that's good. When I look at my career right now, I think...either I'll die...or I'll just get so sick of traveling that I'd wrap it up.

I used to listen to Chick and I would think, "How is he doing this?" He still had that rapid-fire style. Chick was just a marvel. He was in his 80s and these guys were landing in places at 4:30 in the morning. This is crazy. It's the same thing—I listen to their voices. Chick's voice stayed so strong...and Vinnie's still does.

I'm not so sure it's just the voice, but it's your whole body. I try to be sure to get enough sleep. I think by extension the rest of you will be okay. That's the key. I've never had—knock on wood!—a voice issue. It's long hours...time changes...getting up early for meetings and things like that. That's the hard part.

I think Vinnie made a conscious decision about staying with one team instead of going with the networks. The *Game of the Week* is *not* what the *Game of the Week* was. We didn't know that. The network television contracts right now are all about post-season. That's what you're giving up if you don't want that. Vinnie had the chance to do his own thing. There's no such thing as Game of the Week anymore. If you have the Extra-Innings Package, you get to watch every game played. There's nothing special anymore.

> Chick was just a marvel. He was in his 80s...

I don't want to speak for Vin, but when he left the network, the network wasn't what the network was when he was doing baseball.

WASHINGTON:
FIRST IN WAR, FIRST IN PEACE
LAST IN THE NATIONAL LEAGUE

CHARLIE SLOWES

Charlie Slowes was born in Yonkers New York. He went on to graduate from Fordham University. He worked at WFUV 90.7 FM, the 50,000 watt campus radio station. Shortly after graduating Slowes got a job at KMOX radio in St. Louis. He did "everything" at KMOX—working alongside Bob Costas and the late great Jack Buck he did a variety of on air-func-tions including Cardinal baseball and Cardinal football. He is currently the play-by-play announcer for the Washington Nationals.

Vin and I do a pre-game show every other year. We have the same alma mater—both went to Fordham...many, many years apart. We had a connection in 2005 when the Nationals came into being. He was very excited that D.C. had a team. The station we're on was owned by the same company that owns the all-news station WTOP. That was Vin's first job as a summer replacement announcer in D.C.

He asked me a lot of things about whether it was located in the same place, which it wasn't. Unfortunately he hasn't come back to Washington because he doesn't travel east of the Rockies. He gave us some good memories of his time in D.C. He even had a few different commercial lines and tag lines that we used. That was a big hit with the people in D.C.

This year, when I interviewed him, we were talking about how weak the Western Division was. He had a great line. He said it reminded him of a book that was written by a Hollywood writer, *Treadmill to Oblivion.* I asked him if he missed doing the network games, and he said the only thing he missed was the chance to have a weekend where Saturday he might be doing Yankees-Red Sox at Fenway Park, and then the next day he's back with the Dodgers at Wrigley Field. He said that if you could do Fenway Park and Wrigley Field on consecutive days, that's not too bad. He said that doesn't happen very often.

Wrigley Field still has nothing but **THE ORGAN*** player and none of the crazy, loud music we have today. I'm a big fan of the old-time ball park atmosphere. I'm not into all this new entertainment stuff where it's everything but the game. We talked about that, and we have a common dislike for some of the things that go on now. But that's a sign of change and the times and all that. You almost feel like you're at an indoor laser-light show from MISL with all the stuff that goes on now with the electronic boards and the crazy music.

> I'm a big fan of the old-time ball park atmosphere.

The Vin Scully Lifetime Achievement Award, is a new honor bestowed by WFUV Radio at Fordham University. Vin said that he had won a lot of awards, and it's ironic that "they're giving me awards for my performance when my job is about describing the performance of others." I said, "How about that. We get to do this and hang out and our job is being at baseball games in these great ball parks in all these different cities." He said, "Yeah, how about that. It's a great place to hang out!"

I get along really well with the guy I work with on our broadcast. The obvious difference from Vin is that it is two people as opposed to one. When Vin stops doing it, there'll never be another one-man broadcast. The old school is if there are two people, when I'm doing my part of the broadcast, I'll see you later. They still put on a one-man show, even with two people. There are still some broadcasts like that out there now.

---

*In 1970 every major league park except two had <u>ORGANS</u>. Today less than half the parks have organs.

Tom Paciorek was an outfielder with the Dodgers in the 70s, when Walter Alston was managing. Back then, there was no such thing as headphones and Walkmen and all that. Everybody brought a transistor radio to the ball park to listen to Vin. The players on the field could hear him. If it was a sell-out crowd, there might be 30,000 radios. Manny Mota was in the on-deck circle to pinch-hit. There's one out with nobody on. The second batter makes an out so now there's two out and nobody on. Alston called Mota back to save him for when there's men on base and sends up Paciorek. As Paciorek is stepping out of the dugout for the on-deck circle, he could hear, throughout the stadium, "Well, now, with two out and nobody on, and no chance to score, Alston will switch from Mota to Paciorek." I guess Tom didn't feel too good to hear that.

> ...they have a better pool of selections of people in L.A. to sing the National Anthem than most cities...

Another time, the hitter at the plate could hear Scully saying, "It looks like they're going to throw him the fast ball." That's how bad it was with the radios on in the 70s.

One thing about going to Dodger Stadium that's different than anywhere else: they have a better pool of selections of people in L.A. to sing the **NATIONAL ANTHEM*** than most cities 'cause you've got more people there trying to have a career in entertainment than anywhere else. Anyone who sings the anthem can't go a cappella, they all have to do it with the organ player. One thing that drives you crazy now in stadiums when you're there early doing what we do is that right in the middle of the home team's batting practice, the person who sings the anthem gets to rehearse on the PA system. They might do it a couple of times. If they're bad, you've got to listen to it two or three times before the game then you hear them "be bad" for the actual National Anthem. In Dodger Stadium, they don't come down to the field and do it on

*Before Super Bowl XI, there was no "NATIONAL ANTHEM." Vikki Carr sang "America the Beautiful."

the PA system, they go to the organist's booth and do it in there with the organ player so you don't hear it in the stadium. You don't have anybody trying to do one of these three-minute National Anthems like they're on American Idol trying to start their careers. They sound better too, with the organ. The organ player pushes them along. If they're not very melodic, they are with an organ. It comes off better in Dodger Stadium.

Vin's great. He has no ego whatsoever. Houston's Milo Hamilton is completely about Milo. He's got this chair in the booth in Houston—a big leather chair he sits in—and on the back, embroidered in, it says, "HOF X 4," which means he's in the Baseball Hall of Fame, the Texas Hall of Fame and a couple of other ones. Who would put that on their chair? Also, he's made a big deal about having broadcast in the most stadiums of anyone all-time. He doesn't travel anymore, but he came on the road to D.C. because he wants to say he broadcasted in every Washington D.C. ball park. We heard earlier in the year he was concerned that Vinnie might travel to D.C. and then would eclipse him.

> Vinnie said he had no idea how many stadiums he had broadcast in, "nor do I care."

Vinnie said he had no idea how many stadiums he had broadcast in, "nor do I care." We told him Milo got all bent out of shape because "he thought you might beat him to D.C." Vinnie doesn't travel anymore—he's never even seen Milo's chair. We're in the booth at Dodger Stadium and he goes, "I guess my chair is the same as everybody else's." I said, "It is. We have the same chair." He goes, "That's a good thing."

When I saw Vin at the end of July, we were in the booth talking during the Hall-of-Fame induction ceremony on ESPN. It's going on and on and on with speeches. Bowie Kuhn steps up. The player inductees go last. Dick Williams was going in as a manager, not as a player. Vinnie was telling me, "I can't believe he's going into the Hall of Fame. I remember riding a bus with him in Spring Training. This is the guy who was the cut-up doing all kinds of goofy stuff.

Now here he is, manager of world champions, great leader of men...going into the Hall of Fame."

I've been asked to be on the selection committee at Fordham to select their next award winner. Bob Ahrens has talked to me about doing that. I said to him, "You mean you want me to select somebody after Vin. That's a Vin Scully Lifetime Achievement Award. There's nobody that's accomplished that."

In 1993, Mike Piazza's father, Vincent, and his partner in a computer company wanted to invest $27 million of the $115 million needed to move the Giants to Tampa Bay. The move was blocked by MLB. The two sued to overturn baseball's antitrust exemption. MLB paid Piazza and his partner $6 million in settlement.

MILO HAMILTON IS ONE OF THE GREATEST ANNOUNCERS OF ALL TIME. I THINK I'M QUOTING HIM CORRECTLY ON THAT

MILO HAMILTON

*Milo Hamilton was born in Fairfield, Iowa, and graduated from the **UNIVERSITY OF IOWA*** in 1949. He got his first Major League baseball job with the St. Louis Browns in 1953. When the Browns moved to Baltimore the next year, he joined the St. Louis Cardinals. He has announced for seven different big league teams. Hamilton's style can be described as enthusiastic, but not "over the top." He was the recipient of the Ford C. Frick Award from Baseball's Hall of Fame in 1992. Hamilton is also in the Radio Hall of Fame and soon will be inducted in the Texas Radio Hall of Fame. He has broadcast in 57 different Major League ball parks.*

I remember Vin first from 1954 when I was with the Cardinals, and we would travel to Ebbets Field. Harry Caray, Jack Buck and I were doing the Cardinal games. That lasted one year because the Cardinals wanted to hire Joe Garagiola. They'd been very successful with a player, Gabby Street, back in the 40s and 50s. They'd been without a player for a couple of years. Garagiola was retiring as a player so they wanted to go with him. In the meantime, the Cub job came open...so I moved to Chicago.

I came to Houston in '85 and have been here ever since. Houston has been great to me. I've gone into four Halls of Fame since I got

*Mark McGwire's brother, Dan McGwire, once a starting quarterback for the Iowa **HAWKEYES** and a former # 1 pick of the Seahawks, is the tallest NFL QB ever at 6 feet 8. Former NBA star and Toronto Blue Jay, Danny Ainge, is the tallest major league second baseman ever.

here, and it was the right move. I got the Ford Frick Award in '92, and am in the Baseball Hall of Fame.

Much like Vinnie and Jack Buck and Ernie Harwell, I made some other decisions about travel. None of us wanted to do TV because we felt that radio is a job where you're painting a picture, and you have a chance to weave some stories in if you choose to. The problem with a lot of us was that, in TV, the truck does the game...the announcer really doesn't do the game. It was funny that Buck and I decided, almost simultaneously, to leave television at the same time. I've been happy about that and Buck was also.

Vinnie, oddly enough, went the other direction. That surprised me when it happened. I thought radio was his strong suit. Of course, I'm not speaking for him. One time I asked him, and he said, "I just feel more comfortable now, not moving from one booth to the other." He has more latitude on television than a lot of us did. He has more of a say about what gets shown than we did. I don't think he's beholden to the truck like we were. It's the "Vin Scully Show." I don't think that's a slam at anybody—they want him to be comfortable. He's been with the same team for such a long time—in Brooklyn and in Los Angeles.

For Vin and me, the only difference in our careers was that because Red Barber took a liking to him, he never had to go to the minor leagues. I spent three years in the minors, '50, '51 and '52. That got me to the big leagues better prepared because we had to re-create road games. I'm not sure that Vin—and you'd have to ask him—ever re-created a baseball game. In the minor leagues, you did have to do that. Even after I got to the big leagues, both with the Cub broadcasts at WIND and later with the White Sox we still did re-creation. They had big networks in the Midwest and there was a company called General Finance Loan Company, that brokered the re-created broadcasts into the small towns.

When I was with the White Sox, for instance, in the sixties, we had 90 stations all over the place. There was nothing in Houston yet. There was nothing in Atlanta yet. Obviously nothing in Florida yet. If we were playing a night game at Old Comiskey, I had to go in that afternoon and re-create another American League game for the network for programming. If there wasn't another game, we did two hours of music and sports news. I was doing re-creations clear up to 1965 which was the year I left the White Sox to travel to Atlanta when the Braves made their move. I was the original Atlanta Braves play-by-play guy. I went there when they moved from Milwaukee.

It was a great move for me. It was all new. I had a chance there to do the **HENRY AARON*** 715th. That's my call that's played in commercials. In 2006, the All-Star campaign for State Farm Insurance used that call. I thought it would just be used around the time of the game, but they kept using it and using it, months afterward. I never understood it except that I loved it when the checks came in. It's a talent thing, and if they use my voice, they have to pay me. In the early part of this year, Hallmark did a line of memory cards, one of which is that Aaron call. These are similar to the cards they sell around Christmas that play seasonal songs. That turned out to be a nice contract. Curt Gowdy called that game too for Monday Night Baseball on NBC, and Vin called it for the Dodger broadcast. Although Vin Scully also called #715, Milo Hamilton's call of Henry Aaron's record-breaking home run is usually referred to. "He's sitting on 714. Here's the pitch by Downing...swinging...there's a drive into left center field. That ball is gonna be...outta here! It's 715! There's a new home run champion of all time—Henry Aaron!"

There were other announcers who did the Bobby Thompson call, but you couldn't name them. You only heard Russ Hodges because he was the Giant announcer.

My deal with the Astros is that I don't travel. I did go to St. Louis when they opened their new park, giving me three parks in St. Louis. I went to Tampa, having never been there. After going to D.C. and then next year the new Mets Park will give me 58 total.

*Former Notre Dame quarterback Tony Rice has been on more covers of Sports Illustrated than **HENRY AARON**...when Aaron headed the Atlanta Braves minor league operations, he cut off the pockets on the players' pants so they couldn't carry tobacco products.

As far as I'm concerned, Vin is the best ever. I don't think there's any other way to carve that. His style...his knowledge of the game...his great voice—I don't think there's any way you can not say he is the best ever. Vinnie and I have both been lucky that our voices have held up so well. We're both in our eighties. You could play a tape of us in our sixties and you couldn't tell the difference. We both have taken care of our voices. You never hear Vin use a voice that isn't his. His voice is always the same. Vin Scully knows that you just raise your voice a decibel or two, but some of these announcers who scream abuse their vocal cords.

> You could play a tape of us in our sixties and you couldn't tell the difference.

My training as a singer as a youngster and later with my courses at the University of **IOWA***, I knew you did not speak through your throat, you speak from your diaphragm. There's a difference. If you count on your whole throat to do it, you're abusing it. There have been guys in our business who have had to have nodes taken off their vocal cords and their voice started going. Vinnie and I, with some common sense, took care of our health— we weren't out closing bars after games. You never heard of a story like that about Vinnie or me because we are family men.

When I was going to stop traveling, Vinnie knew it, and he wanted to have our picture taken together in his booth. He autographed it for me.

Every time I would go to Dodger Stadium over the years—and it was a lot of years—or when Vin would come here, we made it a point to see each other and "how are you; how's your family; and #3—what about your ball club?" We picked each other's brain. We didn't have an ego that we knew everything. We weren't ashamed to say to a fellow broadcaster that we need information. I think Vinnie appreciated that, and I know I did. When my wife Arlene

---

*Between his junior and senior years at Van Meter (**IOWA**) High School, Bob Feller struck out 15 St. Louis Browns in a regular season game. Two years earlier, Feller's catcher in American Legion ball was Nile Kinnick, the 1939 Heisman Trophy winner at Iowa.

died, one of the first phone calls was from Vin Scully. And again, when my daughter died. And last fall, when I had a heart attack, I was in the hospital and my son was there monitoring the calls on our cell phones and the hospital phone, I wasn't taking any calls. The phone rang, and Mark handed me the phone and said, "I think this is a call you want to take." It was Vinnie.

> "Vinnie, Jeff Kent was with the Astros and broke Rogers Hornsby's record for home runs by a second baseman...."

Recently I called him and got his answering machine. I said, "Vinnie, Jeff Kent was with the Astros and broke Rogers Hornsby's record for home runs by a second baseman. I went up to shake his hand, and he wouldn't shake my hand. He said, 'Who was **ROGERS HORNSBY***?'" Another time, he broke the Astros' single season hitting streak record, and I went up to him and said, "Will you shake my hand now?" He said, "What for?" I said, "You just set a new franchise record for a hitting streak." He said, "I don't care about that."

Vinnie handled it just the way you knew he would. He never even acknowledged it.

Taking on Vin Scully is like taking on the pope.

Back in the 80s, when things were really hot and heavy between the Dodgers and the Astros, the fans had the little fold-out fans. These had "Beat L.A." on them and the chant. Not to put Lasorda in the limelight but a lot of people resented Lasorda. Astro fans did, and they loved to get on him when he came here.

I think the fans felt Lasorda was the "show" part of their team. When he'd go out to argue, he was a Leo Durocher in disguise. He went out and raised a lot of hell, and it made the fans get on him even more.

Leo Durocher was the "manager" here long before this time, but it may be stretching things to say he managed. He went to sleep in

---

***ROGERS HORNSBY** holds the highest single season batting average for **three** different teams: the Braves, Cubs and Cardinals.

---

the dugout.... This was when the ball club was in a lot of trouble. Spec Richardson was the general manager, and he didn't know the left-field foul pole from the suicide squeeze. He was a friend of Judge Hofheinz so the judge made him the general manager.

Walter Alston was a stern taskmaster, and a lot of people probably don't realize he was a very tough manager. I don't think the fans ever knew that. When a player got out of line, he went down in the runway and he knocked their block off. He was a tough manager. Walter was a quiet guy who didn't say a lot. I got to know him a little bit because he was a big quail hunter and so was I. When I'd see him I'd say, "How'd your bird hunting go this winter?" He'd ask me about mine. He was a great guy to talk to. You could stand around the batting cage with him. Frank Howard would put one in the upper deck, and Walter just looked at you and said, "You know. I'd like to slice that into four singles." That's the way he survived 24 years of one-year contracts!

Alston never gave the fans from the other team a chance to get on him like Tommy did. I think Tommy loved it and thrived on it. He probably wasn't even saying anything to the umpires. If truth be known, he'd say, "Boy, I've really got those fans going now."

> **Walter Alston was a stern taskmaster...**

THE POISE THAT REFRESHES

JOE MORGAN

Joe Morgan was born in Bonham, Texas. He was raised in Oakland and was a standout at Castlemont High School. He signed with the Houston Colt 45's in 1962. Morgan played well for Houston, but was traded to the Cincinnati Reds in 1971. That was the beginning of the Big Red Machine. He was ranked 60th on the Sporting News list of the 100 greatest baseball players. Currently Morgan broadcasts Sunday Night Baseball on ESPN.

Vin always had the reputation of being very fair. You knew he was rooting for the Dodgers, but you never got the feeling from the booth when you were on the field that he was really pulling for the Dodgers. He would never be biased in his calls. If I made a good play on the field, or had a good **AT-BAT***, or whatever, I know he'd always speak well of it. He would never knock an opposing player or team.

Growing up, I was always a Giant fan. I listened more to Lon Simmons and those guys, but I was a baseball fan in general. I was a small guy and never really knew I would play well enough to make the Majors, much less be the kind of player I was.

I brought that into broadcasting. I paid attention to broadcasting because I always thought I had a chance to be a broadcaster.

I didn't talk to Vin much when I started my broadcasting career. I knew more and more athletes were becoming broadcasters, but my point of view was that I always worked very hard to be a ball

---

*When the George Brett "pine tar" game was concluded, Ron Guidry was the centerfielder, and Don Mattingly was the second baseman . . . In 1974, Graig Nettles had a broken **BAT** single and six Superballs bounced from inside the bat.

player and I knew very much that I had to work hard to be a broadcaster. It wasn't going to be easy. It was a different challenge altogether. I always had a good work ethic for being a player, knowing I had the physical limitation of being a small guy. I knew I was going to have to work hard to be a broadcaster and that's the way I approached it.

The way I feel is that I'm a broadcaster *who happened to have been a player*. There are young players now who don't even know that I was a player—they don't remember me playing. I'm proud of that because I consider myself a broadcaster now. I'm 65 years old and my playing days are long gone. I think the fact that people don't even know I was a

> Growing up, I was always a Giant fan. I listened more to Lon Simmons...

player is a compliment to me. They know that I didn't get that job because I *was* a player—I got the job because I am a good broadcaster.

I was friendly with guys like Jon Miller who I work with at ESPN. He knew I was going to try to be a broadcaster. I went to **LITTLE LEAGUE WORLD SERIES*** games. I did some minor league games just to see if I was any good at it. I found that I liked it, and I found I was good at it, and I worked at it. I didn't have a very long apprenticeship because I was pretty good at it right off the bat.

Vin Scully is the Babe Ruth of what we do. The fact that he has been doing it so many years is an incredible run—for anybody in any walk of life. To still bring the freshness and the enthusiasm he has I only hope I can do that. He has such knowledge of the game. He's probably got more knowledge of the game than any other broadcaster. He's seen every possible situation. There's nothing that he sees now in a game that he hasn't seen before.

---

*At the **LITTLE LEAGUE WORLD SERIES** in Williamsport—for $16 total—a family of four can each get a ticket, program, hot dog and soda.

When I'm doing a game in L.A., Vin and I see each other and speak. We're busy preparing for our game on **ESPN***, so I'm busy with Jon Miller and don't have much of a chance to see Vin. The fact I'm working the game with Jon who, to me, is a great broadcaster by himself—that's a thrill for me. It's like working alongside two Hall-of-Fame broadcasters, being on the same level with them. I think the fact that I'm working with Jon has made me a better broadcaster 'cause he's extremely good in his own right.

> "You kept me from winning another World Series when you hit that home run for the Giants..."

One thing does come up—more with Tommy Lasorda—is the home run I hit for the Giants in a game that knocked the Dodgers out of the pennant one year. Tommy always kids me about it whenever I see him. He says, "You kept me from winning another World Series when you hit that home run for the Giants which knocked us out of the pennant."

Sparky Anderson always figured that he was the total opposite of Vin. Sparky could barely speak. Most of the time he spoke with us players, he was using curse words but he knew he couldn't do that on the air. Working with Vin was a great thing for him because he brought a lot of color to the broadcast. Vin was so straight-laced, and Sparky was just the opposite. He was a guy who knew the game inside-out and could bring a certain color to the game.

I know Vin has agreed to sign on to do another year. I'll bet he walks in there and they give him what he wants. He's been so much a part of the Dodger family, I wouldn't even think he'd need an agent. I'd think it would basically be a hand-shake situation between the Dodgers and Vin. How could you have the Dodgers without Vin Scully? It'd be like having the Vatican without the Pope.

***ESPN** debuted September 7, 1979. ESPN2 debuted October 1, 1993.
ESPN The Magazine made its first appearance on March 11, 1998.

Jeff Kent has been the same everywhere he's played. For him to belittle a guy like Vin, that's unbelievable. I can see where he's coming from, but he has no call making any disparaging remarks about Vin. What has he done for the game that exceeds what Vin has done?

I know Vin usually works alone so when he worked with Sparky, he didn't want anybody talking over him so he told Sparky that when he wanted to say something, to use a signal, and that will tell me you have something to say on the air. Jon and I don't have to do that, but I usually nod at John when I want to say something, and he will usually defer to me if I have a comment to make. We work together very well.

When I was a player, Vin would always come down around the batting cage and would chat us up. Many of the opposing team's broadcasters didn't come down on the field, Vin always was there. He would make conversation with us. He didn't get in anyone's way. He was always pleasant. You knew he was a Dodger, but you didn't care because he wasn't going to be a guy who would bring secrets back to the Dodgers...because there were no secrets. We were all doing our job—batting-cage stuff. He would talk to the players about how they'd been playing and that kind of stuff. He was almost like a fan—down there talking and interested in everything that was going on because he liked the game so much.

It meant a lot to me have role models like Vin Scully and Jon Miller, probably the two best guys in the business.

WHY CAN'T SUGAR BE AS SWEET AS VIN SCULLY?

JIM HILL

Jim Hill was a first round NFL draft pick in 1968. He played with the San Diego Chargers, Green Bay Packers and Cleveland Browns. After his playing career ended, he became an analyst and play-by-play announcer for CBS. He has worked as a sports anchor in L.A. for over 30 years and is currently with CBS 2 in L.A.

I've been around Vin for all the years I've been in Los Angeles. When Vin did the show with John Wooden at the Nokia Center, I brought 20 teen-agers from my church in Los Angeles. They had never met Vin or John Wooden, and they were in awe of meeting two people they had heard about all their lives. They were amazed at the personalities and the enthusiasm that two guys like Vin and John Wooden still had after their many years in L.A. To see Vin Scully, whose voice they had only heard before, was exciting. Vin was extremely cordial and friendly to them.

We were at the ball park one day, 10-15 years ago, in the dining room. We were all laughing and joking. I was joking with this guy, and we were laughing and horse-playing around. During the process, as we were laughing and joking, I turned away real quick. Behind me was Vinnie, who had a cup of coffee in his hand—*I spilled coffee on Vin Scully.* It was one of the most embarrassing things that has ever happened to me. In typical Vinnie fashion he said, "That's all right, Jim. It'll be okay." And then he went into the booth and did his game. Thank goodness it was on the radio!

Vinnie is everything and anything that's good about our business. Even today, I jokingly say to him, "I came to get my dose of reality." I sit on the steps right next to him, and we sit and chat for a little bit about anything and everything before the game starts. We could talk about the game...it could be sports...it could be about anything. In talking to Vin, it really does get me a dose of reality.

I remember when I was doing play-by-play for **NFL FOOTBALL***, I asked Vin, "What's the most important thing a play-by-play man should know?" Without even hesitating, Vin said, "Names and numbers." He said he would wake up in the middle of the night reciting names and numbers. He would shave, on the morning of a game, looking in the mirror, reciting names and numbers.

> Vinnie is everything and anything that's good about our business.

Being in the same town with Vin all these years has been special. When I was given a star on the Hollywood Walk of Fame a few years ago, Vin sent down a taped message to congratulate me on that. That was very memorable that Vin would take time out of his schedule to do that for me. That's one of the greatest honors I've ever received—to have Vin tape a tribute to me when I was given that star.

When I interviewed Vin, he was talking about the beginning—'58 and '59. He said, "First of all, the stage was perfect. We were in the Coliseum, and it was the birth of the transistor radio. Then the fans who came to the ball park—most of them were so far away, looking down on the field—needed a radio. All those conditions fell together and I happened to profit by it...so God has been good to me. What God did, which really overwhelmed me because I had not done anything to deserve it—he gave me the job I wanted. When I was eight years old, I wanted to do sports. He gave me the job with the Dodgers at such a young age. He allowed me to have

---

*More **NFL GAMES** have been played in the Meadowlands than any other stadium. Until 2003, Wrigley Field held the record even though Wrigley had not hosted an NFL game since 1971.

---

the health to be around as long as I've been around. I owe God everything. Really, I say that from the bottom of my heart."

Then I asked Scully where this gift came from to turn words into pictures. Vin said, "I love to read—not necessarily high-brow books—but I just love to read. When we're on the road, a good book is like having your wife with you because you look forward to getting back to the room, and you don't want to leave to go to work." The one thing I tell people—"Remember I haven't accomplished anything. Really. What I do is spend my time talking about the accomplishments of others." That's my job.

> I went on to ask him where, "pull up a chair," came from.

I went on to ask him where, "pull up a chair," came from. He said, "I don't even know how it evolved where one day I was just speaking and I said 'Pull up a chair.' After I said it, I wondered 'Gee where did that come from?' But that's kinda nice. You're saying to someone, 'Hey, sit down. Let's chew the fat. Let's watch the ball game together.' Where that came from I don't know. Once in a while, I kick myself in the fanny because a lot of times you get in the car going home and you're thinking, 'Gee, man, I really blew that. I should have done.... I should have said....' One of my favorite writers was a humorist who appeared in movies in the thirties, Robert Benchley. He wrote a small piece one time years ago, and it was called, "Take the Witness." He had been on the stand and had just blubbered and made a complete mess of things. Going home, he's dreaming about how it should have been on the witness stand...but of course, the moment is gone. I've always related to that."

Vin mentioned one of his very early games: "Years ago, when I was single and going out with a lot of college guys and girls, I did some game and then went to a party. One of the fellows said, "Boy, I heard your broadcast today. That really must be hard. *You go hard!*" It's not supposed to sound hard. It's supposed to sound like the easiest thing in the whole world. Just sitting there talking—and that's what you try to do."

Vin ended the interview with something Vince Lombardi wrote on the wall in Green Bay, "I believe in God and human decency, and I firmly believe that any man's finest hour to total fulfillment, to all he holds dear, is that moment he lies on the field of battle exhausted yet victorious." Then Vin said he knew Vince reasonably well. Vin said, "Lombardi went to Fordham. He was one of the 'Seven Blocks of Granite;' I went to Fordham. When I was there, he was the quarterback's coach of the Fordham football team, coming from St. Cecelia High School in New Jersey. The head coach at Fordham in those days was Ed Danowski who had played very well for the New York football Giants. Vince was totally unheard of. Then of course, he went to the Giants and Green Bay and the Redskins and he became bigger than life."

THE GIANTS THINK THAT BASEBALL IS LIKE GOLF: LOW SCORE WINS

LON SIMMONS

Lon Simmons came to San Francisco in 1957 as the color announcer for the 49ers where he worked with Bob Fouts, Dan Fouts' father. He took over play-by-play in 1958. Simmons started calling San Francisco Giant games in 1958. He received the 2004 Ford C. Frick Award—given by the Base-ball Hall of Fame. In 2006, he was elected to the Bay Area Radio Hall of Fame. His trademark home-run call was "tell it goodbye." He semi-retired in 2002 and now lives in Maui.

When we were both broadcasting, I would talk to Vin every time our teams played. When he was working with Jerry Doggett, he would play golf whenever they came to San Francisco. We also played together down South. Vinnie would sometimes round up some celebrities, but it was usually Vinnie, Jerry and me.

A few years ago, I walked into the cart shop and the guy said, "Hey, your cart is over there, and Mr. Scully's bag is on the cart." I went over and it had a ball retriever in it. I told the guy, "Tell Vinnie if he doesn't have enough golf balls, I've got plenty of extra ones if he needs some. I didn't know he went around with a ball retriever." I was on the fourth hole, and he was over on the fairway. I yelled at him and said, "I didn't know you had to have a ball retriever." He said, "Yeah. In fact, I've had to have it re-gripped three times." In the early years, when the Dodgers would come through Phoenix in the spring, Vinnie, Jerry, and Ross Porter and I would play.

I remember when Fresno State played Bowling Green in a foot-ball game in the L.A. Coliseum for the benefit of the Cal-Poly team after their plane had crashed. Vinnie and I announced the game. Each of us did a half. This must have been in the early or mid-sixties. I was doing the 49ers at the time and was the only one of us doing football. Up until this time, I don't know if Vinnie ever did a lot of football. He came on and did his half and it sounded like he'd been doing football his entire life. I was really impressed at how he did.

Vin went over and played St. Andrews in Scotland. It was raining and the wind was blowing. His caddy had a big wool coat on. They played several holes and the **CADDY*** said, "I'll tell you, laddie, if you were back home, would you be playing in weather like this?" Vinnie said, "No." The caddy said, "Well, why don't we go to the bar?" So that's what they did.

> He came on…and it sounded like he'd been doing football his entire life.

When the Dodgers and Giants announced they were coming west—'57—I got the job to work with Russ Hodges. Vin had already been working in Brooklyn, and he came out with the team for the '58 season. The Dodgers didn't use television much when they started out here. They only televised from San Francisco. At that time, the transistor radio was becoming popular and people would bring them to the ball park. I have heard when a guy would even bring his transistor to the opera and listen to Vin do the Dodgers. People also brought them to Giants games but nothing like the people in L.A.

One time Vin and I were playing golf at my home club, California Club, up in the Bay area. The ninth hole there is a fairly long, par-four dogleg up a hill. If you hit it up on top of the hill, you have a level shot into the green. It's a pretty good drive to get it up there. We all hit our balls and they appeared to be in the fairway. We went up there, and we found three of them. We didn't find Vinnie's golf ball. We looked and looked and looked. Finally we went driving off because we gave up on finding it. About 75 yards farther down the fairway was Vinnie's ball. We said, "Damn, we

*The Professional **CADDIES** Association (PCA) has 2,800 members and is headquartered in Palm Coast, Florida. Until 2002, the PCA's Hall of Fame was located in founder Dennis Cone's Winnebago.

knew you hit it good, but we didn't think you hit it that good." We're praising him for hitting his drive that far...it turns out that our caddy-master who was sort of a jokester was up there. We couldn't see him because he was up on the hill. He didn't know whose ball it was, but he picked it up and threw it clear down the fairway. Here we thought Vinnie had hit about a 350 yard drive. The caddy-master told me about what he had done the next time I went to the golf course to play. I asked him, "Do you realize we were playing for money?" It didn't bother him...he didn't care. He was a character! I don't remember if I ever did tell Vinnie what happened. We knew he had hit a good one...we also knew he didn't hit it *that* good! So Vin had this nice easy shot onto the green while the rest of us were hitting a fairway wood to get there. He probably hit a medium iron. So the caddy had a pretty good arm; he threw it a long way.

> I could hear Michaels' voice and it sounded just like Vinnie's.

When I was living in Palm Springs, after my first wife passed away, I went over to Dodger Stadium. Scully was in one booth, and there was an empty booth, and then the Giant broadcast booth was over to the left. I sat in the booth in between. I could hear Al Michaels and I could hear Scully. I went to Vinnie and said, "You know, Vinnie, this is the first time I've ever heard you broadcast in stereo." I could hear Michaels' voice and it sounded just like Vinnie's. After that, Michaels worked on his style so that he did not sound like Vinnie, but when he first started, he sounded a great deal like Vinnie.

I was driving to Los Angeles and was going through Fresno, where I'd done Fresno State sports previously. I turned on the Fresno station, and I heard Vinnie doing the Fresno State baseball games. I said, "What's going on here?" I listened to an inning, and the guy didn't say his name. But I thought everything sounded exactly like Vinnie. I called my friend who lived in Fresno and said, "What's going on? Did Scully come down here and sit in and do a couple of innings?" He said, "No, the guy who does the Fresno State baseball sounds so much like Scully that when you tune in, you'd think it's Scully." It sounded like Vinnie to me as I was driving through there. I thought maybe he'd stopped by and was just doing a guest spot or something on the broadcast.

Scully has a very distinctive style. The kids who are impressionable grow up listening to him. If they grow up to be broadcasters, they capture his rhythm and his style and his expressions. They have developed that listening to him. Consequently, there were a lot of them who sounded like Vinnie. Michaels—he'll never admit it—did sound like Vinnie. Al got away from that. I don't know whether he got away from it just because he dropped into his own way of doing things or he deliberately did it. I never questioned him about it because I knew it was a sore spot with him. He did sound like Vinnie. That time when I was at Dodger Stadium, I could listen to one side and then the other, and both of them sounded like Vinnie.

I interviewed Vinnie two years ago and questioned him about people and asked if imitation was a form of flattery. I asked him if he was flattered by the people who imitated him. He said, "Well, I do, if they're not making fun of me." I didn't take it any further than that.

> He does a Japanese announcer doing Vin Scully.

Jon Miller, who does a good imitation of Vinnie, is a great broadcaster and is a great mimic. He's highly talented. He does a Japanese announcer doing Vin Scully. He does an exaggerated Vin Scully.

Vinnie has been able to step into any venue and do his own unique style. There's no doubt about it. He brings a more erudite approach to "broadcasting" than most people do. He does a heck of a job. He works at it, and it shows that he works at it. The man is just great—that's all. Vinnie does several innings of simulcast. Vinnie works by himself—he doesn't want two voices on the air. When he was in the broadcast booth, he wanted one voice on at a time; consequently, he didn't want anyone else with him.

He's the tops in his field, and I would say, at the moment, Jon Miller is probably number two to him.

WHY DOES HAWAII HAVE INTERSTATES?

MARK ROLFING

A 1972 graduate of DePauw University in Greencastle, Indiana, Rolfing has worked as a golf reporter for NBC and ABC since 1988, when he provided commentary for the coverage of the Bob Hope Chrysler Classic. He began his commentating career at ESPN in 1986. He hosts Golf Hawaii, a 30-minute magazine format golf and travel show, on the Golf Channel. Following a successful high school and college golf career, Mark turned professional in 1973 and spent two years competing on professional tours in Europe and Asia.

When I started as a golf commentator, I was scared to death. Vin was like a father-figure to me in a lot of ways because I was a little bit ahead of the curve in terms of a player who didn't have a great playing record to become an announcer. Back then, you pretty much had to have won a major championship...even the on-course guys, Bob Goalby, for example, and Bob Rosburg. It was a little bit of a risk on NBC's part and was pretty much uncharted territory.

Vin was great. He couldn't have been more helpful and kind to me. He was always concerned about how I was doing. He went out of his way constantly to help me become a better communicator.

We had official production meetings. We had some dinners where there was business done and some socializing. Vin always took the time, one-on-one, to help me. He always encouraged me to ask him questions if I had any concerns. The biggest thing I needed to learn was how the television part of the business actually ran. I didn't even know what an IFB was. It is a sound system that allows you to hear the program and the producer at the same time.

I remember having a discussion with Vin about "learning how to talk while you were listening." A lot of times your producer or director or maybe even a couple of people, at the same time, will be talking to you, and you have to continue your conversation while you are listening. So talking and listening at the same time is an art. Nobody listens as much as they should. Vin helped me with that a lot.

The first time I was in a booth with Vin was in Hawaii, and that was before I went to work for NBC. That was in the mid-eighties, and that was my big break. The round was on a Friday. Back then, the announcers announced on ESPN as well as NBC. Vin and Lee Trevino were in the booth.

> When I started as a golf commentator, I was scared to death.

I shot a pretty good score that day and, being a local guy, it was a good story, so they brought me up to the booth for an interview. Back then, you didn't have guests in the booth. That's not what they did. If you shot a good score, they asked you a couple of questions about your round by the 18th green and sent you on your way. In this case, being a local guy, and involved in putting the tournament together, Vin was thinking there may be a story here. He invited me up to the tower.

When I got up there and we were talking, there was a ruling to be made on the course. It was the 16th hole, and there was a lateral hazard that goes right up the middle of the hole. There were questions as to what was happening and what the rule was and what the options were. I basically sat in there and talked about it, which was pretty unusual. It was Vin that led me into it.

In the middle of the interview, they had to cut away to go to this ruling, and I think normally they would kick the guy out of the booth at that point, "See you later—we're done." But Vin didn't do that. We talked about it a little more, while they were still making this ruling, about the uniqueness of the course. It was a good 15 minutes, which is a lot. Vin, Lee Trevino and I just sat there all that time and had a three-way conversation. I don't remember that having ever happened in televised golf before. It may have, but I hadn't seen it.

After the ruling, I came down from the tower...they were still on the air. I went ahead and did the things I had to do. Don Ohlmeyer called me not an hour after they were off the air and said, "Will you come back up tomorrow? You were fabulous." I said, "Okay...like, no matter what I shoot?" He said, "No matter what you shoot. I want to see you up there tomorrow." That was the first guest appearance I can remember, not only for me, but for anybody.

> **Don Ohlmeyer called me not an hour after they were off the air...**

I shot something "not very good" the next day. I went up to the booth and did two segments with them. Then the next day, Sunday, I did it again. I was a guest analyst, sitting right next to Vin both times.

Vin Scully is one of my idols. I was so nervous filling in there. I thought, "Why would he ever agree to do this? Why would he ever want to have a guy whose biggest win in his golf career is the Hawaii Assistant Professional's Championship?" For some reason, Vin and I connected. It's all because of him. He took me in.

When the week was over on Sunday, Don Ohlmeyer asked me to go to work the next weekend for him on ESPN on the World Cup. He hired me for this one-event deal...and after that event, he hired me for the whole year. I told him, "Don, I'm a nobody. This is not the way this business works." This was breaking old tradition. Don had a lot to do with it...but so did Vin.

When I left Vin on that Sunday, I went to work for Ohlmeyer at ESPN. I was there a year and a half before Larry Cirillo called and hired me for NBC. The first event I worked was the Bob Hope in 1988, and Vin Scully was the host. I remember him saying, "My God, you've done it." He hugged me, and I probably hadn't seen him in more than a year. When I was working at ESPN, he was working for NBC.

Vin Scully and I did Senior Skins in Hawaii. We must have announced that four or five years from 1992 to '95. Back then, we only had two announcers—there was no analyst. It was Vin and Mark—Mark was on the course with the players, and Vin was in the booth.

Vin and I had some amazing times with the Senior Skins. These were two-day deals. It was always Arnold Palmer, **JACK NICKLAUS*** and either Trevino, Floyd or Player, depending on who had won the year before. We all hung out together. It was phenomenal. That was on The Big Island.

I was in college at DePauw University with Dan Quayle, who still is one of my best friends. When he became the Vice President, all of a sudden his college career was better than it really was. I still see Dan every year at the American Century Celebrity Championship in Lake Tahoe, Nevada. I continually say to him, "The older you get, the better golfer you were." I spent a lot of time in Washington when he was the Vice President, and he and I went to a lot of places. The problem was that I had the key to the treasure chest for Dan Quayle stuff. When he got nominated in '88, I was in Montana—and I'll never forget it as long as I live—I had *Time Magazine, Newsweek,* everybody, because they knew that I knew a lot of stuff. I made a pact with myself that I was going to forget everything I knew. A couple of guys sold him out, but I was never going to do that.

I don't see Vin much anymore, because we go in different directions. He helped me a lot in the early years. He may not realize that, but he really did.

> Nobody could describe it *like him.*

Vin loved being out there, but golf was never really his game. The thing I liked about playing golf with Vin was listening to his commentary. Listening to his reaction to what he was doing was just out of this world. Nobody could describe it *like him.*

*Only three people have ever appeared on Scotland's five-pound note: Queen Elizabeth II, the Queen Mum, and JACK NICKLAUS.

WORKIN' WITH VIN WAS LIKE PLAYING HOOKY FROM LIFE

TOMMY HAWKINS

Tommy Hawkins was born in Chicago and went to Parker High School before playing basketball at the University of **NOTRE DAME***. *He was selected in the first round of the 1959 NBA draft by the Minneapolis (later Los Angeles) Lakers. Hawkins had a productive ten-year career. He later spent 18 years with the Los Angeles Dodgers serving as both VP of Communications and External Affairs.*

Vin has always been the darling of the community. He was immediately adopted by Greater Los Angeles as the voice that ushered the Dodgers into the community, and it was Vin who made sure that the team became an integral part of everything that was going on. You didn't move without Vin Scully.

The Lakers came to L.A. in '60. As a matter of fact, the Dodgers came here in '58. They came well equipped with everything they needed to succeed...but they didn't succeed in '58. In 1959 they won the World Series title against the **CHICAGO WHITE SOX***, which was my team. I loved the Sox players: Minnie Minoso, Luis

---

*The Oakland A's copied their green and gold colors from **NOTRE DAME**. When LaPorte, Indiana native Charles O. Finley bought the Kansas City A's in the 60s, he changed the colors to honor his friend, former Irish coach Frank Leahy...The Green Bay Packers took the Notre Dame colors because Curly Lambeau played at Notre Dame.

---

*In 1944 the Chicago White Sox played forty-three doubleheaders. Last year, they played one...In March 1954 the Lakers and the Hawks played a regulation, regular season NBA game using baskets that were 12 feet high rather than the usual 10 feet...the next night they played each other in a doubleheader. True facts, believe them or not!

Aparicio, Jungle Jim Rivera, and Nellie Fox—my favorite tobacco-chewer—he always had that big wad of tobacco in his jaw. When the Dodgers won the Series, they flew back on a private plane, which was met by tens of thousands of people at the airport, and were given a ticker-tape parade up and down Broadway in downtown Los Angeles. They got an official welcome on the steps of City Hall. The year after they won the World Series, we came to town. We being The Lakers.

No announcer. New head coach. We drove in through San Bernadino at midnight in our individual cars and no one knew we were here and nobody gave a damn. The first year, we didn't even have radio coverage. It wasn't until the end of the year, when we made the playoffs, that we finally got radio coverage, and Chick Hearn was hired to do the play-by-play—at the *end of the year!*

The Dodgers came with great reputation. And they came with a young Vin Scully, who was then already eight years into his broadcasting career and was the hand-picked person of Red Barber and had secured his position. Vinnie ushered the Dodgers into Los Angeles from a broadcasting standpoint and solidified their position as a major factor in this community.

> Chick Hearn was hired to do the play-by-play— at the *end of the year!*

When I worked for the Dodgers, I saw Vinnie every day during the season. Tommy Lasorda, Vin Scully, Jaime Jarrin, Don Drysdale and I would all sit together at dinner before the game. I was vice president of communications. We had the deployment of the press box and everything else.

Vinnie would see me and would always have that warm, ingratiating smile. "Tommy, my boy, how we doing?"

Vinnie would laugh at the players, the coaches, Tommy Lasorda—he's a master storyteller, a master talker and broadcaster...he's also a master listener. He wouldn't interrupt you while you were telling your story, and you'd love to be quiet while he was telling his.

> **If he had been a writer, he would have been a Shakespeare.**

I've probably seen Vinnie outside of the broadcast booth about as much as anyone else.. Tommy Lasorda and I were doing 80 or 90 speaking engagements a year. On many of those occasions, we shared the podium with Vinnie. I've never seen Vinnie mess up—never. Vinnie is a verbal artist. If he had been a writer, he would have been a Shakespeare. If he had been a painter, he would have been a Rembrandt. That is the art that Vinnie possesses within himself. He's a verbal poet. I've interviewed Vinnie myself when I was with KABC and was doing Dodger Talk, Dodger Confidential, Baseball Spotlight—all those different shows.

I look at it this way. Basketball is 82 games a year. Football is 16 games a year. Baseball is 162 games a year, plus post-season. No sport is in our lives to the extent that baseball is. Vinnie describes baseball as America's favorite pastime because baseball, he said, is a universal experience. He said everybody has thrown a baseball, caught a baseball, swung a baseball bat. He said most of the nation has probably never picked up a hockey stick or shot a hockey puck. Few of us really know how to kick a football. Few of us are adept at passing a football. "What's the first game that's played at a picnic?" Vinnie paints these verbal pictures for you, and he'll put them out there so you can see them...a part of his success is that he paints these pictures. He's telling me why baseball is so universally admired and accepted, and he said, "What is the first thing that is usually put in a baby's crib?" A ball or a small plastic bat the baby can swing and tap with.

"What is the universal game that most of us, sometime in our life, have played?" He also said another thing, "Baseball allows the viewer, the fan, a chance to totally involve themselves in the game. Everybody who watches a game knows that they can manage better than the manager. They don't necessarily coach the football team or the hockey team or the basketball team, but the baseball manager is probably the most questioned person alive?" He says that baseball provides the fans a socialization that most sports don't. If you're sitting at a basketball game, if you take a break, you miss a play. If you're at a football game, you're cold and you're watching and there's not that much time for great social exchange. In baseball, you can sit and visit with your neighbor.

Who are the people who are most remembered in terms of calling games? Baseball announcers. The king of that group—Vin Scully.

I would tell people that, if a dog got loose and was running across the baseball diamond, I'd want to hear Vinnie call that action because I know I'm going to get that action in a way that's accurate and personable and entertaining. You could take it to the bank every time.

> **You treat every game as if it were your first.**

Vinnie told me something that I tried to incorporate into every broadcast. You treat every game as if it were your first. You never cheat on your profession. Vinnie never comes unprepared. Vinnie always gets there at a certain time that allows him to do the things that he needs to do to be ready to call that game.

There are rules about who can come into the press box. Everybody wants to meet Vin Scully. We hear that request all the time. Vinnie is very professional and would say hello to people as much as he could, but never to the point that he was going to let it distract from what he did. Everybody wants to see, touch or meet Vin Scully.

I have had the pleasure of being associated with the two greatest announcers that any city could ever have—Vin Scully and Chick Hearn.

CANDLESTICK PARK: WHERE THE DODGERS PRACTICED FOR THEIR REALLY IMPORTANT GAMES

HANK GREENWALD

Hank Greenwald, a Syracuse grad, became the "Voice of the Giants" in 1979. Perhaps to repay a debt to Satan, he did a two-year-stint with the Yankees in '87-'88. After eight more years with the Giants, he retired in 1996 and was replaced by Jon Miller.

Like everybody else, the first time I met Vin Scully, I was in awe. I had met him briefly a few times before I started with the Giants as a broadcaster in 1979. I was always impressed by the way Vin made you feel...as if you were one of his colleagues. He never made you feel like you were just a young guy starting out in the business. He'd come over and talk to you like he had known you. He'd ask you questions. He made you feel very welcome and a part of the business. There were a great many people with lesser credentials who didn't have the ability to do that. It certainly made a lasting impression on me—his personality and his kindness—and one that I feel even transcended his work as a broadcaster. That's the first thing that comes to mind about Vin.

I worked at Candlestick Park, which may have been the worst place in the world, not only to play a game, but certainly to broadcast, as well. I thought it was a terrible place. We used to work with the windows open. It was one of those traditional things you did...to get a feel for the game. At night it was cold...it was windy, and it blew your papers all around. It distracted you constantly as a broadcaster.

I'd been with the Giants about four years. We were playing the Dodgers on a Friday night at Candlestick. All of a sudden, during one of these typical Candlestick nights, I look over at the booth to my right. There's Scully -he's got the window closed. He's comfortable. He's broadcasting the game. No papers are blowing around. He's doing his work. I'm thinking to myself, "Now I know why this guy is in the Hall of Fame, and I'm going to be working the rest of my life." He's figured it out—*to heck with this*. I'd rather be comfortable than to sit there, for the sake of being macho, with the windows open at Candlestick Park. From that point on, I thought, "If it's good enough for Vin, it's good enough for me."

All that matters is the finished product. For the guy sitting at home listening...he doesn't care whether you've got the windows open or have the windows closed...he just wants to hear the broadcast. He wants to hear the best effort you can give. If you can do your best job with the windows closed, close the windows.

> ...the first time
> I met
> Vin Scully,
> I was in awe.

Even to this day, there are guys who still believe you "gotta feel the action." Well, that's a lot of baloney.

From time to time, Vin and I have sat in the press room at Dodger Stadium and eaten together, but we never played golf. I don't think, all the years I was around, that I played much golf in Los Angeles. I used to take my clubs to cities where there was less to do. I didn't bring them to L.A. very often.

I guess one of the drawbacks to working baseball is that you don't get to hear your colleagues because you are generally working at the same time. Having grown up in the East, as I did, and having gone to college in the East, I did have the opportunity, as a young person, to listen to Vin back in the Brooklyn days. It was obvious from the start that this guy was a cut above everybody else.

He started out with Red Barber and was working in the same market as Mel Allen, and, even in the midst of those all-time greats, Vin still managed to make a name for himself...which was quite an accomplishment.

I always get to the ball park three hours before game time. I would see Vin around the dugout and the batting cage before the game.

He said, "The O'Malleys have been like family to me."

Since I have retired, I've had the opportunity to listen to Vin on XM radio and on satellite TV. I'm totally impressed with how contemporary Vin remains to this day. Obviously, an announcer has to know the names and information about the team you are working for, but Vin is really up on things. He's not a guy who is living in the past. It's easier keeping up with what's going on now, but, Vin remains very much on top of what is happening today...all the more credit to him.

There are times when the announcers work in booths next door to each other, and will look at one another and shake our heads or roll our eyes. We see things at the same time and probably share the same thoughts about it.

One time, Vin and I were talking. I would get a little bit frustrated from time to time about things that would happen—not so much during games, but maybe with the state of baseball or travel—things like that. I remember one day in Los Angeles saying to Vin, "How do you keep going?" He'd been doing it about 50 years by then! I said, "How do you do it? How do you just keep going?" He said, "The O'Malleys have been like family to me." This was when Peter still was running the club, many years after Walter had died. "Peter is like a brother to me. They treat me very nicely here. They make my life a lot easier."

Vinnie did PGA Golf during the off-season. He did football, much of which would also have been off-season. He may have missed a weekend game occasionally, possibly, but I don't think he missed many. He told me one time that he had six kids to put through college, so....

I'll always think of Vin as a guy who "what you see is what you get!" There's no pretense about him. He's just a good guy...and a great broadcaster.

I'm totally retired. I think we can safely say I've finally found something I do well! Doing nothing. More than anything else, I listen to my son's game on the Internet. He's broadcasting in Fresno. That keeps me going.

When I first started working full-time, I worked with Lindsay Nelson for the first three years. One of the things he told me was, "Don't get caught up in wins and losses, because if you've got a bad ball club, you're going to sound the way they play. You can't let that happen to you." You hope your team does well...you just can't let that creep into your broadcast. You can't get down. You've got to be better than they are on the field. You've got to be better in the booth than the team is on the field because you have no control over what the team does on the field, but you do have control about what you do in the broadcast booth. Just because it's a bad game, doesn't mean it has to be a bad broadcast. Your job is to make it a good broadcast.

> You've got to give people a reason to want to listen.

You've got to be able to do that outside of the performance of the club. Once you learn that, then you can survive bad seasons. You've got to give people a reason to want to listen.

WE'LL BE BACK RIGHT AFTER THIS

CBS hired Vin Scully to do just about everything on their sports schedule, including golf. Vinnie went right to the 18th tower and became my anchor man. He worked with Ken Venturi.

I had a few problems with Vinnie in that he was not exactly a "picture" person. Vinnie was a radio guy. I had some words with him early on about this being a visual medium. Sometimes what you're saying is obtuse because the viewers can already see what you're talking about. In other words, I had some very firm rules about what you never were allowed to say. For instance, "He missed the putt"...because everybody at home is saying "really?" They already see that—you don't have to tell them that. Or "The ball is rolling across the green." These were little things that I had to get through to Vinnie.

> I had a few problems with Vinnie in that he was not exactly a "picture" person.

Vinnie, early on, was at Fordham. Two of his mentors were both named Red. One was a writer and one was a broadcaster. Red Barber was the broadcaster; Red Smith the writer. They were the types of people that Vinnie patterned himself on. He became a wordsmith. Sometimes, on television, that gets in the way, even though Vinnie still has that great ability to turn a mundane fact into something interesting. He's a poet laureate in broadcasting...there's no question about that. He's an absolute joy to work with. Too many broadcasters today have a tendency to inundate the airwaves with clichés and mundane statements. This is something Vinnie never did. Vinnie was very particular about the usage of the English language, thank God!

All broadcasters have monstrous egos and any instruction and/or criticism you would give them would be private. Talent without ego is not talent.

—FRANK CHIRKINIAN, retired legendary Director of Golf at CBS

Vin Scully was always extraordinarily cordial. He fit very well into the team. There was a lot of controversy about his being brought in. It caused a lot of friction because the other guys who got displaced, namely Pat Summerall and Jack Whittaker were annoyed. Whittaker left and went to ABC. It was a troublesome move in one sense, but Vinnie was such a good guy that he fit in. I personally had a delightful relationship with him; although he upset me at times because he wasn't really a golf man like he is a baseball man. I don't think I've ever heard anybody better because I didn't know Red Barber. I wasn't around long enough here to appreciate him....but I do appreciate Vin Scully on baseball. I never heard anything better—and I love baseball, by the way. Unfortunately, I love the Braves, but....

Production meetings for us were dinners with the finest wines. Vinnie fit in well. We discussed our differences and discussed what was important to us *over dinner*. It was a very civilized existence. Mr. Frank Chirkinian was again to thank for that. We used to call him "our American Express card,"—*don't leave home without him.* He would buy us the finest

> We used to call him "our American Express card,"— *don't leave home without him.*

wines and the finest foods at the best restaurants. We didn't really have production meetings. People who didn't fit in and who didn't want to come out drinking with us were not included in these dinners, so usually we only had six or eight people there.

I worked every tournament that Vinnie worked at CBS, but I can't remember how many years that was.

Vinnie must have had a "sweetheart" arrangement with the Dodgers that enabled him to work the summer golf tournaments. I don't know any of the arrangements, but at times the sports were not compatible. We would do 10-20 tournaments a year and would be on the road for weeks on end.

I played golf with Vinnie a few times. He was left-handed, and he was not very good. He sprayed the ball all over Bel Air. I regarded all left-handers, in those days, as a bloody nuisance because you're always standing on the wrong side of them. In those days, left-handers were very rare...there was no one on the tour that was any good at all. Have you ever seen a left-handed female golfer?

Back then, we played all the Pro-Ams we were going to broadcast that week because they put us in to bring in people. We'd sign a lot of autographs and get to know the golf course. Then, when the financial thing became a little tighter, they gave all the Pro-Am spots to the Sales Department so they could give them to their best clients....so we got the "bum's rush." Vinnie played in those earlier Pro-Ams. We played in President Ford's tournament among things on the side. Verne Lundquist was another bad golfer that we tried to avoid.

There was a lot of talk about Vin, a baseball man, being there on the golf scene. He had to suffer that. What can you do? He has a job to do...and he did it...and he did it very thoroughly. No one ever was better researched than Vinnie. He would do his homework with a

religious fervor. I liked that very much about the man. He never, never came to the tower unprepared. The fact was, of course, that he wasn't intimately in the golf game, like we were, people like myself who'd been around the game all my life, brought up in it, came through the International boys' ranks and stuff like that. Vinnie was, in a sense, an outsider. You did sense that attitude, "What's this baseball guy doing here?" That was fairly prevalent.

But you're going to get that. They said it about Summerall, the football guy. They also said it about Lundquist being a jack-of-all trades. There were fewer golf people. For instance, Whittaker in horse racing. Melnyk and I were the only guys out there who did nothing else but golf. We basically drafted in people from contractual obligations, as they said. On occasion, they drafted in people like Gary Bender who knew very little about golf.

The point was that Vinnie stayed longer than any of them because he was so well-prepared.

>   —BEN WRIGHT, a native of England, he broadcast golf on CBS
>   for 23 years and now lives in North Carolina

In the 1992 season, the Dodgers lost 99 games. I used to write for a Dodger newspaper called "Big Blue Review." It was a monthly publication, and I did a feature column in it.

When the Dodgers were coming off their 99-loss season, the following spring training, I wrote an article about the fact that as much as I was upset about the Dodgers poor season, when I hear the voice of Vin Scully, it revives me. I was born in 1958, the year the Dodgers came to Los Angeles. I can honestly say that I have listened to the Vin Odyssey my entire life.

About two months after the article was printed, I get a card in the mail from Vin Scully. I was still relatively new in the business and had never met Vin outside of passing. In the card, Vin thanked me for the kind words I wrote about him in this article. I was just flabbergasted that: one—he had even seen the article; and two—that he would take the time to write me a thank-you card.

One day, I left my briefcase in an outdoor patio area where I used to do my radio show in Santa Monica. Somebody stole it. The only item in there that I was upset about losing was the thank-you card from Vin.

Fast-forward to about 10 years later. Jim Hill and I are doing Sports Central on CBS 2, in Los Angeles, and Jim had done an interview with Vin Scully. After we played the interview, I talked about what a wonderful man Vin Scully is, and how it is that someone of his stature could be so nice, while other people of far less importance in our business seemed to think so much of themselves.

About two weeks later, in my mail, I got a card from Vin Scully which said, "Dear Steve, Once again I find myself thanking you for your kind words. Life is too short to not say "thank you."—Vin Scully." I had that card framed, and it is in my office right now.

These are the kinds of things about Vin Scully that I make clear to everybody. This is such a genuine guy, such a wonderful man—beyond, obviously, being the best of all time in what he does. That card is in my office and definitely is a reminder to me that life is too short to not say "thank you."

I had been so sad when, 10 years earlier, I had lost that first card he sent me. I thought how could I ever replace something like that? It's not like, "Hey Vin, can you write me a thank-you card?" Without even mentioning anything about it, it just so happened that he wrote me a second card...this time I was not going to lose it.

—STEVE HARTMAN, Trivia Expert, former Los Angeles
Raiders Executive, Radio Sports Talk Show Host

Tom Harmon was on a plane flying to Minnesota for a World Series, seated next to Vin Scully. The stewardess asked Tom, "Aren't you on television?" Tom Harmon said, "No. he is," and pointed to Scully. "You mean you don't know who this man is?" interrupted Scully. He nudged his seatmate, "Go ahead. Tell her." "All right," said Tom Harmon, importantly, "Ricky Nelson's father-in-law." He also was Mark Harmon's father, John Delorean's father-in-law and the 1940 **HEISMAN TROPHY*** winner at Michigan.

I was on the field gathering information for Chris Schenkel's nightly radio show on ABC. I was doing actualities. I would write all five shows on Sunday, and Chris would come in on Monday and tape them. I went up to Maury Wills and asked if he would mind doing a little bit for Chris Schenkel's show. He said, "Okay." I asked him a question—but I used a very big word in the question and he turned around and walked away from me.

Here is my reporting of it: Maury Wills, the temperamental shortstop of the Los Angeles Dodgers, was in the process of setting a Major League base-stealing record. We were in the dugout before a game, and I explained the format of the Chris Schenkel show. Holding the microphone up to him, I asked, "Is your acute facility in getting a jump on the pitcher due to an innate anticipatory sense?" He either didn't understand what I said or misinterpreted it. He quickly wheeled and walked away without another word, leaving me with an empty mic and an interview lesson— Leave the polysyllabic palaver to **HOWARD COSELL***.

—MURRAY OLDERMAN, 86, author, retired columnist for the
Newspaper Enterprise Association

> *What HEISMAN TROPHY winner has made the most money? The 1959 winner, Billy Cannon of LSU, was arrested for counterfeiting in the early '80s and spent almost three years in jail. Technically, he is the only Heisman Trophy winner to ever "make" money.

> *When former ESPN and current NFL Channel anchor Rich Eisen was in college, his standup comedy routine included reading "Letters to Penthouse" using HOWARD COSELL's voice.

When you work with Vin, you knew you were going to be a part of a broadcast that was a level above most because when he came on the air with his voice and demeanor and with the background that he brought to it, you just knew you were part of something that was special. Vin's abilities and his talents made it a better broadcast. He always was rooting for all of the announcers and complimenting us and suggesting things. He was not only a broadcaster but at the same time when you were doing something like golf, which requires so much teamwork in covering so much of the event that was over 150 acres and strung out all over the place, he was remarkable in how he brought it all together. Another thing about Vin, he made the transition so seamlessly from radio to TV. He taught me a great deal about trying not to talk so much on TV. He is such a great storyteller. I think of Jim McKay's passing recently. McKay was one of the great storytellers. He was there at the beginning of the renaissance of sports television and so was Vin. Baseball is a radio sport really, but Vin has done both, and he's still just mesmerizing to listen to on a Dodger game. He's a terrific human being. I'm a better broadcaster from just being with him and listening to him and understanding his great ability. He was a terrific help to me, and he's been a wonderful friend.

> ...began to do the golf broadcasting, people asked what these football and baseball guys were doing there.

I played golf with him a few times. I played at Bel Air with him a number of times. He played a couple of times with us on the road. He doesn't play anymore, but he certainly understood the game, studied the game, and although he was not a great player, he didn't get in your way or anything like that. He was always a joy to be with.

When Pat Summerall and Vin Scully began to do the golf broadcasting, people asked what these football and baseball guys were doing there. But Pat played golf and Vin played golf. When you're anchoring a golf tournament, you're relying, as an anchor, on the fellows who are in the field and on your analysts and other reporters who might be working in towers, and people who are on the ground. Your most important job is to pull the whole thing together. Vin did a marvelous job of that, telling the stories, tying it together. You're working with as many as six other announcers sometimes who are doing different jobs, either reporting from the towers or analyzing and being able to pull that all together, and be the captain of the ship—I don't know that anybody did it any better than he did.

At the network level, you always had production meetings because the producer was *expected* to have a production meeting. I would say that, for the most part, there wasn't a lot of production meetings that had to do with how to broadcast. All of our group—Vin, Jim Simpson, Cary Middlecoff and most of the people who were doing golf in my day, not so much today—knew what our jobs were. Vin was the ringmaster, the interlocutor, so to speak. He tied it all together. The producers worked extremely well with him. Vin didn't need much direction. He always seemed to have a feeling for the flow and how it was going. He always could take a dramatic moment and spin it with the right verbiage. He was remarkable with his talent.

A lot of the golf tournaments were in the baseball off-season, from January to March and from October to December. He took some time off for baseball games. I must tell you that I don't know of anyone who has been more dedicated to his primary job than Vin is. He had the opportunity many, many times over in his career to skip a game because he was doing a tournament for NBC or for CBS. I'll tell you this, there's never been a man who was more dedicated to serving his #1 master, so to speak—the Dodgers. I've seen him bust his butt to get to games when he didn't have to.

> I don't know why Vin wouldn't do another year with the Dodgers.

For those of us who are dedicated to our craft, sometimes we're not any more appreciated by the listeners than the guys who aren't, which is a shame. Certainly Vin has set a standard that is really almost unattainable by most guys, no matter how much talent they have.

I don't know why Vin wouldn't do another year with the Dodgers. Knowing him as I do, and knowing how much he enjoys it, if it got to the point, for some reason or other, where his health was a problem or where he wasn't enjoying it, I think he'll be a lot like Harry Caray and Jack Buck and some others. He'll go until they carry him out of the booth.

I've never known anybody who was more dedicated to doing their job than he is. He is remarkable.

> —JAY RANDOLPH, St. Louis veteran network baseball and golf announcer who once sat on FDR's lap as a child. His father was Jennings Randolph, at one time the senior Senator from West Virginia.

Vin Scully has been the crème-de-la-crème of broadcasting. He could do anything he wanted to do in any area, any phase of sports, any phase of any public work. He could go on the Tonight Show or he could do anything. He just has that great gift of word usage. He's a very bright guy. His vocabulary is exceedingly good. Not many broadcasters have what Vin has. His style has been very paced and deliberate and understandable so the people listening to him know exactly what is going on out on the field.

Jerry Coleman

I do one inning of play-by-play, which goes by so quickly. Broadcasting is a flow that you take from the beginning of the game to the end of the game. You jump in and do one inning and... ground ball to short, got him, fly ball to left field, that's the inning. You really don't get into a flow of commentating or being a person on the broadcast the way you would if you were doing all nine. You're in and out pretty quickly.

But I'm happy they gave me a job. I have another year coming up next season. For them to keep an 85-year-old guy on the broadcast is a miracle in itself. I don't know how old Harry Caray was but I'm pretty close. Now Vinnie is just a kid.

Howard Cosell and I were very good friends. Because of my position as a player-representative, I helped him out with a lot of things. Our families socialized together. Howard was one of

> **Howard Cosell and I were very good friends.**

the guys who, if anybody had an inferiority complex, he did. He carried articles that had been written about him around with him. He was very sensitive about some of the things they said about him. Howard was really brilliant in what he did. When Howard's wife died, that finished him.

—JERRY COLEMAN, former Yankee infielder, long-time San Diego Padre announcer

I grew up in Brooklyn listening to a young Vin Scully. My first recollection of Vin Scully was on radio in 1956 or '57. I was a very young baseball fan. I was spoiled in that area because the Yankees had Mel Allen and **PHIL RIZZUTO*** and Red Barber. The Dodgers had Vinnie and Connie Desmond, and Russ Hodges was still doing Giants baseball. I was really spoiled listening to baseball on radio. I grew up addicted to baseball on radio.

I first crossed paths with Vin Scully when I worked in Phoenix. We were the Dodger flagship station for the state of Arizona. We carried Dodger baseball for a long time—about 22 years, before the Diamondbacks moved in. I had access to listen to Vin every night.

One of my big thrills is the first time I interviewed Vin. The first time I went to Vero Beach, I sat down and spent 20 minutes with him...strolling down memory lane. Vin is such a great gentleman. If I were looking for one word to describe Vin Scully, it would be honest.! He paints a picture...tells a story...smooth. I could sit in the back yard under a palm tree and just listen to Vin on radio forever. He's one special guy.

One of the greatest speeches I've ever heard was Vin at the Baseball Hall of Fame. Right out of his mouth, words to live by, "When things are going bad in life, you always ask the question, 'Why, me?'" And as he stood on the steps at Cooperstown, he asked the question, "Why, me? Why do I deserve this honor?"

---

*PHIL RIZZUTO is the only baseball person to earn a Gold Record... his game calling was in the background of Meat Loaf's *Paradise by the Dashboard Lights*....Rizzuto was also the first-ever "Mystery Guest" on *What's My Line*.

I've had Vin on the show two or three times in recent years. He does not do very many outside interviews. He's a very private person. I guess that comes with stardom. His work speaks volumes for him. He's an artist. If he's not the greatest of all time, he's right there with whoever is the greatest.

I remember, as a kid growing up on Long Island, on Sunday afternoons, we'd usually go to the beach. I remember walking along the beach, hearing Brooklyn Dodger games on the radio because everybody had brought their transistor radio. We'd walk from one end of the beach to the other end of the beach and, with the waves crashing, you'd hear Vin Scully and Connie Desmond and, I believe, Jerry Doggett was also with them  then doing Brooklyn Dodger baseball on the radio. It was really something. That was before TV took hold. Baseball on radio was really special. To be able to walk up and down Jones Beach on the south shore of Long Island on the ocean and hear Dodger baseball wherever you walked was pretty impressive.

Before games, in the press room, Vin is very personable, says "Hi" to people, sits and chats. He's very accessible for the media. There's a lot of respect for him. I don't think the media bothers him. We all allow him to "have his space." He's not standoffish by any stretch. To people he knows, he's very open and cordial to them.

> —LEE "HACKSAW" HAMILTON—spent his early adult years in Northeast Ohio listening to the irascible Pete Franklin on WEEE. Hamilton moved to KTAR in Phoenix thirty years ago where many Arizona sports fans, to this day, consider him "the greatest sports talk host" in Phoenix history.

I did not work with Vin Scully in Brooklyn. My real claim to fame is that he took my place. I came up to the Dodgers in 1948. Then the Giants came and wanted me to come work with Russ Hodges so I began to work with the Giants. In the meantime, when that vacancy occurred, Red Barber had to find somebody to replace me...the man he replaced me with was Vin Scully.

The only time Vin and I really met was when I was doing a Game of the Week for CBS Radio several years ago. The Dodgers were playing the Braves in Atlanta, and the Dodgers pulled a triple play. It was the first time the Dodgers had one since 1949. Vinnie and I were working in adjacent booths with a glass partition between them. He leaned over and said, "What do you think about that?" I said, "Well, I saw the last one in '49." Then he put something on the air about that. They sent me a cassette of that.

> ...nothing happens in a baseball game until the announcer says it does.

That's about the only time Vin and I have gotten together. Once in a while, when I was doing the Tiger games, and he might be doing an exhibition game in Lakeland, he'd come over, and we'd have a little chat. I'd see him in Vero. I talk to him over the phone every now and then.

I think Vin would agree with me that us old-timers prefer radio announcing to television. There's a saying in radio: nothing happens in a baseball game until the announcer says it does. That is not true in television.

Vin followed me into the Hall of Fame—the year after I made the Hall of Fame, 1981, he went in.

—ERNIE HARWELL, Hall-of-Fame announcer for the ORIOLES* and Tigers...second to Vin Scully in longevity among all play-by-play announcers.

Vin is at one hundred percent while the rest of us are at seventy-five or lower....

I was in musical comedy on Broadway. I grew up in Brooklyn, listening to Red Barber, who was Vin's mentor. That was even before air conditioning, which means you could walk down a street in Flatbush on a hot summer's afternoon. All the windows would be open, with people trying to let air in, and you could hear a Dodger game without missing a pitch. That would have been in 1940.

—GIL STRATTON, long-time L. A. sports anchor (now deceased)

*Since 1977, John Denver's "Thank God, I'm a Country Boy" has been sung at the seventh inning stretch of every ORIOLES home game.

Because I'm in the American League, the only time I see Vin Scully is when we play the Dodgers and that hasn't happened for 3-4 years. Vin Scully is the poet laureate of baseball—no doubt about it. He's probably the most valuable man in the history of the Dodgers in Brooklyn and Los Angeles. Everybody knows what an icon he is. Everybody who is in this business—Vin Scully is their idol.

He's had the press box named after him at Dodger Stadium. I just had the broadcast facility named after me in **SEATTLE***. When they surprised me with that, I thought of Vin immediately. He's such an incredible storyteller, a master. He works hard, even at his age he hasn't missed a beat. He sounds as good as he ever did. He's the best. You can't come up with enough platitudes about Vin. I don't know if there will ever be another like him to come along.

I'm 73 now and Vin is older—we were trained in radio. This was before the days of television. You could create something with the English language and Vin certainly does that. That's the reason I call him the poet laureate. Now he's simulcasting, but you become a slave to what's on the monitor. Baseball is a radio game more than anything else. You can take your radio wherever you are—beaches, boats, mountains. Radio made Vin...and

> He's probably the most valuable man in the history of the Dodgers...

here he is ending his career doing television. He has become, like we all have, so much a part of your family because we're on from March until October. If you're in the pennant race, it's an incredible story. You come into people's lives every day for six months out of the year. There are generations who have grown up with Vin. It's addictive.

> —DAVE NIEHAUS, Hall of Fame Seattle Mariners announcer since 1977...former color man on Rams telecasts...also with Angels team of Buddy Blattner and Don Wells, starting in 1968.

*During the **SEATTLE MARINERS'** first year in 1977, the distance to the fences was measured in fathoms. A fathom is 6 feet. For instance, whereas one park might have a sign that denotes 360 feet, the Kingdome sign would have the number 60...

Vin Scully personifies the mold of making a television show about a broadcaster. If you want somebody to look the part...sound the part...dress the part...use proper words for the part...you'd have to get Vin. He'd be the model. He sounds like a Shakespearean actor. He dresses neatly all the time. He uses words well. He shows excellent judgment. He fits the mold of what you'd like to be. If he were in the Olympics, he'd be getting 10s in all categories.

> If you want somebody to look the part... sound the part... dress the part... use proper words for the part... you'd have to get Vin.

Vin is the ideal radio announcer. He loves to paint word pictures and he intones them in his delivery with the cadence and rhythm of his voice. It's a soothing, pleasant sound. Very newsworthy. For radio, Vin was the ideal person. As the times have gone by, the standards for TV and radio broadcasting have changed, particularly in the sportscasting field. After many years, they started bringing in athletes as color commentators. The athletes came in because they could talk about inside techniques of baseball and football. They were there to provide extra content other than the description of the game. At that time, voices weren't as important as how much knowledge they had. As a consequence, the standards for voice and word use were down. Content became more important. Vin didn't need any analyst to work with him. He preferred, as far as I know, to work alone. He didn't need somebody intruding on the rhythm he had developed himself on the air—the pacing and other things. In most cases, he did the shows by himself. Nowadays, what they look for is somebody who is excited on the air, somebody who had content, somebody who bandies with his booth-mate. On the networks now, they even use three announcers, which makes it even more of an entertainment spectacle. I'm not used to that one yet.

Very few people were good enough to make the demand that they be in the booth alone. Vin was given that privilege when he asked for it because he was that good. It's all subjective of who's good and who's not good. There are no tests you take to see who's the most proficient. But if you mentioned baseball and say, "Who are the all-time greats?" you gotta put Vin Scully on top of that list. Vinnie personified class as a person. It was in the way he carried himself. He was a star...still is.

—BOB WOLFF, the first broadcaster to do play-by-play of the championship series of the four major sports....Voice of the Washington Senators from 1947-1960.

I've been listening to Vin Scully for 54 years. I consider him a friend now. I went to Vin when I started broadcasting for the Padres in 1970 and asked him what suggestions he would have for a budding young broadcaster. I remember him telling me that he didn't listen to other broadcasters because he had gotten some advice from Red Barber, his mentor with the Brooklyn Dodgers, who told him, "You want to be yourself on the radio." So, Vin was afraid if he listened to other broadcasters, he might pick up inflections or something.

I listen to broadcasters all I can. I do pick up ideas from them and pick up new information. Vin is the best because he is "pure" baseball. That's what works for me, but, obviously whatever has worked for Vin Scully has worked out very well for him.

One year in the off-season, I was covering the annual San Diego Open golf tournament. Vin was broadcasting it on CBS. I did an interview with him and asked him if he thought that if the Padres challenged the Dodgers that a Padres-Dodger rivalry would some day be a bigger rivalry than the Dodgers and the Giants. The Giants geographically were much further north and San Diego is just 120 miles to the south. I remember Vin saying that he didn't think so because of the great tradition of the two teams when both played back in New York and Brooklyn.

> **Vin is the best because he is "pure" baseball.**

I was working for a TV station in San Diego when the Padres came to town. We carried the Padres telecast. In those days, 1970-1971, no satellite was available—we had to use the telephone company's long lines. The only games the station could afford to do were the ones in Los Angeles and in San Francisco. We did nine games from L. A. and nine games from San Francisco.

Buzzie Bavasi hired Jerry Coleman and me as the Padres broadcast team starting in 1972. Jerry Gross was one of the original announcers. It was Jerry Gross, Frank Sims and Duke Snider.

When the Padres played in L. A., we would go to do the broadcast and would always see Vin. You can actually learn more from the other team's broadcasters about what's going on with their team than you do from anybody else. I would always talk to Vin and to Jerry Doggett and get some stories from them and get ideas on who is doing well. They would do the same with us. We'd go down by the batting cage and try to talk to the players and coaches. You might get an occasional story there, but you really get more from the broadcasters than from the players.

—BOB CHANDLER, native of Newport, Rhode Island, Padres
    announcer for over 30 years

I got the Dodger job after taking my tape recorder into an empty booth at Dodger Stadium on the final weekend of the 1976 season, and recording an inning or an inning and a half of play-by-play of an L.A.-San Diego game. There were 200 candidates for the job. That was on a Friday night, and by Monday night, I had a deal.

Vin was going to do network events for CBS in 1977 and they needed a third announcer. I had known Vin for close to ten years because I was a sportscaster for Channel 4 (NBC) in Los Angeles.

I see Vin from time to time at certain social events, and we talk on the phone and exchange e-mails.

—ROSS PORTER, retired Dodger announcer

I interviewed Vin and asked him about the move from New York to Los Angeles. He said that no one could really say they *hate* Los Angeles. They can only dislike a part of it...because it's too big to hate the whole thing. That was a little bit different from New York where you have so many millions of people in a small area there.

It's always great to see Vin down at Dodgertown. Down at Vero, a couple of years ago, there was a game which Vin was televising. The Cardinals were playing the Dodgers. Most of the crowd was wearing red. The Cardinals had a pretty good following that night at Dodgertown. Vin looked out and said, "It's great to see the Dodger fans all wearing their Dodger red!"

—JOHN ROONEY, Popular St. Louis Cardinals announcer

My recollections of Vin Scully would go back to being five years old, growing up in the San Fernando Valley. My dad was a huge Vin Scully fan, and he would come home from work and say, "Oh, Vinnie's great tonight." Maybe Koufax was pitching or Drysdale... together we heard so many tremendous moments, just like everybody else who grew up in Los Angeles. We had those little records—the 45s—that played Koufax's perfect game and we had different souvenirs we would get over the years.

Vin has been doing the Dodgers longer than I've been alive... and that's hard for me to believe. As far as working in the same town, Vin is always so gracious. There's no competition because you don't compete with Vin Scully. He's in a class all by himself. I have tremendous respect for everything he's done.

One time, I went into the booth to thank Vin. The Dodgers were playing the Angels at Dodger Stadium. I just wanted to thank him for all the memories he has given me and all the years of greatness he's given to all of us. He said, "Well, you know, I got lucky. I came along about the same time as the transistor radio." I thought, "He's right." I immediately flashed back to being about 10 years old and sitting down by the foul pole at Dodger Stadium and hearing him from some radio a couple of rows away. I thought that was a great observation. All of us kids put their transistor radios underneath our pillows, so our parents wouldn't know, so we would be able to hear the end of the games...but, my dad knew that and didn't mind. My dad, Gary, was a TV director and directed the news back in the days when Brokaw and Tom Snyder were local. I have many a memory of falling asleep with my head on his lap driving home from Dodger Stadium listening to Vinnie's post-game show on the car radio.

To me, Mike Scioscia—who I think is the best manager in baseball—is the one who got away from the Dodgers. I worked in the Pacific Coast League for six years. Albuquerque was the Dodgers affiliate. They always had tremendous teams. There was something about the Dodgers. They just had this *class* about them. We never called them "the Dukes"—we were going to play *the Dodgers.* I think that in the last eight years, Mike Scioscia has  converted the Angels to that. Now, from rookie ball on up, it's, "Oh, here come the Angels," because the organization is so good now. The players know what's expected of them. They do it right. They play the game the right way. The Angels now have what the Dodgers had back then.

The Angels took some of the best of what the Dodgers had to offer and moved it down the freeway a little bit. Scioscia already gets the respect from other baseball people. Now the national media is starting to catch on and realize he has done an incredible job....I never could have imagined being Vin Scully's friend and colleague. It's an honor for me.

—RORY MARKAS, Angels play-by-play announcer

Vinnie has lasted so long, because he's always taken care of himself. Baseball is a game that requires the knowledge of knowing how to handle redundancy because basically it is a redundant exercise over a period of time, interrupted by occasional "great moments of excitement." No one handles that better than Vin Scully. In realizing that one must be a storyteller to do the game of baseball for a long period of time, he's devoted a lot of attention to it and done very well with it.

> I love radio, and a man like Vin makes it magic.

In Vin's formative years, he was surrounded by a bunch of Southerners—most notable was Red Barber. I don't understand how it was that Vin escaped picking up a little bit of Southern twang. You can go back across the years, and many, many of the sports announcers, national as well as local...and the more colorful ones were out of the South. Vinnie avoided all that. He probably absorbed their intent but put it in his own words and became inexplicably successful. It's astounding how well he has held his position and can still tie you to the radio. It's a wonderful thing. I love radio, and a man like Vin makes it magic.

I did baseball for ABC from '76 to '86. When I was a student at Washington State College, I used to drive down the hill to Lewiston, Idaho on weekends and do Western International League games for the Lewiston Broncs and was paid $35 a game in 1950-51, which I thought was pretty good.

— KEITH JACKSON, 80, native of Carrollton, GA and ABC's voice of college football; one-time announcer for the Seattle Rainiers of the Pacific Coast League

"Vin Scully's best work combines aspects of journalism, history, entertainment, drama, and a quality of expression that at times approaches literature. It is a combination of qualities that make him unique among baseball broadcasters."

— BOB COSTAS, St. Louis, NBC and HBO Sports

Vin Scully's only home run against CCNY

OFFICIAL NCAA® BOX SCORE   Game 1 of DH (both MBC)

Date 5/28/1947 Time _____ Stadium Fordham Field _____ City Bronx, NY

Fordham		AB	R	H	RBI	BB	SO	PO	A	CCNY		AB	R	H	RBI	BB	SO	PO	A
Lamena	3B	4	0	0	0		1	2		Greico	CF	2	0	0	0			0	0
Quinn	SS	5	1	1	0		2	6		Seaman	PH/6th	1	0	0	0			0	0
Lyons	2B	5	0	2	1		6	0		Coronberg	CF/7th	1	0	1	0			0	0
Cusmana	LF	4	1	0	0		1	0		Samson	3B	3	0	0	0			2	2
Barigo	CF	5	1	2	0		3	0		Perlmutter	RF	3	2	2	0			0	0
Morreale	1B	4	0	0	0		6	2		Ludwig	2B	5	1	1	2			1	4
Scully	RF	3	1	1	1		2	0		Levy	1B	2	0	1	0			7	1
Bloemen	C	3	0	0	0		1	2		Brecenberg	1B	3	1	1	0			6	0
Arbuclo	PH/8th	1	0	0	0		0	0		Shapiro	LF	3	0	1	1			1	0
Rehn	C/8th	1	0	0	0		0	0		Las Places	SS	3	1	1	1			3	1
Suchowiecki	P	2	0	2	0		0	1		Elkind	C	4	2	2	1			6	1
Kaminski	P	0	0	0	0		1	1		Satin	P	1	1	0	0			1	4
O'Connor	PH/8th	1	0	0	0		0	0											
Weiderecht	P/8th	0	0	0	0		0	0											
TOTALS		38	4	8	2	2	3	24	13	**TOTALS**		31	8	10	5	8	1	27	13

SCORE BY INNINGS		1	2	3		4	5	6		7	8	9	10	11	12		R	H	E.
Fordham		0	2	0		0	1	1		0	0	0				—	4	8	3
CCNY		0	2	1		0	1	1		2	1	X				—	8	10	4

E— Lyons, Morreale, Kaminski, Las Places, Elkind, Samson
DP— CCNY 1   LOB— Fordham 8, CCNY 7
2B— Perlmutter, Quinn   3B— Elkind
HR— Scully
SB— Perlmutter, Shapiro, Lyons, Ludwig, Elkind, B CS—
SH— Samson   SF—

Fordham	IP	H	R	ER	BB	SO	CCNY	IP	H	R	ER	BB	SO
Suchowiecki	6.0	7	5		3	1	Satin	9.0	8	4		2	3
Kaminski	1.0	2	2		3	0							
Weiderecht	1.0	1	1		2	0							

WINNER— Satin   LOSER— Suchowiecki   SAVE— _____
WP— _____   PB— Bloemen, Rehn   BK/IP— _____
HBP— _____
U— Bergen, Brown   T— 2:55   A— _____

NCAA 1987.s/bg   Copyright 1996 National Collegiate Athletic Association

Chapter 2

Put Me In Coach

It was a Ball

THERE'S NO EXPIRATION DATE ON DREAMS

ERIC KARROS

Eric Karros graduated from UCLA before playing 11 years with the Dodgers. Karros was named NL Rookie of the Year in 1992. His best year was 1999 when he hit .304 with 34 home runs and 112 runs batted in. He is the Los Angeles Dodgers career home-run leader with 270. He now works as a color commentator for Fox.

For their honeymoon, my dad took my mom to go see Koufax and Drysdale pitch at Dodger Stadium. That's how much the Dodgers meant to him. When he grew up and went into the Marines, he asked to be stationed at Camp Pendleton because that would be near the Dodgers.

My dad was born in Brooklyn and grew up in a Masonic Home in Utica, New York. Most of the boys there were Yankee fans, and my dad was one of the few Dodger fans. He had a ball that he had caught when Don Newcombe hit a home run off Sal Maglie in one of the games he had gone to as a kid. When I signed with the Dodgers, I brought that ball to spring training because I knew Don Newcombe would be there. I had him sign it and told him the story.

I don't know how many guys you are going to run across, player-wise, who can say that their interaction or their relationship or their introduction to Vin Scully happened much before the ages of 6-7-8. Growing up, we listened to games. My dad listened to Dodger games every single night. It was Vin Scully and Jerry Doggett. We were in San Diego, and we could only get the reception on the radio in my dad's office. He had a small transistor radio. It had to be held *a certain way* to get the reception. Every night, he was listening to the Dodgers...and Vin Scully. He'd come home from work...we'd all eat dinner...then he would go into his office to do his work, but he'd have the Dodger game on, and he would have to be holding that small transistor radio in one hand so he could get the reception.

For me, growing up—and I didn't get it at the time—all I knew was that there was this voice talking about the Dodgers. It was powerful enough to have my dad listen to it every evening. I grew up with Vin Scully.

To eventually play for the Dodgers...and to meet this man who had this power over my father...was interesting. It wasn't like some religious experience or anything like that, but this man was there at seven o'clock—the time for Dodger baseball. That probably had more of an impact on my life than any passing experience I had with Vin while I was a player. His impact on me was much more powerful as a child through my experience with my father. My dad is still alive and is still a huge Dodger fans. It's bizarre or ironic or whatever word you want to use that I ended up getting drafted by the Dodgers and playing for the Dodgers. My dad took early retirement and traveled with the team some. A lot of people knew that my dad was a long-time, huge Dodger fan. We used to come up to Dodger Stadium from San Diego for the Dodger-Reds series in the 70s because I was a Reds fan.

> For their honeymoon, my dad took my mom to go see Koufax and Drysdale pitch at Dodger Stadium.

I was a Cincinnati fan—a big fan of the Big Red Machine with Johnny Bench, **PETE ROSE***, Joe Morgan, Tony Perez.... I never in a million years knew I'd be playing for the Dodgers. We always had to listen to the Dodger games. It must have rubbed off on me because, even though I was a Reds fan, I admired Vin's doing the games. Later on, when I got to play for the Dodgers, it was a great thrill that my games were called by the guy I grew up listening to at home as a kid in San Diego.

*PETE ROSE is enshrined in the Summitt County (Ohio) Boxing Hall of Fame.

When I started in broadcasting, I didn't go to Vin for advice. I don't think he has any tricks—he's just Vin Scully—the greatest. He has the most soothing voice, the most calming voice. He could tell me a thousand different things, and every one of them would be good, but I'm not going to be Vin Scully.

> The one thing I can say that I marvel at is that he never—when he does a broadcast...ever displays any favoritism.

The one thing I can say that I marvel at is that he never—when he does a broadcast, no matter what the sport is—ever displays any favoritism. That, to me, is unbelievable. You can turn him on, and you have no idea if he's rooting for one side or the other, or if he's pulling for one guy or another. That I marvel at because he's a human being first, and we all have our preferences and our likes and our dislikes, and he never displays that. I think that when someone is describing a game, that's what they are there to do—describe the game, help paint a picture. I would like to be able to emulate that from him. I try to.

When we're doing a game at Dodger Stadium and I see Vin, sometimes I call him "Vin" and sometimes I call him "Mr. Scully."

Thank you very much for allowing me to participate in this book.

HOOSIER DADDY

CARL ERSKINE

Carl Erskine played his entire 12-year Major League career with the Dodgers 1948-1959. He pitched two no-hitters. Erskine was born, and still lives, in Anderson, Indiana. He served as player representative for eight years. Erskine once struck out 14 in a World Series game—including Mickey Mantle four times. He coached Anderson College for twelve years following his retirement.

The first time I met Vinnie was in 1950 just after he had graduated from Fordham, when he joined the Brooklyn Dodgers at Ebbets Field. When I saw Vinnie with Red Barber, both redheads, I made the comment, "This kid is a pup out of Red Barber." It turns out I think I was right. Vinnie learned a lot from his mentor, Red Barber, and then he added all of his own skills and became one of the all-time greats.

In the early years of our acquaintanceship, we were still riding the train. We hadn't gone to commercial airlines yet. On the trains, you had a lot of time to visit and get acquainted riding hours on end. I got to know Vinnie that way, plus I used to pick his brain once in a while. I have a few books on my shelf—I had asked Vinnie to

> "This kid is a pup out of Red Barber."

give me the name of a good book that I could read. Vinnie over time has steered me to some pretty nice literature that he likes and recommended, so I pull a book now and then off my shelf at my house and I have a notation in it, "Vin Scully and I bought this book in Grand Central Station, New York, 1953," or whatever. I have some of those good memories of Vinnie off the field.

My seat-of-the-pants opinion about Vinnie—what made him special was he broadcast like he was talking to you and nobody else. He was telling you the story, and you felt as if he were talking directly to you. He just had that skill. He had a romance about baseball. It wasn't just reporting a "line drive to right field" or something, Vinnie described it in a poetic way. He was very poetic. Red Barber was that way also in his own style. But Vinnie could describe a sporting event with a literary view. It lifts him above the stock-in-trade sports announcer who gives you a good description of the game. Vinnie was more poetic. He touched a lot of people in ways that other sportscasters never did.

When the team came out to California, that was down to the last couple of years of my career. I got selected to pitch the opener in L.A., the first game we played in the Coliseum. I got to be the starting pitcher there, and we did win that game against the Giants. That's one of my fond memories of being able to be a transition player and move from my 10 years in Brooklyn and then come to L.A. and be a part of that historic beginning of the L.A. era. I was very fortunate to do that.

> He "sold" the Dodgers to Southern California.

Vinnie is a professional. He kept his personal feelings out of the whole picture of the move. He became the identity of the Dodgers to Southern California. His voice— he and Jerry Doggett in the early years, the voice of the Dodgers. He "sold" the Dodgers to Southern California. Vinnie can take credit for that. We were a new team—there had never been big-league baseball on the West Coast—no team west of Kansas City. People might have been a little standoffish with all these "big" names coming from New York. They were not acquainted with that team. Vinnie, as a real pro, was able to communicate to this new fan base in such a way that I think the Dodgers should have him through perpetuity...whatever that means. I don't think they ought to ever let him go. He has the identity of being the voice that kids have grown up with. That will be with them the rest of their lives—Vin Scully's voice will be part of their years of maturing—these kids who grew up hearing him broadcast. He's really a special guy.

I wrote a book called *Tales from the Dodger Dugout,* and Vinnie did the foreword for me for the book. In the foreword, he mentioned two things that I remember him so well for. In 1952, I was getting ready to start a game against the **CUBS*** in Brooklyn. I had the warm-up ball on the bench and was getting ready to go out to warm up. Vinnie was sitting beside me, and we were chatting before the game. I tossed the ball up and down and said, "I wonder what this little pill has in store for me today." I ended up pitching a no-hitter against the Cubs that day. Vinnie remembered that and just before going out, I said to him, "I wonder what this little ball has in store for me." He tells that story often.

In a World Series game in 1952, I started the game and had a 4-1 lead. A telegram had come for me before the game from a friend in Texas, "Good luck in the World Series on this fifth day of October, the fifth game of the World Series and congratulations on your fifth wedding anniversary." I showed that wire to Vin in the club house in Yankee Stadium. He said, "Let me have that. I want to take it up to the booth." I handed it to him, and then I forgot about it. I went ahead and pitched my game, and I got to the fifth

> "I looked at the stadium clock... and it was five minutes past five."

inning of that game—remember all the fives now—and the Yankees got five runs off of me. I thought they were going to take me out, but they left me in. The game went 11 innings, and I retired the last 19 in a row and we won it 6-5. I pitched a complete game. Vinnie said he was up in the booth looking for any other fives—it was such an unusual set of fives that were developing here. The Yankees had five runs and five hits on the fifth of October, fifth game, my fifth wedding anniversary. When I struck Yogi Berra out to end the game in the bottom of the 11th inning, so help me, Vinnie said, "I looked at the stadium clock...and it was five minutes past five." That's one of his favorite stories.

*When Chicagoan Joe Davita, 78, died in 2001 his obituary read: "Memorials to **CUBS** so they can acquire a qualified relief pitcher."

That ties me to Vinnie forever. Those were great experiences. My association with Vinnie was over a period of 10-11 seasons. That's a lot of games—a lot of travel together—a lot of memorable things, World Series. I don't think Vinnie and I necessarily separated out as buddies on the team. He was open to everybody—the stars, the guys who didn't play a lot or didn't have the big names. He was a cordial friend to the players. If you were in that Dodger uniform, you were held in high esteem by Vinnie. I wouldn't want to ever claim that I was a better friend than anybody else. He was close to Pee Wee, Snider, Campanella—you name them. And Newcombe is right there in California, and he can tell his own stories.

> That ties me to Vinnie forever. Those were great experiences.

Vinnie never talked much about being a broadcaster during the days of baseball being integrated, but Vinnie brought a positive link to that also. In 1950—Jackie had been in the league since '47, but all the hotels hadn't accepted black players yet in 1950 so there were still things to be done to integrate baseball. Red Barber, of course, was the older sage, but Vinnie was an important part of helping what was happening on the field with Jackie and other black players who came after Jackie. Roy Campanella was there when Vinnie got there and Don Newcombe. Joe Black came later and Jim Gilliam and Sandy Amoros. Vinnie was there describing baseball as it integrated.

Vinnie was a cordial man...and he still is. There is no pretense to Vin. He never held himself out to be "the best broadcaster" ever. In the meantime, he can be in the Hall of Fame three or four times. Vin is a neat man.

EXPERIENCE IS WHAT YOU GET WHEN YOU DON'T GET WHAT YOU WANT

RALPH BRANCA

Ralph Branca pitched for the Brooklyn Dodgers from 1944-1953. Branca was a three-time All Star and won 21 games in 1947. He is best remembered as the pitcher who gave up Bobby Thompson's "shot heard round the world" in 1951. He entered Game Three of the playoffs in the ninth inning and gave up the walk-off home run. Branca is a member of the Italian-American Hall of Fame. He was a contestant on the game show Concentration *where he won 17 straight games. His daughter, Mary, married former Dodger player, Bobby Valentine. Branca lives near the Westchester Country Club in Rye, N. Y. where he has been a member for 40 years.*

Vinnie was a nice young man starting out as the third announcer for the Brooklyn Dodgers behind Red Barber and Connie Desmond. Being New Yorkers was the thread that bound us together even though he went to Fordham and I went to NYU. We went to church together. We bonded together. We were both young guys, New York City guys, both Catholic.

Vin would come into the dugout and would sit and talk to the guys—doing his homework —learning something about the players, what was going on in their lives. On the road, we gravitated together. In fact, it was just a friendship that was there. We had dinner on the road. We rode trains and would be together then.

Vin had played baseball at Fordham so he didn't have to be briefed about the game. He knew enough about the inside of the game. He already had a basic knowledge of the game.

I signed out of NYU after one year—1944. I played basketball, baseball and football. In football, I couldn't run very fast but I could catch the ball. I could have been a specialist. I could kick field goals and extra points—points after touchdown, they called extra points in those days. In fact, Pat Summerall's first name is actually George. He kicked for the New York football Giants. The scoring in the paper would show "P.A.T.-Summerall." The P.A.T. stood for "point after touchdown." Summerall also played minor league baseball against Mickey Mantle.

With Vin and me—it was an instant thing. Vin and I were the same age and were New York City boys, both Catholics, both going to local colleges. It was natural for us to be friendly.

I was dating Ann, who was going to Marymount. Her suitemate at college was a beautiful girl from Cincinnati, Patsy Roche, so Vin and I doubled-dated several times. Ann and I have been married for 57 years.

Vin doesn't come to New York much anymore. I used to go to games and see him and talk to him or I'd call him at his hotel.

> Vin and I were the same age and were New York City boys...

The Dodgers went on a trip to Japan in '56. I was making a comeback then so Ann and I went to Japan too. Ann's father suggested that we complete a trip around the world. So we went on to Hong Kong, Pakistan, Rome, Paris, Ireland and London and took the Queen Mary home. Vinnie and Ann and I did all of that.

We got to see Pope Pius XII when we were in Rome. Vin's mother said, "Tell me everything the Pope said to you." The Pope said, "Are you with them?" That was it. Ann and I talked to the Pope for a while, and then Vinnie came in and the Pope said to him, "Are you with them?" Then, he walked away—so he told his mother, "Are you with them?"

We had left on our trip right after the World Series—mid-October—and didn't get back to New York until the first week in December.

I saw Vinnie in spring training in '57 and would go to games that year and see Vin some. Then the Dodgers moved in '58. Absence didn't diminish our relationship or my respect for Vin—he's still the best announcer of all of them. He's absolutely terrific.

We had nicknames. Vin was "Vinnie Red." I had black hair with a brown spot in it, and he called me "Ralphie Brown."

Vin has a very good sense of humor. It's tough for me remember specific things but he was fun to be around. Being on the road and being a very close ball club—we had a lot of laughs.

> I'm the oldest guy in the group of Dodgers who were born in 1926.

I'm the oldest guy in the group of Dodgers who were born in 1926. There were a ton of guys on that team—Newcombe is June. Rube Walker was June. Bobby Morgan was August. **CLEM LABINE*** is August. Duke was September. Erskine's December.

When I saw Vin at the Fordham dinner, it was the first time I'd seen him in a long time. I used to go to old-timers game out there, but I haven't gone to one in at least 15 years. I would see him when the team came to New York to play the Mets.

Vin let friendship overtake his reporting job for me, and that still means a lot to me. That is very nice—a nice tribute. I know Vin had great respect for me 'cause he knew enough about the game to see how I pitched. Nobody talks about it, but I was leading the league in ERA at the end of August in 1951 before we lost our huge lead to the New York Giants. The guy doing the story for American Express about people who had belonged to American Express for 50 years, and I'm one of them, was doing a booklet with 20 people. He came back with the stat that I was fourth in strikeouts per 9 innings...fourth in hits allowed per-nine innings. I went, "Holy Smokes," because I knew I did not have a good September. We didn't get any runs—every game I pitched I got one run. I went from 12-5 to 13-12. I won one game and lost seven

*Dodger relief pitcher **CLEM LABINE** once retired Stan Musial 49 times in a row.

with two of them in the playoffs. I'd go six innings, and we'd get one run, and the other team would get two or three. I was really having a big year in '51. If the Giants don't do what they did—don't steal the pennant by stealing our signs, we would have gone on to face the Yankees. I told this to Giants back-up catcher, Sal Yvars, "You deprived us of a chance to beat the Yankees. And you deprived the fans of having the Dodgers represent the league." That's a despicable act to go off the field into the sanctity of your locker room and look through a telescope and hook up a buzzer system. That's not part of the game.

> He knows what he's talking about. He understands the game. He loves the game.

People ask me, "How come you kept quiet about the Giants' cheating?" I said, "I wasn't a crybaby. I wasn't going to cry over spilled milk. What was was...and it wasn't going to change the outcome."

A kid interviewed me on radio recently. Then he sent me an email and apologized for talking too much about '51. I wrote him back, "It doesn't bother me. I didn't cheat."

It might have been at the next spring training when I heard what Vin had said on the radio at that game where **BOBBY THOMPSON*** hit his pennant-winning homer, "Oh my God. Poor Ralph." Vin and I were close. And even though I don't see him, there's a great respect. It's a mutual respect and friendship. It's one of those things guys work out.

I was in the harness racing business until 10 years ago. There was so much involving chemicals. It is in every sport. I'm convinced there are players who are back on it only they've got something to keep themselves clean—something to cover it up.

The thing about Vin, to me, is his love of the game. He knows the game well enough. His love of the game keeps him going. He's

---

*In an Old-Timers game at Shea Stadium in the 60s, <u>BOBBY THOMPSON</u> homered into the left-field bullpen off of Ralph Branca.

---

such a natural...but he does his homework. He's so glib. It's like you and I talking and no pressure. He knows what he's talking about. He understands the game. He loves the game. It's all combined into making him what he is. Normally when we watch a game, we don't have the sound on...when it's Vinnie...we have the sound on!

I did some broadcasting with Howard Cosell for two or three years. I live in Rye, N. Y. and have for 82 years."

The first $100 million contract was given to Kevin Brown by the Dodgers in 1998. Ten years later 15 players had $100 million contracts.

AH, A FEMALE DODGER FAN— NO MAN IS WORTHY

JOAN HODGES

Joan Hodges is the widow of all-time Dodger great, Gil Hodges. Hodges died April 1, 1972, at spring training while managing the Mets. He is buried at Holy Cross Cemetery in Brooklyn near the Hodges' home.

Joan Hodges has two great passions in life— baseball and the opera. She has been a volunteer at The Metropolitan Opera for 34 years. She has four children, six grandchildren and four great-grandchildren.

All of us immediately took to Vinnie back in 1950. He was so special. He was absolutely wonderful. He was so refreshing. It was different in the beginning. He was great, and we fell in love with him immediately.

Vin was around the team a lot, and Vin would socialize with us sometimes. He was always at the ball park. The announcers got there early to talk to the boys on the field and in the clubhouse. Vinnie was very, very sociable.

> ...Carl Furillo's wife and I fell in love with Vinnie immediately.

Fern Furillo, Carl Furillo's wife, and I fell in love with Vinnie immediately. We all had quite a close friendship. We were at a dinner one time and Vinnie was sitting with us. He was being acknowledged that night. Vin got up and when he was speaking, he mentioned that he had gone to Fordham and that before he came to the Dodgers...he was a long-time Giants fan. Fern Furillo and I, sitting at the table, just for the moment, lost our composure and yelled out, "Giant fan? How could you say that and do that to us?" Vinnie got as red as a beet. He said, "No, wait a minute. I said I *was* a Giants fan. I didn't say I am."

After the Dodgers won the '55 Series, it was not to be believed. When we got to our house, there was police assigned there. They had to form a human chain line for about two blocks so that we could get into our house. We went home to change and go back to a party at the Bossert Hotel in downtown Brooklyn. We went into our house. I had a housekeeper at the time, a nurse, who was taking care of the children. My son, Gil, Jr., had already been showered and was in his robe. He was five years old and loved to watch a popular children's show, *Ramar of the Jungle*. We walked in and with all that was going on outside, we had to close all the Venetian blinds so people couldn't stare into the house. Frank Slocum, who was with the commissioner's office for 19 years, brother of Bill Slocum, the great sportswriter, who was our dearest friend, came home with us and then was going to the party with us. We walked into the house. My son was sitting there watching television. He looked up and said to Gil, "Oh, daddy, I'm so happy you're home. You can watch *Ramar of the Jungle* with me." He wasn't aware of what was going on outside the house and had no idea of what had happened.

I can remember when I had my third child, on August 19, 1956, I was in the hospital, and the Dodgers were playing in Philadelphia. I was still under sedation when they took me back to my room. When I woke up, they had the radio on in my room—my doctor was a big Dodger fan. I woke up to Vinnie's voice saying, "And that, ladies and gentleman, was a home run hit for Cynthia Hodges, who was born today at 12 o'clock noon." That's how I found out I had just had a baby girl. Cynthia is 51 years old now....so I just closed my eyes and went right back to sleep. I was so happy.

I was at the ball park when **DON LARSEN*** pitched the perfect game on October 8, 1956. I'll never forget that day. I remember

*In the Yankee locker room, on the day of DON LARSEN's perfect game, Larsen was served divorce papers. . . .Years later Don Larsen threw out the first pitch the same day David Cone threw his perfect Yankee game. . . . Larsen and David Wells, another Yankee with a perfect game, graduated from the same high school in San Diego, Point Loma.

the magnificent catch that Mantle made on a line shot. Taking nothing away from Willie, a great, great ball player, and they speak so often of the catch Willie made in centerfield in '54. The Polo Grounds was the ideal stadium for anyone to be able to run and make spectacular catches. I take nothing away from him, but I have to tell you the catch Mickey Mantle made that day on Gil's fly ball is right up there. If I would have to say that I witnessed any magnificent catch—Mickey Mantle made a spectacular catch. He had to run a long way to get it, and it was over him and was magnificent.

Two times in that game, Gil hit balls that were the only two chances the Dodgers had of getting a base-runner that day. You want to win—maybe I shouldn't say this, but I will—I've never said this to anyone—I was at the game when Gil spoiled Lew Burdette's no-hitter with two outs in the ninth inning at Ebbets Field. We left right after the game to go home. We got in the car. Gil said, "What's the matter?" I said, "Nothing." He said to me, "I can tell there's something." I said to him, "Why did you do that?" He said, "Why did I do what?" I said, "Gil—that hit meant nothing in the ninth inning." He said, "I can't believe you're saying that." I said, "But he worked so hard for nine innings. I feel so bad. I really do. I wish it had been someone else who got the hit." He said, "I can't believe you're saying that." I said, "Well, don't take it that way. I don't mean it that way." I just was so sorry and felt so bad for a person who had worked so hard for nine innings, and two outs....

> Mickey Mantle had to run a long way to get it, and it was over him and was magnificent.

In 1951, the Dodgers went through a few blows. The real big one was when we lost it after being thirteen and a half games ahead in August. I'll never forget that as long as I live. Larry Goetz was the home plate umpire the day of Bobby Thompson's home run. At the Polo Grounds, you had to walk underneath when you went to the dressing room. I was hysterical. All the wives were. There was Dottie Reese, Fern Furillo, Millie Walker and Helen Pafko with me. The newspapers wanted to take a picture of us before the game of us cheering with our arms up like we had won. We all said, "No, we don't do that. If you want to take a picture of us cheering, we hope it happens and we'll see you at the same place." When we were walking through, I was hysterical and crying. Larry Goetz was just walking through. He put two hands on me—one on each arm—and said, "Joan, hold that in until you get in the car if you possibly can," because, of course, it was absolute bedlam. It was something you could never imagine.

I've heard so many things over the years about that season and that game, but what's the difference? It happened. It's in the record book and so what difference does it make? I always feel that's not going to prove a thing.

> I'm very superstitious at a ball game. I shouldn't say that, as a Catholic, but I am.

On August 31, 1950, I was there in Brooklyn when Gil hit four **HOME RUNS*** in a game against Boston. Gil hit them against four different Boston pitchers. I was sitting at the ball park next to Don Newcombe's father. I wouldn't look when Gil got up to the plate. I'm very superstitious at a ball game. I shouldn't say that, as a Catholic, but I am. I wouldn't look when he got up to the plate that fourth time. All of a sudden, I heard Newcombe's father yelling, "Joanie, Joanie, open your eyes, girl, it's going to centerfield!" I did. I opened my eyes. Then my cousin and I were walking to the elevator after the game that night. We had to go upstairs to where they were doing radio after the game. Gil and I were going to be on the post-game show. A man walked over to me and kissed me. He had a sweater across his shoulders and said to me, "Mrs. Hodges, I just want to congratulate you. I'm so happy to have been able to be here tonight and to see history." We walked away toward the elevator. My cousin said to me, "Who was that?" I said, "I don't know. I think I met him some place, maybe in a store somewhere. I

*Ten players named Homer have played in the majors, but only four hit a **HOME RUN**.

have no idea who he is." We went upstairs—it was Anthony Quinn! He happened to be at the game, and I saw him upstairs and I said to him, "Forgive me." He said, "That's all right."

When Gil passed away in 1972, I got so many calls and messages. I even heard from the Emperor of Japan. It was unbelievable. I had come home from Florida on Good Friday. Gil was to come home later. He called me Easter morning at 10:20, and, as he usually did for any little occasion, he sent flowers. He was going to play golf with the boys and I was going to my mother's house with the children for Easter Sunday. He was with the Mets at spring training and they were not playing—that was when they were on strike.

When Gil found out he was coming back to manage the Mets, he was a little nervous about it. I said, "Honey, I can't believe that." He said, "You don't understand. I don't want to disappoint those people." I could cry now even talking about it. I said, "Gil, they prayed for you, and cheered you when you were in so many slumps, and I mean that most respectfully. They know whatever you do is going to be your best." He said, "I know that, but I don't want to disappoint them." You have to understand the Mets didn't have what you could call a good record when he came in and inherited the Mets in 1968. The next year...the Mets win the World Series.

> The next year... the Mets win the World Series.

He was 0-21 in the 1952 World Series. It was unbelievable. He'd get standing ovations. If he'd strike out or fly out or whatever, it was like he hit a grand slam. He was that beloved. I was at all those games, and I'm such a baseball fan, I wanted to ignore it as much as I can. I tried to avoid the newspapers being there in time for him to have his breakfast in the morning. He'd say, "Why are the newspapers delayed?"

Since all the games were played in New York, we were there every day. Anyone you'd meet, or anything you'd do, or anyone who comes through the door would be saying, "Don't worry about it,

Gil. Don't worry about it." Even if you didn't want to think about it, you had to.

Gil attended church every single Sunday of his life. When I was expecting my first child, I was very, very sick the whole nine months. In my ninth month, I developed pneumonia and pleurisy before I had the baby. My labor pains started at 5:15 in the morning. When the pains started, I said to him, "Gil, I think I'm going into labor." He looked at his watch on his arm and said to me, "Okay, honey, I'm going to get up and make six o'clock Mass." That was the last thing on this earth I could possibly have wanted to hear. I said to him, "What?" He said, "Yes, I'm going to make six o'clock Mass. I'll be home by quarter to seven." He got up and went to Mass. He wasn't going to miss that. We were staying at my mom's house at the time. We had plenty of time and didn't have the baby until 10:21 that night.

> ...the popularity of the Dodgers is related to the way Vin introduced Major League baseball to the Los Angeles area.

You could say that the popularity of the Dodgers is related to the way Vin introduced Major League baseball to the Los Angeles area. Vinnie has a special calling. He does. I can still hear him and I still have the utmost respect and admiration for him.

Vinnie used to make one road trip to New York so when the Dodgers come in, I call to see if Vinnie is coming with them. I would always leave a message for him to let him know that I've called and that I love him. When he gets a chance, he leaves a message for me. If they make the playoffs and come out here, you know I'll be there.

We kept our home here when Gil went other places so I still live in it now, and Mayor Rudy Giuliani renamed the street to Gil Hodges Way.

QUICK HITS AND INTERESTING BITS

Vin was 15 when I was 17 in high school. We had a big assembly. He was sitting right behind me, and he grabbed me by the shoulder, and he leaned over and whispered, "Some day you're going to be in the big leagues. The first time you hit a home run, I'll be announcing to the world about it." That's what he said.

Sure enough, on my first big-league trip to Brooklyn, with St. Louis in 1952, Eddie Stanky, the manager put me in the lineup. All my family and all my friends came to the game. We hadn't beaten Preacher Roe in three years. We didn't beat him that day either. I did hit a home run off of him. Sure enough, Vin was on the mic when it happened, and he told the story on the air. I heard from people in Germany. I knew that Vin was doing the broadcast but I didn't get to see him or talk to him that day.

> Vin was 15 when I was 17 in high school.

Later, when Vin was inducted into the Hall of Fame, they asked him about the highlights of his career, and he told that story. A friend of mine had taped the ceremony, and he sent me a copy. I couldn't believe it. Vin must have seen 10,000 big league games, at least, and this was the game he talked about.

I have a son who teaches in Potomac Maryland, at a private school. He told me that one of his fellow teachers had a brother who graduated from Fordham University. It was the year Vin was given the honorary doctorate and was speaking to the graduates, and Vin told that story.

When Vin would come to Houston, I would see him before the game. I would talk to him about him telling the story. He said, "I got a B.A. degree from Fordham, so what can I tell these people? They've all got Masters and PhD's so I figured I could do one thing. I could put something out there—something that could happen—it might not happen...but it could happen and give them something to shoot for in their life."

I didn't play much after that. We had two Hall-of-Famers in the outfield, Stan Musial and Enos Slaughter, Peanuts Lowrey played centerfield, and there was no way I could break in there.

I hit a home run off Warren Spahn—my second home run. Twenty one years later, my friend Charlie Fox and I went to a ball game in New York. We were sitting by the dugout and who walks behind us? Warren Spahn. I told Charlie that in 1952, I had hit a homer off him in Boston. He said, "You did? Spahnie, come over here." He came over and said, "This character claims he hit a homer off you in Boston in 1952." Spahn said, "What's his name?" He told him, and Spahn said, "I remember it. It was a 3-1 fastball." And it was!

In 1950, I was playing in Columbus in the International League. It was a tight ball game. I'm playing left field. The batter hit a shot down the left field line, which went over the fence on the fly. It hit out but it bounced back in. I ran over to the corner where there was a four-foot cyclone fence. I jumped up and got the ball. I came down and turned around, threw to second base as the guy slid into second. He was called safe by the umpire. Everyone in the ball park knew it was a home

Larry Miggins

run except the ump. The whole team came out chasing the umpire. It was hilarious. All of a sudden, the manager said to the umpire, "Listen. I know that kid in left field, and he'll tell you the truth. Go out and ask him. He'll tell you what happened." My manager was standing about ten feet behind him and heard this so he shook his head at me telling me not to tell the umpire anything. The umpire walked out where I was and the first thing he said, "Larry, they tell me you're an honest man." He said to me, "I lost the ball in the sun. There was a man sitting out there with a white shirt on, and I couldn't see so I'm going to ask you man-to-man. Tell me the truth...was it a home run? Yes or no." I said, "Well, I don't get paid to umpire. I get paid to play left field...." So, anyway he called it a home run, and they beat us by two runs. I wound up getting booed all the way into the dugout. I got to the dugout, and nobody would talk to me. They gave me the silent treatment—just ignored me.

Every time the Dodgers came to Houston, I would get to talk to Vin. He used to travel all the time, but now he doesn't go farther than Denver.

—LARRY MIGGINS, high school contemporary and baseball teammate of Vin Scully

Usually on the plane on our road trips, the press stayed together and the players stayed together. On some of those flights, 30 years ago, we had a lot of time because it would take 12-13 hours to go across the country.

From time to time, before games, Vin Scully would walk around the club house and the field talking to players. Vinnie did his homework, for sure. He did his homework on the opposing players better than anybody else. He'd spend time there because, though he obviously worked for the Dodgers, he would be able to paint a real good picture of the opposing team and players.

Vin was never negative, and I don't see how anybody could say anything bad about him. He's an amazing guy.

> Vin talked about that on the radio and had the crowd saying, "Get well, Bill Singer."

I had pitched a no-hitter in the minors so Vin nicknamed me "No-No." It carried over and there were three or four different versions as to how that came about. One version was that the name came from my shaking my head while running wind sprints.

One time I had hepatitis, and I was in isolation at Santa Monica hospital. Vin talked about that on the radio and had the crowd saying, "Get well, Bill Singer." I was in the hospital listening to that and that helped my spirit, for sure. He was very thoughtful to think of doing that.

I listened to Vin when I was in junior high and high school. I grew up listening to Vin Scully. I was a Hollywood Stars fan and an L.A. Angels fan. When the Dodgers came out to the West Coast in '58, that was a big thrill for me. Vinnie sold baseball...his voice...and his painting the picture of the game really sold the Dodgers and sold baseball big-time here.

The Hollywood Stars were the farm team of the Pittsburg Pirates and the Angels were a farm team of the Chicago Cubs. In '57 they became a farm team of the Dodgers, which was in preparation for moving out.

I was born in Los Angeles and grew up in Pomona. I was 17 years old when I signed and went to the instructional league. Then I was in big-league camp when I was still 17.

    —BILL SINGER, won 20 games for the Dodgers in 1969, won
    20 games for the Angels in 1973

I listened to Vin Scully do his broadcasting of games before I played...and I hear him now. It's the same. He's the best.

I was a rookie and the team was taking their first trip to San Diego. We had a day game and got into San Diego that afternoon from L.A. I went down to the restaurant/bar area where Vin was sitting by himself. I went up to order something at the bar and Vin said, "Tracy, sit with me." I sat down next to him and had a sandwich and a drink.

Vin asked me personal questions so he would know more about me for his broadcasts. There I was, a rookie, sitting there with Vin Scully by myself...me knowing who he is and him hardly knowing me at all...yet trying to learn everything he can about me.

My **FIRST BIG-LEAGUE HOME RUN***, Vin called it, and the radio station brought that tape down to me two days later. I distinctly hear his voice saying, "Tracy Woodson, a tall good-looking blond from Richmond, Virginia...," and then you hear the crack of the bat. Just hearing him calling my play! Vin has these things that he says about the players all the time. I'm just wondering if he does this with all the players—tries to get to know them so it helps him with what he says on the radio.

Vin is always so fair to the players. You always have players who complain about radio guys. Wherever I went, guys would get mad because the broadcaster said this or that. Sometimes guys would even sneak back into the clubhouse to listen to see if the broadcaster was badmouthing the player. Vin never did that.

    —TRACY WOODSON, Baseball coach at Valparaiso University,
    Valparaiso, Indiana

*Fewer than half of the 17,000+ major leaguers have ever homered.

Vinnie and I had this thing going, especially in L.A., the day I was pitching, I'd always see him and educate him on some stuff. He always had a show at the end of the game and his guest was the star of that day's game. I'd always say, "I'll see you on the post-game show." He got a big kick out of that. And in '59 I was on the show a lot of times.

I remember one thing Vinnie said one time—that he was in love with the English language. He studied it. That rung a bell with me. It was true for him—he not only had a great voice but his vocabulary was neat. He always seemed to say the right thing. Whereas when I was coaching and managing and playing, I studied the game. I never thought I was going to be a manager. I loved being a pitching coach and loved teaching.

Vin was *one of the guys.* If you would see him after a ball game, he might ask you to go have dinner with him. He was close with all the players, and yet he still would say what he thought on the air. He never really second-guessed us or anything like that. He was just a class act. He always was, and he always will be.

Back in the 50s, the Dodgers would take the train to away games. I loved those train trips because we were all in the same couple of cars. We'd be together and would sit around and talk and played a lot of bridge. Vinnie and all the announcers and some of the writers would be there with us. It was a close-knit thing. Now you get on a plane and everyone goes to sleep, or the stewardesses are bothering you all the time.

> Back in the 50s, the Dodgers would take the train to away games.

Vinnie had a way, and still does, of announcing a ball game that captivates you. When I'm traveling now, if I can catch him on the radio, I always listen to him and he still amazes me with the way he calls a ball game. He calls a game like it should be called. The fans don't want to hear if somebody is up there who says, "If I was managing, I'd do this or do that." They want you to call what you see and describe what happens. Vin was so good at that. Nowadays you hear all these talking heads and most of them have never managed, and they want to sit up there and manage. Vin doesn't try to impress you—he wants to let you know what he sees on the field and not so much "what I would do if I was the manager," or "I would hit and run," or "why did he take this guy out?" He just tells you what he sees on the field.

In spring training when I first went to Vero Beach as a kid, we were assigned four to a room. We all ate at the same place and we stayed there all the time. They had a swimming pool and ping-pong tables and we were a close-knit Dodger organization. Mr. O'Malley used to have a big St. Patrick's Day party with everything green. He had the Major League and the minor league players there. There was a theater, and Mr. O'Malley had

Roger Craig

movies every once in a while, and they had church services. They made it almost like a little city there in Vero Beach. There were great facilities plus we had six diamonds. Vin was always there too. If he'd walk in for dinner, he might sit down with anybody. Three or four players might go to eat at the same time, but he'd just come in and sit down anywhere. Everybody accepted him and wanted him to sit with them.

Vinnie was very popular on the buses. We'd land at the airport and take a bus to the hotel and all the guys enjoyed sitting with him and listening to him tell his stories. I don't mean that he would just start talking, but if you asked him something he would tell you. Vin was so much fun to be around. He was one of the guys.

Vinnie was a real Dodger. He typifies the Dodgers. He's been with that one club all his life. Even though he wasn't a player, he was just as good or better than the players 'cause he spent his whole career doing the same thing.

Walter Alston was the exact opposite of Tommy Lasorda. Lasorda was clapping his hands and would do whatever he was doing, but Alston would just sit there. One thing Alston did—he was thinking he had a lot of good players, a lot of good players, and he handled them really well. One reason the players respected him so much, he would go up and ask players, "What do you think? Should we do this? Should we have done

> **Walter Alston was the exact opposite of Tommy Lasorda.**

that?" He didn't always use their advice, but he asked them about it…and he considered it. That was one thing that made Alston a very, very good manager.

  —ROGER CRAIG, former Dodger pitcher, Major League
   pitching coach and manager

Transistor radios first came in when we were playing in the Coliseum. Everybody started taking their radios to the ballpark. Vin Scully sold the Dodgers to the people because that's all you heard. When I was out in the bullpen, I never missed a pitch. Everybody in the ballpark had a transistor radio there with them.

  Vin was terrific. His voice is great. He's knowledgeable. I think he made all those people Dodger fans.

  People have told me Vin gave me some credit for the improvement in Sandy Koufax—I did catch Sandy in the bullpen, and we talked…. I'm not going to take any credit for that. Sandy had a lot of talent, and after a few years the light went on, and he pitched his way into the Hall of Fame.

  I live in San Diego now so I never get to hear Vin because no one carries the Dodger games down here.

  —NORM SHERRY, graduated from Fairfax High in L. A.….
   Back-up catcher for Dodgers from '59 to '62

I have never listened to Mr. Scully's broadcast of the Dodger games. I have never had a conversation with Mr. Scully about baseball. Therefore, other than to state the general platitudes that people say when asked questions in situations like this, I have nothing to say to you.

  —DR. MIKE MARSHALL, former Dodger star relief pitcher

Vin was a great announcer. I remember when Vin first came to Brooklyn back in 1950 and remember him as a young announcer for the team. I was impressed with Vin's voice and impressed with Vin personally. He's got to be pretty darn good if he's been with them for 58 years.

  —YOGI BERRA, legendary Hall-of-Famer

Don was from Van Nuys and was a Southern California kid. To come back to the team he played for and work as a broadcaster for the O'Malley family was special to him. To be able to work side-by-side with Vinnie and Ross Porter—it was a wonderful threesome.

My relationship with Vin has always been warm and cordial. When I'd go on the road with them, I'd go to church with Vinnie—we were Catholic.

While Don was playing, he aspired to do broadcasting. Don and I got married in '86, after his career was over. Don was already working for the Angels then. It was a treat for him to come back full circle to work for the Dodgers. Sadly, he was on a trip with the Dodgers in Montreal when he passed. Vin was unbelievably gracious and spoke at Don's funeral.

> Vinnie is a very private person. He doesn't let a lot of people in.

Vinnie is a very private person. He doesn't let a lot of people in. He keeps his emotions in check. He's a class guy. He's always been very supportive of our family and remembers the children's birthdays and talks about them on the air, as Ross Porter did. The O'Malley's made the Dodgers a family. Don had the utmost respect for Walter, and always called him Mr. O'Malley, and I think Vinnie did too.

I remember the night Don passed away and how Vinnie held everything together.

—**ANN MEYERS-DRYSDALE**, widow of Don Drysdale; first
   female ever drafted by the NBA (Pacers)

Back in the 70s very few games were televised in Los Angeles. As a matter of fact, there were only nine, and those were the games in San Francisco. As a result, everybody brought their transistors because they wanted to listen to Vinnie do the games. There are times when there could have been 30-40,000 radios in the ball park. You could hear Vinnie broadcast the game even when you were on the field.

Listening to Vinnie is like listening to the greatest poet in the world recite his poetry. I always think of Vinnie, "Well, the azure blue skies meet the billowy white clouds as the sun comes cascading down and the sea of blue at Dodger Stadium," 'cause that's the way his voice sounded. It was like the greatest poet in the world.

One night, it was the bottom of the eighth inning. I can only tell the story in Vinnie's voice. "It's the bottom of the eighth inning, two out and nobody on, no chance to score so Manager Alston will use Tom Paciorek and save Manny Mota for the ninth inning when the Dodgers do have a chance." As you can imagine, I'm flipping off Vinnie from the on-deck circle 'cause I've heard every word he's said.

> I'm flipping off Vinnie from the on-deck circle 'cause I've heard every word he's said.

The next thing you hear around the ball park is, "Here's the pitch to Paciorek, and I'll be back with the top of the ninth inning right after these words from Farmer John, bologna and Kielbasa." I remember Vinnie used to close out, "Farmer John—bologna and Kielbasa."

It was really funny. One time Andy Messersmith was pitching. Vinnie was doing the play-by-play, and it went like this, "Well, the Reds have the bases loaded. Tony Perez is the hitter, and Steve Yeager puts down the sign for a fastball. Messersmith shakes him off for the curve." Here's Andy on the mound, hearing all this and he knows Tony Perez can hear it too. They call time out and change the signs with Yeager. He comes to the dugout and says, "Vinnie's calling my pitches." He's telling Perez what was coming.

That was a standard joke back then.

I remember back in the 70s, to be interviewed after the game by Vinnie was the greatest honor a player could have. Nowadays you see these guys blowing off national TV. You're at the World Series and guys are blowing off people. The few times I got interviewed by Vinnie, we used to sit in the dugout maybe a half-hour before he got to us. We welcomed it because we got $10 of Union 76 gasoline. We'd sit there for a half-hour just panting—couldn't wait to talk to Vinnie on the radio...and we got ten bucks for it. You'd wait there all night if you had to 'cause it was Vinnie.

Vinnie is amazing. I was listening to a game a couple of years ago. A Braves pitcher was pitching against the Dodgers. Vin was talking about his grandmother, "From Guadalajara, she took a bus to see her grandson. She took three hours to get to Tijuana, and then she transferred over to San Diego, off to the Harbor

Freeway, and here she is tonight to watch her grandson pitch for the first time in a Braves uniform at Dodger Stadium." He'd give you background on people.

When you've got everybody impersonating you, you've got to be good. I don't know where the heck he gets all this stuff. You listen to him and you hear all you ever wanted to know about that guy 30 seconds into his appearance at home plate.

When I was traded to the White Sox from Seattle in 1982, Don Drysdale was doing television for the Chicago White Sox. I knew Double D from Dodger days when I was coming to spring training. He was a great guy, a great teammate. You want him on your team, that's for sure. If he wasn't your teammate, you didn't like him too much. He was a wonderful guy—wonderful person. That was a great loss to baseball as well as to the Dodger organization. He was a great broadcaster too.

> —TOM PACIOREK, played in the Dodger organization for eight years with three seasons on the parent club...later a successful announcer with the Chicago White Sox. His brother, John, holds the Major League record for most at-bats in the big leagues without making an out. John Paciorek was 3-3 in his Major League career.

I was having dinner with Vin and a bunch of other guys at the press room at Dodger Stadium. At the time I was scouting for the Pirates. He told us a story about when he interviewed with my grandfather to be the Dodger announcer. This was in 1949, and he was prepared to go in and have Branch Rickey ask him questions about baseball. Instead, he was asked a lot of questions about his family and what kind of upbringing he had and what kind of family background—was he married? At that time, Vin was not married. He was asked how he grew up and what his values were. He was very impressed by that. He told us the story that he was very impressed by the fact that Branch asked him questions about things that weren't related to baseball, but were more about people and what kind of a person he was. Branch was a teetotaler...did not drink, and Vin was very impressed by that. He felt that Branch was more concerned about him as a person than as a guy who knew baseball. Red Barber had put in a good word for Vin to my grandfather. Red was a very strait-laced kind of guy. Branch thought Vin was like Red Barber, and that was very important to him. He always felt that was an attribute to his being hired to be the broadcaster of the Dodger games at a very young age.

The story goes that Branch, Sr. told Red Barber a couple of years before he integrated the Dodgers that he had his eye on a black player without naming the guy. He said he wanted to do the integration of baseball and wanted to get Red's feelings about that because Red was a Southerner, and he might have felt uncomfortable about being a broadcaster of a team that brought in a black player. He told Red to sit on this information and not tell anybody else. Branch, Sr. told Red this a couple of years

before he brought Jackie Robinson into the picture. It is a very important story that not too many people even know to this day—that Branch gave Red a chance to get out of announcing the Dodger games if he had any uncomfortableness about a black player. Red apparently resolved that this was not going to be an issue. He welcomed Jackie Robinson to the Major Leagues and to the Dodger organization when he signed with Montreal in '46.

That's always been a very important story in my family's background. It has always colored the way I felt about Red Barber that my grandfather gave him two years of preparation before Jackie Robinson integrated baseball, and he was okay with that. That was the kind of guy Red Barber was and the kind of guy Vin Scully is.

—BRANCH RICKEY, III, grandson of Branch Rickey, President of the Pacific Coast League

Vin Scully is one of the great, great baseball announcers. I got to know him first when we played the Dodgers. When I was at Kansas City, sometimes I had him on the play-offs. He is a wonderful, wonderful announcer and a very fair guy. I always thought he was one of the fairest guys in the world.

They talk about **HARRY CARAY*** and what he did for the Cardinal organization. Everybody listened to Harry in the Midwest, Oklahoma, all over. I think when the Dodgers moved west that Vin Scully was so popular on the West Coast that he almost did as much for the Dodgers as Harry Caray did for the Cardinals. I believe that.

Vin Scully drew people into the ball park. And the away games were on so early in California that people driving home from work weren't able to watch TV so they listened to Scully on the car radio.

Scully never did the interviews on the field. The other guys always came down and got the interviews, but I would see Vin quite often in the press room afterward. He knew the game. He knew the personnel on both teams, and he was very fair to everybody.

> —<u>WHITEY HERZOG</u>, Long-time Major League manager, the
> "White Rat" built the 1969 Amazin' Mets and remains the
> most popular manager in the history of the St. Louis
> baseball Cardinals.

I was hired by Branch Rickey in 1952 for a player-manager job in the Pirate organization. I felt it was an honor to work for him. He was the smartest man I've ever known. He was a genius.

On Sundays, if the Dodgers were playing, I'd take my transistor radio with me and listen to the game while I'm watching our youth team play. One of Vin Scully's remarks when a ball player from either side made a great play was, "50,000 people have just seen one great play." Or when a no-hitter came up, "50,000 people saw a masterpiece." When a boy in centerfield on my club made a great catch, I happened to say, "Yeah, and 50,000 people at Dodger Stadium *didn't* see that play today." To this day, when

---

*In 1949, <u>HARRY CARAY</u>'s first wife Dorothy divorced him. In 1979 Harry wrote her: "Dearest Dorothy, Enclosed is my 360th alimony check. How much longer is this _ _ _ _ going to continue?" Dorothy responded: "Dearest Harry, Til death do us part. Love, Dorothy." Harry paid monthly till he passed away in Palm Springs in 1998.

I'm out there, somebody makes a play and I'll say, "50,000 people at Dodger Stadium did not see that play today." That makes that kid feel good. At the time when that phrase happened to come  up, and I replied to the people around us and sitting in the stands watching our team, I just said, "Yes, and 50,000 people at Dodger Stadium missed a great play today." I've been using that line ever since I became a scout.

I know Vin Scully well. He's a great announcer—he is also very fair. He gives credit to everybody. Another thing about Vin, he is not a mystery guy. What you see is what you get.

—GEORGE GENOVESE, 86, Dodger Scout

I've known Vin Scully in three different dimensions. A lot of the folks who got to know me in Los Angeles as a young Dodger got to know me because of Vin Scully. As I got to be a veteran player and had a chance to chase some of the Dodger records and had grown up a little bit in the organization, our relationship became a little different. And, then as a broadcaster. There have been a number of times I've asked Vin for advice. One of the best pieces of advice he ever gave me was to find out what I am as a broadcaster and to do that.

The Dodgers are having a fundraiser and one of the items being auctioned to raise money is "sit in the booth with Vin Scully for an inning." As of right now, the bidding is at $2,100. I was thinking about bidding on it, but that's a little out of my price range....

I can remember times when I was in the dugout and wanted to go into the locker room to get a cup of coffee. The game is on in the locker room and you listen. I'd be sitting there watching the game and there would be times when I would think, "I'd rather stay in here. I think I'm getting a better picture sitting in here in my chair at my locker than I am out there watching it." That's about the best compliment you can give somebody.

We used to have a Chamber of Commerce luncheon at the beginning of every season in L.A. The players would show up downtown with businessmen and there would be a question and answer session. I happened to pitch the night before one of those luncheons. During the Q&A session, someone brought up a situation from the night before. There was a right-handed hitter coming up, a left-handed hitter on deck, and the Reds had a runner on second. I walked the right-handed batter on four pitches to face a left-hander with the game on the line. Vinnie said, "He's thrown a lot of pitches. Don may be running out of gas this early in the season." Well, I knew that the right-handed hitter was something like seven for nine off me and the left-handed hitter was 0-21. I'm going by the scouting report and the numbers that I knew. In Vinnie's mind, it made sense. It was early in the year. I've stretched out. I've thrown a lot of pitches. When it came to my turn to answer a question, one of the gentlemen stood up and said, "Last night, seventh inning, did you run out of gas a little bit? Get a little tired? Could have been the only reason you walked the right-handed hitter to get to a left-handed hitter?" I said, "No. I did it because the right-handed hitter was hitting me well, and the left-handed hitter was not." He said, "Well, that's not what Vinnie said." I'm arguing with a guy over why I walked a right-handed hitter, and he was telling me, "No, you must be wrong... *cause that's not what Vinnie said.*"

Vinnie has so much credibility and his broadcast has so much substance. It's a remarkable compliment to the man and his way of doing the job that so many of us feel that if Vinnie says it, that's the way it is.

Vinnie is able to point out when a player does something that is not up to big league standards, but he does it in a way that does not personalize it. He's critiquing the performance...not the person. That's a nice gift. It's one that all of us who sit behind microphones try to work on.

—DON SUTTON, Dodger Hall of Famer

A sportswriter for the *Mobile Press* in Mobile, Alabama, Bill Bingham, gave me the nickname "Shotgun," because of my line drives to center field, left field and right field—he said it was like the ball was coming out of a shotgun.

I met Vin Scully when I went to Vero Beach for spring training. He was on the train with us on the way down. I was surprised that he actually was younger than I was, and here he was about to replace Red Barber. I'd heard that he was a pretty good college ball player. They said he was a pretty good fielder, but he wasn't a very good hitter.

He has many stories and facts. I went to an old-timers game in L. A. around 1975 and went out to right field. I took a baseball with me in my back pocket. With one out, a batter hit a line drive to me in right field. It went over my head. I took about three steps, turned around, took the ball out of my pocket and threw it to second base. Everybody couldn't believe what happened because they saw the ball going down the right-field line, and the ball coming in to second. Vin Scully was announcing on the P.A. system and picked up on it very quickly. He said, "Ladies and gentlemen, you will find that play on page 93 of the *Dodgers Way to Play Baseball*." Of course, I threw the guy out. It would have been a stand-up double but the second baseman had the ball waiting for him. Vin was quick to figure out what happened.

In 1985, Peter O'Malley brought the '55 team back to Dodgertown for the 30th anniversary. We were at Vero Beach for about five days. We played golf and had a great time. The wives were there also. We had a banquet the night before we left. Vin started off by saying: "There are three stages in our life. Youth... maturity...and, "you're looking wonderful." You've looked at each other for the past few days and, with a straight face, you're saying to each other, "You're looking wonderful."

—GEORGE "SHOTGUN" SHUBA, 83, utility outfielder for '50s
Brooklyn Dodgers, hit .305 in 1952, born in Youngstown, OH

Credit: UCLA Special Collections

Vin Scully and Bob Chandler

Chapter 3

The Write Guys

The Fourth Estate
Doesn't Take the Fifth

PAY THE MAN, SHIRLEY

NORM CHAD

Norman Chad is a graduate of the University of Maryland. Since 2003, he has appeared on ESPN's coverage of the World Series of Poker. Chad is based in Los Angeles.

I wrote about him a lot because when I was writing a sports media column, it was clear from early on how Vin was above and beyond anyone else who did baseball on the radio in my lifetime.

I wrote about Vin in the Washington Post and the National Sports Daily. I ended up moving to Los Angeles, where I ended up listening to Vin constantly. Vin set a standard that I haven't seen anyone get close to matching. The closest, actually in a different way, was Jon Miller. I used to listen to him do the Baltimore Oriole games, and now he does the San Francisco Giants. Jon has a slightly different approach, but he definitely went to school on Vin's ability to paint the picture on the radio and to weave in stories between play-by-play in almost a seamless fashion.

It's still remarkable to me how you can start to tell a story in a baseball game at the wrong moment, and you don't know it, and something really big happens...and your story is obliterated. Vin has almost a sixth sense of just filling in the empty spots with the stories and nothing big ever happens when he's telling you a story. He's blessed...but there is skill there in knowing how to pick the right moment to either indicate what's happening on the field or to enlighten us with some story.

Vin Scully and wife, Sandra

Vin Scully on a popular street in Dodgertown

Vin SCULLY Way

John Wooden and Vin Scully

Living High in the Early Days

Vin Scully with Gil Hodges

Sharing stories with George Lederer of the *Long Beach Press-Telegram*

JJ "The Bag Lady" and Vin Scully

VIN SCULLY

VIN SCULLY IS THE ENDURING VOICE OF SUMMER IN LOS ANGELES.

SCULLY JOINED THE DODGERS AS A PLAY-BY-PLAY ANNOUNCER IN 1950, WHEN HE WAS 22. IN 1958, HE
MOVED FROM BROOKLYN TO LOS ANGELES WITH THE TEAM. THOSE FIRST FOUR SEASONS IN CALIFORNIA, THE
DODGERS' HOME WAS THE COLISEUM, AND SCULLY WAS THERE FOR ALL OF THEM, SERVING AS OUR EYES AND
EARS, BRINGING A TEAM INTO OUR HOMES AND HEARTS. HIS WORDS EMBROIDERED THE DODGERS IRREVOCABLY
INTO THE FABRIC OF LOS ANGELES.

SCULLY'S TENURE WITH THE DODGERS IS THE LONGEST OF ANY BROADCASTER WITH A SINGLE CLUB IN
PROFESSIONAL SPORTS HISTORY. ON TELEVISION OR RADIO HE HAS CALLED 28 WORLD SERIES, MORE THAN ANY
BROADCASTER. HE WAS INDUCTED INTO THE BROADCASTERS WING OF THE BASEBALL HALL OF FAME IN 1982, INTO
THE RADIO HALL OF FAME IN 1995, VOTED BROADCASTER OF THE CENTURY BY THE AMERICAN SPORTSCASTERS
ASSOCIATION IN 2000, AND NAMED BASEBALL'S ALL-TIME BEST BROADCASTER IN 2005.

FOR MORE THAN A HALF CENTURY, VIN SCULLY HAS BRIDGED THE CULTURAL AND GENERATIONAL DIVIDE.
HIS VOICE HAS CONNECTED US TO EACH OTHER, YOUNG TO OLD, BLACK TO WHITE, LATINO TO ASIAN. HIS VOICE
IS OUR COMMON THREAD.

THE GAMES ARE EPHEMERAL, THE SCORES ARE FORGOTTEN, THE PLAYERS COME AND GO, BUT THE EMOTIONS
AND THE CONNECTIONS VIN CREATED THROUGH SCULLY TO LOS ANGELES WILL LAST FOREVER.

Lucky Strike had a slogan "L. S. M. F. T." which stood for "LUCKY STRIKE MEANS FINE TOBACCO". Baseball people referred to "L. S. M. F. T." as "LORD, SAVE ME FROM THE TEXAS LEAGUE".

In the press box with Jerry Doggett

Vin Scully with Don Drysdale and Sandy Koufax at Dodgertown

Receiving an Honorary Degree at Pepperdine University

Vin is pretty close to the vest on how much longer he plans to broadcast the Dodger games. My guess is that only Vin and his wife know that...or, only Vin knows that! I've talked to people in the L.A. media. They figure it's year-to-year with Vin. For instance, earlier this year there was some talk of him retiring. Not to be too cynical I just figured it was more of a negotiation ploy on Vin's part to get a better contract.

Sometimes you look for somebody to get pushed out because he's been doing it for so long. I haven't ever spoke to anybody who's waiting for Vin to get pushed out. It's just amazing—not at how good he is—how *long* Vin has been this good. In talking with people I haven't heard anyone express concern that he's not doing as well or that he's losing it or

> **Vin has almost a sixth sense of just filling in the empty spots with the stories**

that they hope he's not doing it much longer—that's never been the case with Vin, which is remarkable considering he's been doing it since 1950.

When you do something for several years, you lose your enthusiasm or passion after you've been doing it for 5 years—10 years—20 years, it's amazing he's been doing it for nearly 60 years, *and still operates at that level.*

It's hard to get up in the morning and go do the same thing again and again in any endeavor and do it really, really well. No one has really ever done it better than Vin in his lifetime. I assume the only person who compares to him and the way he does it was his mentor, Red Barber. It's just remarkable.

Although I enjoy him on TV, I'd much rather listen to him do the whole game on radio, and I give him all the credit in the world for having the power and the foresight to keep other people out of the booth with him. He's the only one-man booth in America when he's doing radio and the TV. He's very, very smart to do it that way. There's no reason to take away from his time by having some ex-jock telling us what Vin already has told us, or what he will tell us.

Vin has done golf on TV, and I remember when Vin did football on TV, which is the least skilled thing he's done of the group. You can't beat him for baseball but the way he delivers—his cadence—is perfect for golf. **BRENT MUSBURGER*** is not perfect for golf. With Brent, he's breathless like something has just happened or is about to happen. Golf doesn't work that way. Vin has the perfect pitch, tone, cadence and delivery for golf, and he was very good at it. His first football year he was put with John Madden. It took up too much air space for that type of pairing 'cause **JOHN MADDEN*** was going to be the star in the booth. If you want to call that a failure, that would be Vin's failure that he didn't pair off with Madden all that well. Pat Summerall was a better complement for Madden I'm sure because Pat is very, very spare with his words. Vin obviously is not as spare. For all the words Vin says, he doesn't usually have a lot of extra verbiage in there which is the beauty of what he does.

Vin is associated with baseball so people just think he's a baseball announcer or he's a one-trick pony. Chances are if he can do baseball that well, he can do basketball pretty darn well...he can do golf pretty darn well...he can do tennis pretty darn well. He's able to do any of those things. He understands the preparation. He understands the timing of when he's supposed to come in and not supposed to come in. Sometimes because a person is so good at one thing, we slight him thinking that he probably can't do other things. Scully probably can do the other things better than almost anybody else.

One of the great clichés about Vin's early career is how he taught baseball to Los Angeles because when it came to Los Angeles, no

*BRENT MUSBURGER was the home plate umpire when Tim McCarver made his pro baseball debut for Keokuk, Iowa, in the Midwest League in 1959.

*Golfer John Daly was named to the 1991 All-<u>MADDEN</u> Team. Colts Coach Ron Meyer was going to have Daly kick an extra point in an exhibition game but owner Robert Irsay nixed the idea.

one knew it so people would listen to him on the radio in the park. When I came to Los Angeles in the 1990s, people were listening to Vin on the radio in the ball park, which is the ultimate compliment. It's one thing to paint a picture for us when we're sitting at home and not at the park but people *at the park* are even listening to what he has to say—that's just remarkable. I have never seen that in any other stadium to the extent I saw people listening to Vin on the radio at Dodger Stadium.

In June of 1945, theatrical producer Mike Todd—then with the USO in France—tried to set up a major league All-Star game in Nuremburg Stadium. The stadium had a capacity of 120,000 and Todd wanted American GIs to be able to see major league baseball.

VIN SCULLY MEMORIES ARE FREE AND THEY'RE WORTH EVERY PENNY

STEVE RUSHIN

Steve Rushin was born in Elmhurst, IL and grew up in Bloomington, MN. After graduating from Marquette University in 1988. Rushin began writing a weekly column for Sports Illustrated. *The column ran from 1988-2007. He was named 2005 National Sportswriter of the Year by the National Sportscasters and Sportswriters Association. The* St. Paul Pioneer Press *called him the "best sportswriter in the country."'His 1994 story, "How We got Here" remains the longest-ever published in a single issue of* Sports Illustrated. *Rushin is married to former professional basketball player, Rebecca Lobo.*

Vin Scully is one of the few guys I've written about who has written to me—he sent me a nice note afterward, and I still have that. It's so rare for a sportswriter to hear something nice from someone you've written about. He actually has written to me more than once after I've written an article about him. Not many people have done that in the 20 years I've been a sportswriter.

Everybody has heard his voice. I used the term "drawn butter" to describe it. I was trying to draw an analogy to something that is rich and smooth for Vin Scully's voice, on a Saturday afternoon, from Dodger Stadium. That was the first thing that came to my head.

Drawn butter is probably considered bad for you these days so maybe I should have said something else.

When I got on XM Satellite Radio, I had written of being able to listen to every single baseball game on the radio...and being able to sit home and hear Vin Scully doing a Dodgers game while I'm here at midnight, and he's out there on the West Coast, both on the Internet and on Satellite Radio. The great thing about satellite radio is hearing this voice from a continent away describing things that you can then see in your head. Most of my experience with Vin Scully has been as a listener.

I was sitting up listening to him as he was describing Cesar Izturis going for a ground ball, going to his right like a statue falling over. I was sitting here, 3000 miles away, with a perfect image in my head of what was happening there at Dodger Stadium. We've all seen statues toppling over, and you can picture a shortstop going to his right for a ball and toppling like a statue. I mentioned that in a column, and Vin sent me a note after that as well. He's been a very gracious guy over the years. Vin has such a wealth of experience to draw on. I was a child of the seventies. I somehow became fascinated with the *Boys of Summer* and the Brooklyn Dodgers of the 50s, and to have a guy like Vin who has a connection to that and also has a wealth of his own interests and knowledge of literary references. He has all the books he reads and his own experiences to draw on. He is genuinely one of the guys who has gotten better with age. That wealth of experience he has to draw on brings more to the game.

> I was sitting...3000 miles away, with a perfect image in my head of what was happening there at Dodger Stadium.

Vin called Sandy Koufax's perfect game and Kirk Gibson's home run and other momentous events—Hank Aaron's 715th home run. There are very few guys ever, in any sport, who have been a relic-like figure in all these historical events.

Vin's voice is so distinctive and pleasant on the ears. He's synonymous with baseball to me. I grew up experiencing baseball in Minneapolis, hearing his voice on Game of the Week. When I picture Dodger Stadium, I picture the left field bleachers from watching on TV. When Ron Cey and Steve Garvey were Dodgers and then hearing Vin Scully's voice—those are my associations. I see that orange Union 76 Ball out in the outfield parking lot. Vin Scully is inseparable from those images for me.

It doesn't surprise me to hear that Vin did such a good job when he was asked to sing **"TAKE ME OUT TO THE BALL GAME"*** at Wrigley Field. He has such a beautiful voice...a voice that is very well suited for baseball and golf.

> ...particularly in recent years, he's been the reason to be a Dodger fan.

Vin is a guy who hates to draw attention to himself. When I was trying to arrange to interview him, I thought I had it all set up. The Dodgers kept telling me that he hates talking about himself. On the other hand, he's a nice man whose instinct is to be accommodating. When I went out to Dodger Stadium, I ran into him in the press box cafeteria. I introduced myself and told him, "I'm here for this arranged interview." He had no idea what I was talking about, but he sat there with his cup of coffee and talked to me for an hour—all on the spur of the moment. He mentioned that he was uncomfortable being the focus of attention. For many years, particularly in recent years, he's been the reason to be a Dodger fan. Even when the team is lousy, you can always turn on the radio or TV and hear him and that's worth the price of admission.

If there's anyone in broadcasting who *doesn't* talk too much, it's Vin Scully. When he was calling Aaron's home run, he let the crowd noise do the talking. He went to the back of the booth and drank a cup of coffee for a minute or so. If anybody has a sense of when to talk and when not to talk, it's Vin Scully. He's such an icon, and I can't imagine anyone in Los Angeles making the remark that Vin talks too much.

Vin has such a breadth of interest. One of the things I identified with him was his dread of going on the road. After years and years

---

***"TAKE ME OUT TO THE BALL GAME"** is the third-most sung song in America after "Happy Birthday" and "The Star-Spangled Banner."

and years of doing it myself, I got to the point where I just couldn't stand being in a hotel room at noon knowing that you didn't go to the ball park until 3:30—still 3 ½ hours away, and then the game is still four hours away after that. Vin talked to me at length about how it ate him up being on the road away from his wife. He said that his companion on the road was books. Nobody ever saw him out and about. He never really hobnobbed with players.

A friend of mine, John O'Keefe, who used to work for **_SPORTS ILLUSTRATED_***, and grew up in Westwood, was at a wedding in L. A. that Vin Scully attended. He said everybody wanted to talk to Vin Scully. John, who was probably in his mid-thirties, and a bunch of people his age cornered Vin and were using him like a human juke box—"come on, just do the Gibson call," He said Vin was ridiculously affable and would laugh but he wouldn't do the call. If he were out and about in Los Angeles, he would have to be doing that call 23 hours a day. People always want him to do their favorite call of his or to do their outgoing call message on their cell phones. He did tell me that he got asked that a lot. He said it was all very flattering but he felt he had to preserve some of himself for himself.

A lot of people mention that Vin benefited from the transistor radio, but really the transistor radio benefited from Vin.

When he does just try to fade away, there will be a lot of acclaim and people trying to do tributes to him, and he doesn't want that...but he deserves it—that's for sure.

When you interview as many people as I have, you get a preconceived idea of them and then sometimes they don't live up to expectations—Vin is one of those who live up to expectations and beyond.

*Who was the only Major League Baseball player to grace the cover of the college football edition of <u>SPORTS ILLUSTRATED</u>? Bo Jackson? No. Kirk Gibson? No. Rick Leach of Michigan? Yes.

> He deserves all the praise that he gets. That's not true of everybody.

People forget after a while that the Dodgers and Giants came from New York. Like those two baseball institutions, Vin Scully also comes from New York—Fordham and the Bronx. You think of him as if he were raised in orange groves by Chavez Ravine. To me, these are three baseball institutions who came west and made baseball what it is today—the Giants...the Dodgers...and Vin Scully.

He deserves all the praise that he gets. That's not true of everybody.

WIT HAPPENS

SCOTT OSTLER

Ostler has written his very humorous columns for the L. A. Times, The National Sports Daily *and currently for the* San Francisco Chronicle. *In 2003, Vin Scully was California Sportscaster of the Year, and Ostler was Sportswriter of the Year. Sometimes his column is titled "Answerman," but his funniest stuff comes in his "Deep Thoughts, Cheap-Shots and Bon Mots" segment.*

As a kid, every night in the summer, for two or three hours, I was glued in to Vinnie. I loved it. Vinnie made me love baseball. There are some people who have a gift. You love to sit down with them, have a Coke or a beer or coffee, and you think, "This guy's great. He's got a great personality. I would love talking to this guy." To me, Vinnie was like that. He made you feel like you were spending part of an evening with him. He's an enjoyable guy. There's something about the positive nature of his broadcast and the tone of his voice and just how he made the listener feel right at home and comfortable and made you enjoy the time and brought the game to life. To me, it was magical.

Anybody who follows sports thinks their first announcer is the greatest. I figured maybe I just like Vinnie because he is the first announcer I ever heard. As I got around a little bit, I found out that a lot of people in a lot of other cities thought he was great also. I decided I had just been lucky enough as a kid to be tuned in to him and to have him be a part of my life growing up in baseball. I always looked forward to tuning in the Dodgers just to hear Vinnie's voice.

I covered the Dodgers as a beat guy for only half of one season. Then I was around them for six or seven years after that as a columnist, so I'd be at games on a somewhat regular basis. Vinnie was different than most broadcasters I know. The guy who works for the Giants now, when I go to a Giants game, I see him before almost every game and I chat with him around the batting cage. I never saw Vinnie out there on the field. I never saw him hanging around the batting cage. I never saw him in the club house. He did his work differently. I'm not saying he did it the wrong way or anything, but certainly differently. I think he had people he knew or he was around the team on the road enough so he got to know the guys. He definitely got to know everybody and knew what was going on but he did it without hanging around schmoozing with the guys on the field.

> Anybody who follows sports thinks their first announcer is the greatest.

Tom Candiotti was pitching for the Dodgers back in '92. Jeff Kent is with the Mets. Candiotti is in a fantasy league but he doesn't have Kent on his team. Kent's off to a torrid start, and he's killing him. So the Dodgers are in New York to play the Mets. Ramon Martinez is warming up in the Dodgers bull pen to pitch the series opener. Candiotti strolls to the pen and within earshot so Martinez can hear him, he tells pitching coach Ron Perranoski, "Peri, I just talked to Bret Saberhagen and Saberhagen told me that if Kent gets drilled his first time up, he's mush for the rest of the series." The first inning, Kent comes to the plate and Ramon just absolutely buries one...right in Kent's ribs. Candiotti said it was so bad Kent went down on one knee and had to come out of the game. I sat there thinking, "What'd you just do? You told a complete lie. You got this guy drilled." After that, it was funny. Pedro Martinez, Ramon's brother, started drilling Kent and so did all the other Dominican pitchers. For years, Ramon drilled Kent...every time. That winter, I'm in a charity golf tournament and wind up in Kent's group. We're sitting there together at dinner. He's the nicest guy in the world. I didn't tell him.

How did Candiotti's fantasy team do? When I saw Kent get hit by Ramon, that was the end of my fantasy days. It was out of control.

I ran the story by Kent, and he said, "It's part of the game. I've been hit for many reasons." So, Rotisserie League—no big deal.

I've been in the pressbox when Dick Enberg was broadcasting and Chick Hearn at the Lakers—they were always joking around. Vin just didn't hang out with the writers. That's not necessarily a bad thing.

I knew Vin was angry with me about one of my columns. I mentioned his "non-coverage" of the impending baseball strike. He had probably never had any kind of criticism at all so it probably hit him out of the blue. Before that, there had been two or three occasions where he had dropped me a personal note saying, "I really liked the column you wrote the other day. I really enjoy reading your columns." He was nice enough, after reading those articles, to drop me a couple of personal notes, which I appreciated.

SOMETIMES GOD JUST HANDS YOU ONE

PHIL ELDERKIN

Phil Elderkin was Sports Editor of the Christian Science Monitor *for 5 years—1970-75—and worked there from 1943 to 1989. He was born and grew up just outside of Boston. He is 82 years old.*

When Vin came out of the Navy in 1946, he went back to Fordham. For his first three years at Fordham, he was their regular centerfielder. He was a good college ball player. He didn't have any power—he was a spray hitter. He was good in the field. His ambition was to hit a home run.

The *Bronx Home News* used to cover all of Fordham's home games. They covered the away games too, but on the home games they always sent a photographer. If you hit a home run, that photographer was always at home plate to snap you and you were on the front page of the sports section in the next day's edition. For a long, long time, Scully dreamed he would be able to hit a home run. Where they played, there was no way anybody could hit a home run out of that field. The field went on forever—you had to hit it just over the outfielder's head because the ball would roll forever, and you'd get an inside-the-park home run. Finally the day happened...Vin got hold of one and hit it over the opposing centerfielder's head, and it rolled and rolled. He scampered around the bases—sure enough, as he crossed home plate, Vin Scully was snapped by the Bronx Home News photographer. The next day, sure enough, his picture was on page one. But...he was identified as Frank Scully instead of Vin Scully.

Vin didn't play his senior year. He had some broadcasting opportunities—I think it was more than one station, not large stations, but popular ones—to do some work for them. I'm not sure all of it was sports. Some of it may have been news. Vin knew by then that he was never going to be a big-league ball player. He did see a future in radio and was willing to give up his last year of baseball at Fordham to help his radio career.

Vin Scully never pushes Vin Scully. He tells things the way they happened, and he doesn't embellish them. He doesn't get very emotional about anything. I don't get to the ball park nearly as early as I used to so I don't see Vin as often. I'll see him in the press room for a minute or two before or after a game. So many people want to talk to him—he's always talking with somebody. If you ever had Vin Scully alone, you didn't have him alone for very long because somebody was going to break in—someone who knew him or someone who had a question or had a message to deliver.

I don't think people realize how tough it is to broadcast a Major League baseball game. I was fortunate in that Ernie Harwell allowed me to broadcast one inning of a Red Sox-Detroit Tiger game in 1974. When there are two men on base and there's one out, and the hitter hits the ball between the outfielders, and you've got two outfielders running after the ball, and you've got two guys on the bases trying to get home, it's tough to tie that all together. You'd suddenly forget—were there two men on? Was there one man on? Who picked up the ball—the centerfielder or the right fielder? Is the guy who hit the ball halfway between first and second...is he sliding into second? It's not easy.

My inning was during a game at Fenway Park. It was a fairly routine inning. The Tigers went out 1-2-3. And the **RED SOX*** had two men on with two outs, and somebody drove them in with a single or a double. We got through it easily. They had told me beforehand, "Brother, you make a mistake, you're outta here!" At first, Harwell wasn't going to let me do it. He said, "I've got to call the station." We'd known each other a long time, and he told me

---

*The RED SOX hold the record for most books written about one team followed by the Yankees and the Brooklyn Dodgers.

he'd like to do it, but I'm not sure I can without calling the station and getting permission from the sponsor. Then all of a sudden he said, "Hey, I've been doing this for 20 years. I can make this decision. Let's do it."

It's impossible to overestimate Scully's value to the Dodgers. He's made a lot out of broadcasting. He's a master at distracting attention away from the inept and the boring. He doesn't broadcast a game...he really narrates it. There's no dead-air time when Vin Scully is at the mic. He can make a blow-out game interesting. The way he broadcasts, you don't leave your radio. You don't turn your radio or your TV off. He's always got something to say.

> **Vin Scully was the son Red Barber never had.**

In the winter in '66, Carl Yastrzemski had met a Hungarian trainer who was well known in Europe but not in the United States. They got together and he told Yastrzemski his philosophy of getting a ballplayer ready for the season. Yastrzemski devoted the entire winter to working with this guy. He worked with him every day for hours at a time. During the '67 season, Yastrzemski had a year like few people ever had. His home runs went from 28 to 43. He won the Triple Crown...and nobody's won it since. After the season, I talked to him and asked, "Are you going to do this again?" He said, "No, I will never do that again. I will never put myself through that." I said, "It wasn't worth it?" He said, "No. Even with the progress I made, I punished myself physically and I punished myself mentally. I will never do that again."

Vin Scully was the son Red Barber never had. He saw something in Scully long before other people did. It would have come out eventually, but he was the first to see it. He was never jealous of Scully. He was Scully's mentor...with love. He helped Scully a great deal. Red Barber helped Vin all he could. Vin realized this, and he really appreciated it. Scully gives credit where credit is due.

As a reporter, I would have been in the press box when Vin was doing the games, so I didn't always hear him. It's the same for the players...but the wives who go to the games...the wives know what's going on.

Vin loved one-liners, and they didn't have to be about baseball—the type of thing Jack Benny used to dish out. Vin also was a great reader. He read all the time when the Dodgers were on the road. He didn't read junk. He was very well read. He read a lot of biographies and a lot of books of the month. He's a good writer himself. He wrote the foreword to one of Jim Murray's books. When he was at Fordham, he was the correspondent for the *New York Times*. They had a long-time column there called "Looking Them Over." John Kieran preceded Scully, and preceding Kieran was Arthur Daly, a Pulitzer Prize winner.

Everybody I've ever talked to thought Scully was a great writer. The few things I've seen that he's written are very well done. Scully was an English major since there was no Broadcasting major at that time.

A friend of mine had a son who came from another state to visit him. It turned out the young man was blind from birth. He was a real sharp kid. His ambition in life was to meet and talk with Vin Scully. I knew this guy, and he asked me if I would try to get Vin to talk to his son. I told him I would try. Right away, Vin said, "yes." He talked with his son for quite a while. The young man came out of the booth walking on air.

> Scully was an English major since there was no Broadcasting major at that time.

I have another story that's not really a Vin Scully story, but it is a Dodger story. Charlie Dressen was managing the Dodgers back in the early 50s and was eyeing a utility player dying to be sent up to pinch hit—George Shuba—so Dressen says, "George, grab a bat! Go in the club house and stir that pot of chili I have cooking by the shower."

WE'RE PLAYING BEL AIR SO GET YOUR BALL RETRIEVER REGRIPPED... DOGLEG PAR-3s

BILL DWYRE

*When Bill Dwyre was at Notre Dame in the early '60s, he and his roommate made tapes of the two of them broadcasting a high school football game and sent it to the local hot-shot sports anchor in **SOUTH BEND***. The latter wrote back advising the young men to study hard because they had no future in sports. Dwyre became sports editor of the Los Angeles Times, and his roommate, George Blaha, has been the voice of the Detroit Pistons and the Michigan State Spartans for four decades.*

About two years ago, I was playing in a charity golf outing at Bel Air Country Club, where Vinnie belongs. I didn't even know he was there. I teed off on the first hole—it's up high, a long par-five, and it's right next to the dining room area. I was with my group, and we were playing a scramble. I was a little bit nervous 'cause this is a nice country club, and I didn't want to look like an idiot on the first tee. Out of nowhere, comes Vinnie. He said, "I'm gonna walk with you guys." He starts walking along, talking about golf and telling stories in the classic "Vin Scully intoning voice." I get down there and hit my second shot close and my third shot is within six feet of the pin. They're all in the hole in par. I've got a shot to make a birdie. They're all laughing while we were standing around. Vinnie is making wisecracks about sportswriters who play too much golf and stuff like that. I

*The man who wrote the Michigan fight song, "(Hail to) The Victors," lived in **SOUTH BEND**, Indiana on what is now the site of the College Football Hall of Fame.

made the putt—no big deal—it's the first hole. Vinnie, out of nowhere, says, "Ladies and gentleman, that is, outside of the Kirk Gibson home run, the greatest moment in sports I've ever seen."

It was just one of those moments. Vin said, "I'm going to walk another hole with you." I'm looking around. It's February. We were up on the top of a hill there on the first green at Bel Air. You look down and it's a clear winter day, and you see the whole sky-line of Los Angeles. You're walking along with Vin Scully and Tommy Lasorda telling you stories about baseball, thinking, "This is what heaven should be when you die—how it should be."

It was a time when Vin's wife, Sandy, was very ill. She had some sort of asbestos in her system. They were working on their house. She had to go into a hospital on the West Side two or three days a week for treatments. Vin said he didn't have time to play a whole 18 holes, or even 9 holes, but he'd drop her off, and she'd go through this treatment, and then he had to pick her up.

> "This is what heaven should be when you die—how it should be."

He just wandered by Bel Air. When you're there, you sit down and look around, and pretty soon Al Michaels is sitting on your left and Vin Scully is sitting on your right. You say, "Oh my God!" That's the way it was for me that day. He walked another hole or two with us and told stories. We didn't care about the golf. We just wanted to walk with Vinnie. And then, he had to go pick up his wife. I'll never forget that. He was just like a regular guy walk-ing along...yet the stories were incredible. Everything he tells is so good because of the way he tells it....

There's a guy on first base, and he says, "Now watch Fernando's left foot on the rubber. If he's going to go to first base, he'll just edge a little bit closer, but he'll put his foot on the rubber a little bit closer if he really wants to pick somebody off." Fernando threw a couple of pitches...then the camera guy picked up on what he was doing—he moved his foot closer to first base and went into his stretch and picked the guy off. You think, "Oh my God. He called the shot."

> Everybody was leaning forward to make sure they heard every word and every inflection of what he said.

Jim Murray was one of Vin's best friends. When Jim died, we had a memorial service for him at Dodger Stadium. I was in charge of putting it together. There must have been 3,000 to 4,000 people there. They went from the lower deck home plate all the way down to first base. I had Chick Hearn, Al Michaels, Al Davis, Chris McCarron, Jerry West, and Vin Scully as speakers—now there's a lineup. In planning it, I had to decide who was to be the clean-up hitter, the anchor. Of course, it was Vin Scully. I made the decision rather arbitrarily and everybody certainly agreed with it. All the other guys got up and had their say...Vin got up and told stories about Murray. He talked about how it was an overcast day and he said, "The Irish call this a 'soft' day." The whole place was absolutely mesmerized by what he had to say. He made it a classic tribute to a friend whom he had been everywhere with. We just used one of the corners so there were echoes. Everybody was leaning forward to make sure they heard every word and every inflection of what he said.

Vin Scully always rises to the occasion. He always says the right thing. I've heard him hundreds of times at speeches at the Southern California Broadcasters and there's never been anyone like him.

SHORT STORIES FROM LONG MEMORIES

I was walking out of a hotel, the Chase, in St. Louis, with a couple of engineers who worked for Scully and Red Barber. We had a softball, gloves and a bat. George "Shotgun" Shuba, a pinch hitter and left fielder, said, "Where are you going?" I said, "We're going to a park and play a little ball." "Shotgun" said, "Can I come?" He was hitting about .340 and was leading the league. I said, "Yeah, sure, you can come." We got set up there and he said, "Do you want to pitch to me?" I said, "I'm not comfortable with this. You're going against Major League fastballs now, and I'm going to give you this underhand softball stuff." He said, "Just go ahead and pitch." I pitched, and he hit some low line drives. He didn't hit anything through the box, happily! I don't think Vin went with us to play softball, he went to play golf.

One of the things in St. Louis was that J. G. Taylor Spink—the publisher of *The Sporting News*—had a membership at one of the clubs. Any time Dodger media people wanted to play golf, Spink would make the arrangement. After Scully returned from playing golf, I asked him, "How did you do?" He said, "Well, I didn't get snake bit. That was the best thing that happened."

In Vero Beach, before the games, a lot of us would shag flies, and Vinnie would do that too. We were down there for a long time. Vinnie could catch the ball and could get off a decent throw. When Vinnie was young, Red Barber was the boss of the radio team, which included Connie Desmond, who was a very amiable guy. Red could be quite severe. He was very different in person than he was over the radio, when he was like everybody's uncle.

You always look for somebody to go to the ballpark in a cab with you to split the fare. One time in St. Louis, I stepped outside and Red said, "Are you going to Sportsman's Park?" I said, "Yes." The Mississippi River heat was about 100 degrees. I said, "Oh boy, it's hot." Barber said severely, "You have to expect heat in St. Louis if you're going to be a baseball writer, young man." That was the nature of Red.

Vin was bright and spoke well. He was under Barber's thumb to a great extent. We'd hang around and have a drink after a game. Vin was single, and he was very Catholic. He told me that a priest had once told him that a single couple was making out famously in a car at the bottom of a hill. A tractor trailer came unhinged and the trailer slammed into the car and killed them both, so they met their death while they were sinning. Vin was strongly influenced by the Jesuits at Fordham. He was the junior fellow, but he didn't live wildly.

The economics were different in the old days. The players, the announcers and the writers were in the same economic strata. That made closeness easier than if you're hanging around someone making four million a year.

Vin and I would hang around. One night in spring training, which was interminable, we got to New Orleans, and it was like liberation because in some of these little towns the cooking was terrible. You had the southern cooking, and they would put ham fat in the green beans. You get to New Orleans and it's "restaurant city," so we were going to eat great. Then we decided we would check out the French Quarter so Scully and I went up to Bourbon Street. There would be a jazz joint and then there would be a joint with girls doing unusual dances on the bar top and then there's another jazz joint. We had a wonderful time. We talked about what we were going to do. I was going to write some books. Scully said he'd really like to travel. People say to him, "You travel now." Vinnie said, "But, where do I go? I go to Cincinnati and Milwaukee. When I say 'travel' I'm thinking of Venice and Paris." I assume by now he's been to Venice and Paris.

He told me one story about his college baseball. He said he slid home safely, and it was an important run, and there was a photographer with a speed graphic. He slid across home plate safely, and then he went to the photographer and said, "Who are you with?" The guy said, "*The New York Times.*" So Scully said the next morning he hurried to the newsstand to buy the *New York Times*, and there was his picture on the back page of the sports section, and the caption was, "Frank Sully scored a run."

> —ROGER KAHN, 81, author of *The Boys of Summer,* the best-selling book in Dodger history

They were doing a big fund raiser for Fordham. They were honoring Vin Scully and Charles Osgood. Both of them were in town, and some of us writers were invited to come and talk with them. I sat down with Vin for 15-20 minutes.

Still, such is the reverence for Vin that when *The New York Times* posted a short story about Scully's ambivalence regarding the future, it caused quite a stir in Southern California.

Despite his long association with the Dodgers and thus with Ebbets Field and **DODGER STADIUM***, he retains an emotional attachment to the New York Giants and Polo Grounds, the team and ballpark of his youth.

Vin said, "When Shea Stadium first opened, Mrs. Payson owned the ball club. Where the press box is now was a room covered with oil paintings. I saw one and I felt like I had been kicked in the stomach. It was as if the artist was sitting in a box seat behind home plate at the old Polo Grounds where I really grew up, and it's all dark umbers and dark greens and the eye takes you out toward centerfield because there's a light in the clubhouse. There are two men standing there talking in street clothes. Now the sun is just starting to change the coloration of the sky, so your eye naturally now starts to go up the clubhouse and as the sky is brightening, you realize there is a huge derrick, and hanging from it is the destruction ball, and you realize when the sun comes up they're going to knock down the ballpark. So if you want to talk about how you feel when an old ballpark goes, that's

---

*DODGER STADIUM—since the day it opened in 1962—is the only current stadium that has never changed its seating capacity. Because of a conditional use permit from the city of Los Angeles, the capacity is always 56,000....Fenway Park's seating capacity is lower for day games (36,984) than for night games (37,400).

the way I feel. That really touched me. I couldn't buy the oil, but thanks to Ralph Kiner, Mrs. Payson had a print made and framed and gave it to me and I have it to this day."

Getting back to some reasons he may retire, Vin said "I heard 60 percent of Americans have trouble sleeping. The older you get, the more trouble you have. Travel and time zones affect your sleep. Lack of sleep plays a big part in the way you perform."

On working alone, Vin said, "It goes back to Brooklyn with Red Barber and Connie Desmond and back to New York, period. In the old days, you had Mel Allen and Curt Gowdy, and you had Russ Hodges and Ernie Harwell, and you had Red Barber and Connie Desmond. They worked alone."

"There was never any interplay on the air. I know Red always felt one man, one voice, and the more I thought about that when we were moving out to California, the more I thought that works best."

"If I want to sell you a car, is it more effective for me to talk directly to you about the merits of the car or do you think you'd be more inclined listening to me talk to somebody else about the car? I've found it just makes more sense, one man, one voice and—sell."

Scully on his old neighborhood in Washington Heights: "It was a wonderful neighborhood growing up. In those days it was basically Jewish, European Jews fleeing Hitler. And they were hard-working people. Doors were wide open. It was a wonderful area to grow up in."

Vin says he seldom listens to other announcers. "I'm not a listener. It's not ego at all. But Red Barber gave me a bit of advice when I first joined him. He said you shouldn't listen to other broadcasters because each announcer brings something into the booth that no one else has."

"And I looked at him and I thought what the heck do I have just out of **COLLEGE*** and he said yourself, there's no one else like you. He didn't want me to consciously or subconsciously borrow tonal effect or whatever. So I don't listen. Whatever comes out of me is me. It's pure original, good, bad or indifferent."

*Of the 750 players on Major League rosters recently, only seventeen were COLLEGE graduates.

Scully on being honored by his alma mater, Fordham: "Back in 2000 when they invited me to give the commencement address I was in shock. I did that with kind of a smile in my heart looking at these fellows and girls sitting where I sat a long time ago."

"I'm not really a fan. That has long since gone. I might turn on an SC football game. I watched the last three minutes of the Super Bowl. I have 18 grandchildren and everyone was in one house. As **ELI MANNING*** was performing his magic, everything stopped."

> I thought the No. 1 announcer in tonal quality was Ted Husing.

Scully on Al Campanis: "Al and I roomed together for several years in Vero Beach. It's really one of life's tragedies what happened to him. When you say Al Campanis, my heart winces."

Scully on his favorite announcer when he was a child: "When I was growing up, I thought the No. 1 announcer in tonal quality was Ted Husing. His command of the language really made an impression, even on a little kid growing up."

—**NEIL BEST**, Sports Media Director for Newsday

XM Radio carries every Major League baseball game for all the teams, including the Dodgers. Within the first few months of offering Major League games for fans across the country, the first thing we heard was feedback from folks who say extraordinary things about Vin Scully. It was the first time for many of them to actually be able to hear Vin's voice on the radio. They knew of his reputation but hadn't actually heard him call a game. The excitement and the resonance were exceptional.

Charley Steiner, who also does play-by-play for the Dodgers, does a separate program specifically for XM Radio. He does his show from his home in California. He is reverent as can be regarding Vin.

XM is to radio what your cable or satellite is to your television set. XM offers a 170-channel package that includes every Major League baseball game for every team, thousands of other sporting

---

*The speed limit on the University of Mississippi campus is 18 MPH in honor of Archie **MANNING**'s uniform number.

events throughout the year, college sports, hockey, plus you get dozens of different commercial-free music channels, news radio, talk radio.

We did a survey of baseball fans a couple of years ago asking about great announcers...Vin Scully topped the list! We regularly hear from fans who appreciate XM Radio because it allows them to hear Scully, Uecker and other legendary announcers.

Baseball is the sport most ideally suited to radio. There's something about the directness of radio that brings the sport alive and the ability of legendary announcers like Vin Scully to paint the picture for listeners, even listeners thousands of miles away. He is unparalleled in sports broadcasting. There's nothing quite like listening to baseball on the radio. And there's nothing quite like hearing Vin Scully call a Dodger game....

Vin appeared in the film *For Love of the Game* in 1999 with Kevin Costner. It was different and challenging in ways he had never been challenged before.

> Vin worked on the movie over a period of a few weeks.

Vin worked on the movie over a period of a few weeks. When he did work with the film folk, he put in some very long days. The interesting thing about his working on that was that they, at first, had a script for him. As it turned out, since he's so good at what he does, he was better off—and ended up pretty much discarding the script—watching where the film was showing the game, and he would broadcast, as he normally would, and they recorded it. He was a good friend of Kevin Costner, and that may have had something to do with him getting to do that project. He also seemed to very much enjoy talking with Costner in between takes about what he was doing and how he was doing it. He told us that gave him some keys as to what he could talk about when he was actually doing the broadcast of that fictional game. Penny Marshall and James Earl Jones were in the film.

Toward the end of the production, they had many of the scenes filmed and those were what Vin watched on a large screen as he then did the voice part of that. It was done during the off-season. Vin really ended up adding his own imprint to what the director originally had in mind because he could do it so easily. I recall him telling us he had taken a few lines that he liked from the script, but ninety percent of what he did was just Vinnie off-the-cuff, as he would do any Dodger game.

I have listened to Vin do games on the computer. Every time I'm in southern California now during baseball season, I always turn on the radio during games just to hear his voice. There's something about that voice that means the Dodgers to me. I've been a life-long Dodger fan from the Brooklyn days.

My co-author, Steve Wood, grew up in L.A. in the 60s. He bought LP records—yes, LP records—of Vin calling Dodger games so he could listen to Vin in the off-season.

Vinnie has a way about him that is unlike any other broadcaster. He has a way of capturing and expressing what is going on. It allows the listener to feel as though they are there seeing the game. There's no other broadcaster who I think comes close. I hold Dick Enberg in high regard and a few others who do a very fine job, but they just can't be Vin Scully. That is what makes him so special and so unique.

When Vinnie stops broadcasting for the Dodgers, I will lose much of my emotional attachment to the team. To me, Vin represents the Dodgers right to the heart and soul.

> —DAVID PINCUS, Co-author of *Reel Baseball* and XM Radio
> executive

In my book, *The Giants and the Dodgers—Four Cities, Two Teams, One Rivalry*, I took an unpopular position—that the Giant-Dodger rivalry got better when it moved to California. I don't know if Vin Scully would confirm that. In a way, in 1978, he did—that was a very hot year for the rivalry. The Giants and Dodgers were both in it 'til the end. The Giants would go down to L.A., and the crowds would be very polite and clean and civilized. Then the Dodgers would come to Candlestick, and the Giant fans were just nasty, sometimes even violent.

> ...the Giant fans were just nasty, sometimes even violent.

There was a point when Vin Scully made the remark that I read in a column by Ron Bergman in the *Oakland Tribune*. "You know what they ought to do with the Friday night crowds here? They ought to let them all in, lock the gates and go play the game somewhere else."

Then he said, "The fans at Ebbets Field and the Polo Grounds would never think of throwing things at the players." I loved that quote because, to me, it substantiated the passion of the rivalry in California was just as strong as it had been back east.

Vin Scully emceed the April 10, 1962, Opening Day ceremonies at Dodger Stadium. At the ceremonies, National League president Warren Giles said, "When Mr. O'Malley first asked to move his team to Los Angeles, we never saw anything like this at the end of the rainbow." This may not be a Vin Scully story, but Jaime Jarrin, the Spanish language announcer for the Dodgers, said Fernando Valenzuela was a hero who did not speak English, did not have a good body, came from a humble background and he walked like a general.

—ANDREW GOLDBLATT, author, Berkeley, California

I was a newspaperman and was making my very first trip for the Los Angeles Herald Examiner in 1969. It was a three-city trip. We were in Atlanta. I walked down and sat by the swimming pool. I looked over and Vin Scully was sitting next to me. I was tongue-tied naturally...here's the guy I'd listened to all my life and had worshipped like every kid growing up in L.A. I was quick to find out that he was very unpretentious and cordial. Pretty soon I found myself talking about what books he was reading and what I was reading. We talked about the different authors we liked. I walked away later, and I'm shaking my head thinking, "My God, I was sitting there with Scully." It was hard for me to believe.

Vin said, "I really, truly love the game. I've done football and golf and even a little tennis, but I really believe baseball is an incredible game. The other thing is the roar of the crowd. It still stirs the adrenalin in me. It still gives me goose-bumps."

Other announcers might sound monotonous, but not Scully. He can be plugging one of the team's many give-away nights—this time for free Dodgers noisemakers for kids, then pause and say, "There's something redundant about giving noisemakers to youngsters under 14 years of age."

Vin Scully is still going strong. His play-by-play calls are as velvety-smooth as ever with his storytelling and his wonderfully-descriptive phrases spilling out as easily as your morning orange juice. This is the Babe Ruth of baseball broadcasting. Someday you'll want to tell your grandkids—they'll all be excited about some new announcer they like—you'll smile and shake your head and give them the only answer you can, "You should have heard Vin Scully. He was as much a poet as a broadcaster."

> Vin said, "I really, truly love the game."

—STEVE BISHEFF, long-time columnist for the *Orange County Register*, currently writes "Steve Bisheff Insider Blog" on 710 ESPN, Los Angeles

Vin Scully is arguably Los Angeles' greatest living treasure. He is the one intellectual concept that a fractured, fractious region can agree upon. There is no measurable dissent. He makes Los Angeles a better place to live. It's a little alarming that Scully will be 81 in November. He looks like a much younger man and seems to have the energy of one. Even as he concedes he may have lost a step from his prime. He says he thinks as players slow up, as their hand-eye coordination slows up, also play-by-play announcers lose something. The mind and tongue cannot always be as sharp as it was.

I asked him why he didn't do an autobiography. He said, "Oh, no, no, no. It's really too much trouble. I don't want to spend a lot of time talking about me. I've already spent a lifetime talking. I don't have the drive. To know there's going to be a book with your name on it just isn't me at all. I've had many suggestions by writers that they would like to do a book and I've said, "I don't think so. No."

I also asked Vin if it surprises him that many people cannot envision the Dodgers without Vin Scully. Vin said, "I can understand that. I remember growing up in New York as a kid. The New

York Yankees *were* Mel Allen. The Brooklyn Dodgers *were* Red Barber. The Giants became Russ Hodges. But Allen and Barber were so closely identified with their team so I understood that. I never, ever thought it would happen to me because, first of all, I never thought I would be around doing the games for that long. I went to Los Angeles when the transistor radio was new. People would be sitting a long way from the action so the radio helped them see it. Also the fans had heard of Willie Mays and Stan Musial, but they didn't know many others. Now they had the radio to help them. Otherwise I don't puff up about it. It could have been some other announcer who started in '58, and it would have been his good fortune instead of mine."

Vin does make errors these days during the game. He'll get a stat wrong or the wrong count—things he never did 20 years ago but, my goodness, the man is over 80 years old.

—PAUL OBERJUERGE, former sports writer for the *San Bernardino Sun*

> When Vin uses the term, "ink-stained wretches" …it's a term of endearment.

When Vin uses the term, "ink-stained wretches" to denote the newspaper journalists, it's a term of endearment.

Those of us who are around every day, have a pretty casual relationship with Vin. If I needed him for something, I could just walk up and tell him what I needed. Somebody from outside, who is not around every day, would have to go through the public relations office to set something up.

Vin handled the Jeff Kent remarks just right—not say anything—let Jeff make a fool of himself. Meantime, Vin maintains the same dignity that has marked his career. He does things with dignity and class, and I thought he handled it well. Jeff Kent doesn't do very many things with dignity and class, and I thought Vinnie handled it the way everyone knew Vinnie would handle it.

Nobody could figure out why Jeff Kent took offense about anybody saying those things when it was obvious to everyone that what was said was true.

—TONY JACKSON, *L.A. Daily News*, native of Springdale, AR

I'd run across Mr. Scully a number of times at Dodgertown over the years. It wasn't like we were big friends. He treated everybody like he wanted to be treated. He was a very personable guy. Once he got to know you, he made you feel very comfortable. We cover the Mets and the Dodgers because they're both in our coverage area. I've had dealings with both over the years. The L.A. media is sure different from the New York media. Mr. Scully pretty much typifies the L.A. media in that they're very outgoing, very friendly. Vin Scully, in my book, is one of the greatest announcers of all times. He certainly doesn't come across that way when you are in a setting with him. Of all the guys I've dealt with—and it became a lot less as time went on—those L.A. guys were really nice to be around. I guess I can't emphasize that enough. It was a far cry from dealing with the crew from New York. I think, even though they've taken some shots at Vero Beach and being the small town that it is, over the years, they have enjoyed themselves when they came down, and I know Mr. Scully did. Every day before the afternoon games or workouts, the O'Malley family would be in the main dining room. Lasorda would be there, Scully would be there—all the writers would be there, and various guests of the O'Malleys would be there. It was almost like "All in the Family." They'd also have a big party every year. The media was part of O'Malley's plans and outlines. Once O'Malley sold the team, that changed drastically. Mr. Scully wasn't a guy who was front and center all the time, but he was an easy guy to approach.

The O'Malleys took care of the press probably better than any owner I've ever been around. Everyone was welcome to come. With Vin Scully, it wasn't like he hung out with the beat writers or the print writers a lot, but when he was around he was a very cordial guy. He treated you like he wanted to be treated. He acted no better than you were. You don't always see that, especially in broadcasters of his stature.

—MIKE GRAHAM, Sportswriter, Vero Beach, Florida

Vin's reading habits were very diverse. The one thing that sticks out in my mind was a book about the West, *Lonesome Dove*, which I remember him alluding to.

Talking about reading habits, Tommy Lasorda would always joke about Steve Sax. He would say "I was sitting there reading and Steve Sax gets on the team bus and sees I'm reading the *Wall Street Journal*. He said, 'Hey, Skip, can I see the sports section?'" Tommy would then say, "...and they expect me to win pennants with these guys."

—<u>TOBY ZWIKEL</u>, former Dodger publicist

Back when I started, there was one bus to take people to the ball park and to the airport so we were all on there together. Then, they had to have two buses—one for the players and one for everybody else. Vin Scully always had a book with him when he traveled. I read cowboy novels, and I know Vin was *above* that.

Back in the day—baseball writers were official scorers. I was scoring a Mets-Dodgers game. I made a call, and apparently Vinnie disagreed with it. I say *apparently* because I didn't hear what he said. That particular play was when the Dodgers were in the field. It was a tough play, but I feel they are Major Leaguers and they've got to catch everything. That was my theory then... and still is. It was somebody who really ran well. He'd been hurt, and I think he had just come off the DL, which justified my ruling in a way. I called it an error. Everybody thought it should have been a hit. Yogi was managing the Mets. I remember him saying afterward, "I think maybe they could have given the kid a hit on that one." There was no replay then, not even a TV monitor in the press box in those days. You'd see it once and that's it. After discussing it with everybody, the next day, I reluctantly changed it to a hit. Apparently, Vinnie went on and on and on. He didn't mention who the scorer was. I didn't know anything about it then. The next day at the ball park Joe Hendrickson, wonderful guy, came running up to me as soon as I got there. He asked me, "Were you scoring last night?" I said, "Yeah, why?" He told me he'd listened to the game on the radio and how Vinnie just went off.

What I should have done was just gone to Vinnie, "I'm hearing this. What did you say? What's the deal?" Then, it would have been done. Instead...I was "Screw those radio guys. I ain't talking to them ever again." That's where I was wrong. It came to a head later. Tommy was managing so it would have been late 70s. Before the game, I was in the offices talking to Tommy, just sitting there, and Doggett walked in, and I got up and walked out. That got back to the PR guy, Steve Brener. He called me and I told him I wasn't talking to those guys. This went on for three-four days. Finally, Brener called Vinnie and said, "Call Verrell. Get this thing over with." And, he did. He called me at home and said, "Well, maybe I did go a little overboard on it." And, he apologized for that. Then we discussed the play, and he could then see my reasoning behind making that call. Even my mother called me and asked about it after hearing the remarks Vinnie made. Mom sided with Vin.

My wife Janet, though not a baseball fan, would sometimes accompany me on a trip, and Vinnie made her feel completely at home. We were in New York, Janet had gone with me, and Vinnie was having a conversation with her and asked if she had ever been to New York. She said, "No, it's my first time." He told her to be careful who you talk to, giving her the warning anybody would give any newcomer in New York City. We go to the ball park. Janet didn't go with us out to Shea. Later, she told me that a Frenchman tried to pick her up...in the hotel. She was on the escalator and the guy starts a conversation with her. I get back and we're talking and she says, "I almost got picked up by a Frenchman." She said, "Don't be telling anybody this." I happened to mention it to Scully. The next time he sees her, he says, "Oh, I heard you got picked up by a Frenchman." She was mad at me so I made a quick trip to my florist!!

> —GORDON VERRELL, covered the Dodgers for 26 years, now
> retired in Virginia

Vin was wise to stay with one team and not go with one of the networks. When you do that, sooner or later, somebody knifes you! He was very much aware of that. He's brilliant—a very, very intelligent man. He's also very funny.

Once, Vin was sitting on a couch talking. He started describing Schaefer Beer. He said they wanted to do a commercial, and the commercials were live in those days. Vinnie was explaining how the advertising guy said, "Just sit there and open a bottle of  beer the way you always do and pour yourself a beer and do these few lines." Vin said, "So I do what I ordinarily do. I picked up the bottle of beer, grabbed it by the neck, grabbed the opener and lifted it up." He said they told him, "No. No. Wait. You have to hold it so people can see the label." Vinnie said, "Okay." He said, "So, I took the beer the way I normally do, holding it by the tips of my fingers, facing it outwards and got the opener on it and opened it up. I poured the beer into a glass there." They said, "No, no, you have to tip the glass and pour it in slowly so the head builds up." Vin said, "So, I did it again the normal way I always drink a bottle of beer. I held it by my fingertips, held it sideways, did this, did that, and poured it very slowly into the glass." I swear it was the funniest thing to hear him tell this. Here was this man who lived by advertising but knew what a crock of bologna went on. They kept telling him, "Just be natural. Just be natural."

Back in the sixties, there was a Dodger-Giants series. Drysdale was scheduled to pitch. I was sitting with Vin in the press room, or "the drinking room" as we used to call it. Giants President Chub Feeney came in and came over to sit with us. He stopped at the table before he sat down and looked at Vin and said, "I just came by the Dodger dressing room. I could hear your pitcher warming up. He was saying, 'Oops! Look out. Oops! Look out.'"

If circumstances were that the Dodgers and Vin had stayed in the New York market, Vin would have blown Mel Allen out of the water. Vin was a much better broadcaster. Mel had a personality and a voice, and a lot of people loved him. But, when you get right down to the technical aspect of it, Vin was a much better broadcaster. I liked Mel Allen, but I didn't think he was in the same class with Vin.

—ROBERT CREAMER, 86, *Sports Illustrated*, '54-'85

When it was announced that my husband, Ross Newhan, had been elected to the Writers Wing of the Baseball Hall of Fame, he was away at the **WORLD SERIES***. When I got home from work, there were a lot of messages on the answering machine. While I was listening to the messages, Vin called and I picked up. He said he was calling to congratulate Ross. I told him, "Vin, would you mind terribly calling back so I can have the answering machine pick up, and then he can hear you in your own words." He said, "No, I'd be glad to do that." He called back a few minutes later, but I was so caught up in still listening and writing down messages that I forgot and picked up the phone. He went, "Connie, it's Vin." I went, "Oh, I'm so sorry. Would you call back again?" He said, "Yes, but I'm going to wait five minutes this time." So, he did call back again. He left a beautiful message which I transcribed and put in Ross's notebook.

Vin is so great. Exactly what you hear is what you get. We had a family doctor, Dr. Garces, who went to Fordham. He saw a Fordham pennant somewhere, got it, gave it to Ross on an office visit, and asked Ross to get it to Vinnie the next time he saw him. A couple of weeks later, Vinnie called here to get our doctor's phone number so he could personally call and thank him for the pennant....About 10 years ago, I sent Vin a thank you note for all the years of bringing pleasure. He sent me a thank you note for a thank you note.

I was a Vin Scully fan years before I met Ross. I used to go to ball games with my uncle who had a Union 76 station, and Union sponsored the games. One time we were going to the game, and my uncle said "You know, I don't think Vin Scully realizes that every time he does the Union 76 commercial, he mentions a dealer, Bill Frick, or whatever the guy's name was." When we went to the game that particular time at the Coliseum, we were in our seats underneath the press box. We got there early enough so I wrote a note to that effect. I was about 16 years old then. My note mentioned to Vin, "Do you know you always mention this Union dealer. My uncle is a Union Oil dealer nearby." He read the note

*The last **WORLD SERIES** game played during the daytime was in 1983.

and at the bottom of it—and I still have it—he wrote, "Honey, say it isn't so. Vin Scully."

When our son, David, was first drafted, he was in the Oakland organization in A-ball, I was waiting for Ross one night at the stadium. Vin and I were having a Coke. I told him, "Vin, I never told anyone this, but my fantasy is that David will be in the Major Leagues, and you will announce him entering the lineup." I had never mentioned that. And, I said, "And, of course, here he is in the American League in A-ball." Vin told me, "Well, you never know about these fantasies."

About five years later, when David was with the Padres, they were playing at Dodger Stadium. I went to the game and afterward, I went up to the press box to meet Ross, and Vin came down the corridor and looked at me. He said, "Where were you? I had the cameras looking all over for you." Then, he looked at me...and he went..."I remembered."

—CONNIE NEWHAN, Los Angeles

I was 13, growing up in the Bronx and a huge Giants fan when Vin Scully was a rookie announcer in Brooklyn. We all knew that an announcer that young would never last.

I hated the Dodgers because I was a Giants fan. That was such a great rivalry. They talk about Boston and the Yankees. Come on! It was the Giants and Dodgers. It had been one for 90 years. 50 years? Whatever!

After '51, an uncle of mine had a job with a cereal company who sponsored the Dodger games. He gave me a whole batch of walk-in tickets for Ebbets Field. I'd never been to Ebbets Field. I didn't even know the subway ran that far. Why would I go to Ebbets Field anyway? But...a free ball game is a free ball game, and I had enough tickets for friends. The first time I went there, I found it in time for the first inning. I walked in and was immediately struck by how small the place was. I'm used to the Polo Grounds, which is a big old barn. Now, I'm at Ebbets Field...and it's small. It had a whole new vista—a whole new scenery. The scoreboard where it was. The fence. The various ads. It was interesting.

They were good seats, better than I should have had, and nobody bothered me. I was sitting there, and there was an immediate change in my feeling about the Dodgers...because the fans were so close to the game, unlike the Polo Grounds, unlike any park I'd ever been in. The fans were terrific. They were chatting with me. I didn't let them know I was one of the enemy. You could almost see the players react—that's how close we were. You could see their faces. At one point, I walked down to the bullpen, and the bullpen seats were right next to where the pitchers were warming up. It was an incredible experience. I walked back to the seat I'd taken at the beginning of the game. I watched the game. I felt like I'd made all new friends—baseball fans. I walked out and made sure I came back again. I used every ticket my uncle gave me, and it was a great experience. Everyone knew most of the players. It was almost an All-Star team on the field.

> After the Giants won a pennant, I ran out into the streets to celebrate...and there was no one there.

I don't know if my uncle lost his job with the cereal company...or if the company was dropped as one of the sponsors...or if he forgot about me, but that was my one season with the freebies. I was about 14 years old, and that was my one experience, and it was terrific.

After the Giants won a pennant, I ran out into the streets to celebrate...and there was no one there. Our block was all Yankee fans, and what did they care that the Giants finally won a pennant. They knew they'd win the World Series. That was the trouble with Yankee fans.

—VIC ZIEGEL, 71, columnist, *N.Y. Daily News*

Vin Scully

LONGEVITY:	10	55 years.
CONTINUITY:	10	Brooklyn NL 1950-57; Los Angeles NL 1958- ; NBC-TV "Game of the Week" 1983-89
NETWORK:	10	"Game" 1983-89 (NBC TV), All-Star Game second 1959 and 1962, 1963, 1983, 1985, 1987, and 1989 (NBC TV) and 1990-91 and 1995-97 (CBS Radio). L.C.S. 1973 (Robert World Radio) and 1983, 1985, 1987, and 1989 (NBC TV). World Series 1953, 1955, 1956, 1959, 1963, 1965, 1966, 1974, 1984, 1986, and 1988 (NBC TV) and 1977-83, 1990-93, and 1995-97 (CBS Radio).
KUDOS:	10	"Most memorable [L.A. Dodgers] personality" 1976. Cooperstown 1982. Star, Hollywood Walk of Fame 1982. NSSA 1959, 1966, 1978, and 1982. Sportscaster of the Year and Hall of Fame 1991. ASA Sportscaster of the Year 1985 and Hall 1992. Named top 20th century sportscaster 2000. Ronald Reagan Media Award 1987. Twenty-five-time California Sportscaster of the Year. Sports Lifetime Achievement Emmy Award 1996. "Vin Scully Way" at Vero Beach training site. Press box at Dodger Stadium named in honor.
LANGUAGE:	10	*Nonpareil.*
POPULARITY:	10	Owns Southern California
PERSONA:	10	Baseball's Olivier
VOICE:	10	"The Fordham Thrush," said Murray, "with the .400 larynx."
KNOWLEDGE:	10	*L.A. Times*: "Dodgers fans say they'd rather have Scully managing the club than Walter Alston."
MISCELLANY:	10	Dodgers radio/TV ads place his name above teams's.
TOTAL:	100	(first place)

From author Curt Smith's book *Voices of Summer,* ranking the 101 best baseball announcers of all time. Vin Scully was not only ranked number one, he scored a perfect 10 in all ten catagories.

Smith is the author of a forthcoming Vin Scully biography *Pull Up a Chair,* published by Potomac Books.

Chapter 4

Fandemonium

Twelve Years Old Forever

VIN SCULLY WAS GOD'S WAY OF BEING NICE TO DODGER FANS

JOHN WOODEN

John Wooden was born in Hall, Indiana in 1910. He is a member of the Basketball Hall of Fame as both a player and coach. He is the first person ever enshrined in both categories. After college at Purdue, Wooden spent several years playing professionally. He started coaching at Dayton H. S. in Kentucky. Then he returned to Indiana and coached at South Bend Central until entering the service. After the war, he coached at Indiana State University in Terre Haute. He also coached baseball and served as athletic director. Wooden started at UCLA in 1948.

Vin Scully and I became acquainted shortly after the Dodgers moved to Los Angeles. We lived in an apartment in Brentwood and Vin and his wife lived in an apartment in the same area.

One time, Vin was going in with his arms so full of groceries that he couldn't open the door, so I opened the door for him. He mentions to people that's how we first met. I think both of us knew who each other was at that time.

I knew the Dodgers had just come out here, and I'm a great baseball fan. I knew some of the Dodger players before they came out here, particularly two, Carl Erskine and Gil Hodges, from Indiana. I was also a friend of Walter Alston. I had great respect for him—for his style in particular—and Vin did know something about me too.

Over the years, I had just an "occasional" relationship with Vin—nothing from the social point of view. We saw each other many times at various functions in regard to athletics so I'd be with him at gatherings several times a year.

I listen to Vin do the Dodger broadcasts. I'd rather turn the sound off on my television and listen to Vin do the game. I consider him the greatest individual sportscaster there has ever been. Certainly no one touches him in baseball. I know he's done a few other things that were very good too, but he has primarily stuck with baseball, and his voice doesn't seem to have changed.

Vin paints a picture, which is what I think broadcasters need to do. I'm sure he got part of that when he was broadcasting before they had television.

I've always been a baseball fan. When the Dodgers came out to Los Angeles, that pleased me very much. I was going to the Angel games prior to that and to the Hollywood Stars, in the Pacific Coast League. Baseball has always been my favorite sport.

I didn't play any baseball after my freshman year in college. I hurt my arm the summer after my freshman year and was not able to throw anymore so I gave it up.

> ... I was offered the job as manager of the Pittsburgh Pirates...

After the O'Malleys got out of baseball, I haven't followed them as closely as I did before. Now I follow the Angels more. I know Mike Scioscia very well, from his having been a Dodger. And now **JOE TORRE*** is here, I know him very well. I visited with him a lot when he was broadcasting for the Angels. I've been going to the Angel games for years whenever they've played the New York Yankees.

Many, many years ago, I was offered the job as manager of the Pittsburgh Pirates when Joe Brown, Jr. was the general manager there. I didn't have any experience in pro baseball but he knew of my interest in baseball. I had coached baseball in high school and the two years I was at Indiana State University.

***JOE TORRE** was player/manager of the Mets for eighteen days in 1977. Since 1962 there have been four player/managers with Pete Rose (1984-86) the last...In 1935 there were nine player/managers.

I had a remarkable winning percentage in baseball. I told him after I turned him down, "If I'd have taken that job as manager, who do you think they'd have fired first? They'd have fired you first for hiring me and then would have turned around and fired me." I would get no respect from the players because I didn't play pro baseball.

Vin has been to some UCLA basketball games over the years.

As a neighbor, Vin was a nice, friendly man. We visited with him in passing. He was never in our apartment and we were never in his, but we would see him from time to time and would talk about baseball and basketball. Vin liked all sports.

Vin and I appeared at a fund raiser for a children's home. We appeared there on stage for almost two hours. First, questions came from the audience. Vin's questions were mostly connected with baseball and the ones directed to me were all connected with basketball. The theater sold out, 7,200, and I think they raised close to a million dollars for the hospital. I would think anyone would want to go hear Vin Scully. He's a great announcer and paints the best pictures possible in his announcing. Because of the type of person he is. He's well prepared with information about everything that is going on. So the number of people who were there didn't surprise me...I would go see him any time. The questions were very interesting. We didn't ask each other questions. We made some remarks perhaps, about each other in certain instances.

I was approached about doing another show with someone else. I always try to do things that will help a charity. The audience seemed to enjoy having Vin and me there for the program. There was a youngster, a cancer patient, who was recovering. I showed him how to put on his shoes and socks, which I always did for my basketball team the first day. They got a great kick out of that.

I think Vin paints a picture. He's like many of the broadcasters before we had television—they could paint a picture. You might have a good voice but not have the ability to paint the picture. But with Vin, you don't have to be there. He just paints the picture for you.

As far as the Dodgers are concerned, the most amazing thing to me was when they had the night honoring Roy Campanella at the Coliseum. It was an amazing night, and I was glad to be there. Also I was there when they played the White Sox in the 1959 World Series

When I lived in Indiana, I followed the Cubs, the White Sox and the Cardinals—the ones that were the closest.

Relief pitcher Jeff Shaw represented the Dodgers in the 1998 All-Star game even though he had never pitched for the Dodgers at that time.

HE WORKS FOR PEANUTS

Roger Owens

Roger Owens is the famed peanut vendor who tosses bags of peanuts under the leg, behind the back—even two at a time—all with unbelievable accuracy to people sitting 30 rows away. Roger has charmed and amazed generations of fans with his show within a show at Dodger games for 50 years.

I met Vin Scully in the early 70s. He's someone who has always had a smile for everyone. I've known him for 35 years and see him from time-to-time at various special events outside of Dodger Stadium.

I saw him at the **ROSE PARADE***. I was part of the Dodger float in the parade. In the parade, I was wearing the uniform I wear at the ball park. I was walking alongside the float right near Vin Scully. He was sitting up on the top with some of the ballplayers. We were all waving at the people, and I had some peanuts with me and I was feeding them. You're not allowed to throw things in the parade because fans would stumble over themselves trying to grab them.

Through sheer desire and hard work I was able to work my way up from soda to ice cream to peanuts all in the first year. Now it takes vendors 20 years to work their way up through the ranks to sell peanuts. Vendors are not allowed to sell beer in the stands—so peanuts are the biggest moneymaker for vendors.

> *The **ROSE PARADE** originally had nothing to do with the Rose Bowl football game. It was a celebration in Pasadena for the ripening of the oranges....The 1942 Rose Bowl game between Oregon State and Duke was played in Durham, North Carolina because of fears that the Rose Bowl in Pasadena could be attacked like Pearl Harbor was three weeks earlier....The Rose Bowl has been sold out every year since 1947.

Vin Scully is the Dodgers...and the Dodgers are Vin Scully, in every sense of the word. There is no one like Vin. We all know he's the very best at what he does. He has never slowed down. It's amazing. He's even better, if that's possible. When he describes what is going on at a ball game, you feel like you are right there. You are *seeing* everything the way it is. I got to thinking about this when I was listening to a road game recently—he can tell you more about a player than his relatives know. Vin really does his homework on each member of the team. He can tell you not only what high school and college he attended, but his favorite songs and hobbies and what he likes outside of baseball. It's unbelievable. Vin's memory and knowledge is hard to describe.

At the games, I sell the peanuts in the same section every game so I get to know the fans. I'm #1 in seniority so I'm the only one who gets to do that. Seniority at Dodger Stadium is based on the number of events you have worked for the Dodgers since they came here. There are 81 home games a year. We have rookies from high

> **Vin Scully is the Dodgers... and the Dodgers are Vin Scully...**

school who feel pretty proud who have worked one, two or three years. They have 200-300 events under their belts and will sometimes paste their number on the bottom of their photo on their working badge. Then they will walk by me, and they'll sometimes look over and see my badge—it says 4,580 events! They go "Wow, when did you start here?"

I have "season peanut holders." These are businessmen, season ticket-holders, who sit in my section who own several seats there. They send me checks to my home each year during the month of March before the first game opens in April, and they have me pitch three bags of **PEANUTS*** to clients, friends and relatives for 81 home games a year. I have about 10 or 12 individuals who own their own companies who have me do that. With the price of peanuts having gone up so much through the years, this year I

*Charles Schultz drew almost 18,000 PEANUTS strips and almost 2,000 dealt with baseball.

collected close to $7,000 before the first game of the year. I'm their good-will ambassador. I greet their people. I don't need to know their names. I ask, "Are you guests of...?" They will say yes they are and I let them know the owner appreciates their business.

> There was one couple who would always take me to Lawry's Prime Rib on Fan Appreciation Day.

There was one couple who would always take me to Lawry's Prime Rib on Fan Appreciation Day. They said it was their way of showing their appreciation. They would always remind me to bring a change of clothes and meet them at Lawry's Prime Rib over in Beverly Hills every year. Kiddingly, a couple of years ago, I told them, "I appreciate it, but I don't deserve Lawry's Prime Rib this year. Some of my throws have been way off. Maybe I'm losing my arm here. Maybe I'm developing 'peanut' elbow. A Big Mac will be enough." They told me, "Nope. Show up at Lawry's." I get there, and the waitress is taking our order and this man's wife pulls out a Big Mac and puts it on the table and tells the waitress, "He won't be ordering off the menu. All he wanted was a McDonalds Big Mac."

The **DALLAS COWBOYS*** football team saw me on The Tonight Show with Johnny Carson in 1976. Tex Schram got his PR people to get old Roger and tell him if he wants to come to Texas Stadium and entertain our people, we would love it. They flew me there, put me up in a first-class hotel and treated me like a king. They introduced me to the crowd, before the game started, out on the middle of the field. Then they had a car wheel me around like I was a grand marshal in a parade. I threw out peanuts at the beginning and then I started selling them for charity for that night. I broke my all-time record. I sold 2,400 bags of peanuts at one game. The most I'd ever sold at Dodger Stadium was 1,000 bags. I just shattered my own personal record. It was such a hit that the Cowboys, once a year, would fly me to Texas Stadium for

*When the **DALLAS COWBOYS** cheerleaders started in 1972, each earned $15 per game—the same amount they receive today.

either the Thanksgiving Day game or Monday Night football when it would be on national television for 12 straight years until Tex Schram and Tom Landry were no longer with the team.

I've worked Olympics, Super Bowls, All-Star games and so many others I've lost track. In 1976, the Dodgers gave me the honor of throwing out the ceremonial first-pitch to officially open up the 1976 baseball season. That normally is given to the President of the United States or to a big-time movie star. They wanted me to throw the ball from the top of the loge level all the way to Steve Yeager at home plate. It's the longest ceremonial first-pitch ever. They weren't sure, but they had me come in the day before and make a practice throw to be sure I could make that long of a throw. It had to travel over the loge level, over the field level, over the backstop screen to home plate. I came in, made a practice throw the day before and the next day it was done. The *Herald Examiner* newspaper the following day said, "It was a strike." They put it in the program and ran a picture of me releasing the ball.

> Dodger Stadium is my home away from home.

Dodger Stadium is my home away from home. I don't know what my life would be without working the games. It's become a labor of love now for me, just like it has been with Vin Scully all these years. The fans, I think, certainly appreciate Vin Scully. He's like a family member. Yet the people have treated me like family also.

When I'm working at our home games, I don't get to listen to Vin do the games. I don't have the time because I'm working the crowd. On the road games, I get to listen to Vin. In the seventh inning, we are allowed to check out and leave so we can beat the traffic and get home. Peanut sales slow down by the 5th or 6th inning. If you haven't sold what you're going to sell by the 6th inning, you're not going to sell any more. So when I leave the ballpark and hop in the car, it's usually still the 7th inning, and I can listen to Vin describe the rest of the game.

The only story I remember Tommy Lasorda telling is when he was talking about when Pope John Paul came to the United

States, he was late trying to get to the United Nations to address the United Nations. He hopped in the limo and told the driver, "Could you please really step on it. I know it's not your fault, but the plane was late and I'm late, and I want to be there on time." The driver said, "My boss has told me if I get one more ticket, I'm out the door." Pope John Paul said, "No, I wouldn't want to be responsible for that, but everywhere I go, people provide me with a limo, and I've always wondered what it was like to drive one. Would you let me drive, and you can get in the back. I promise you I won't go over the speed limit. I just want to get there, and it would be a real joy for me to drive a limo." The driver said, "Okay." The Pope was so anxious to get to the United Nations, he was speeding. He got pulled over by a New York PD motorcycle officer. The officer goes up to the window. The window goes down. The officer is face to face with Pope John Paul in the driver's seat. The policeman goes, "Oh, no. Please sir, stay right here." He goes back to the radio on his motorcycle and calls his sergeant and says, "Hey, sergeant, I just pulled somebody over for speeding on the bridge. This is a guy we don't want to give a ticket to." The sergeant said, "Look, if it's Mayor Giuliani, we've given him enough breaks. Write him a ticket." He said, "No. No. This guy's bigger than Giuliani." This was a few years back, and he said, "Is it Frank Sinatra again? I'm telling you right now. We've let this guy go too many times. Issue the ticket." He said, "This guy's much bigger than that." He said, "Who is it?" He said, "Sarge, I don't even know." He said, "What do you mean you don't know?" He said, "The guy is so big, he's got Pope John Paul driving for him!"

> **"The guy is so big, he's got Pope John Paul driving for him!"**

Lasorda talks about his heritage and being Italian. He said, "I'm so proud to be an American, of course, but there are so many Italians in this country. Not all of them, but a lot of them, their first name is Tony. The reason why that is—when the immigrants were coming over here from Italy, they couldn't speak English. They didn't hardly know anything, but they wanted to come to America. They put them on a ship and, so they wouldn't get lost, on their forehead, they penciled in T O N Y (To New York). When they got off the ship, everybody was greeting them, 'Hey Tony. Tony.'"

Vin Scully has been a dear friend. He's always been so cordial to me. He's always shaking my hand and saying, "Roger, it's good to see you." I can remember one time, after I'd been on the Tonight Show with Johnny Carson, Vin bent over in the broadcast booth and challenged me to throw him a bag of peanuts up in the press box. I told him, "Vin, no, you know I am not allowed to do that because of liability insurance." He kiddingly said, "Yeah, I know, Roger." Vin just amazes me how he can get so much information and have it right at his fingertips about any ballplayer ready to give it to you. He has things that probably the player's relatives don't even know about that person.

WHERE THE PAST IS PRESENT

JIM GOVERNALE

Jim Governale is a long time broadcaster and radio host in Southern California. He has done work in voiceovers and narrations for companies, organizations and faith-based ministries. Governale has won the prestigious "Mobius" award for radio advertising and is currently the morning host on KKLA 99.5 in Los Angeles.

My uncle was a big Dodger baseball fan. The team was relatively new to L.A. back in '62. He would have been 14 years old. Like a lot of kids from that time, he was into monkeying around with a big reel-to-reel tape deck that his dad, my grandfather, had. He was recording his voice and having fun with it.

One night he had the Dodger ball game on the radio. Vin Scully was calling the action. He must have sensed history in the making because Koufax was getting later into the game with a no-hitter—not the '65 perfect game. He strung up a tape on the player there and hit "record." He ended up grabbing the audio of the last inning-and-a-half, plus the post-game interview after the game with Jerry Doggett and Koufax.

The tape went into a 7 ½ inch reel box, with a clipping from the following day's newspaper, The *L.A. Herald Examiner.* He cut out the story and taped the clipping to the box.

Fast forward to many years later...probably about 1990, when my grandfather passed away. He lived in Whittier, California. My grandmother, noticing the box of reel-to-reel tapes, asked me if I was interested in taking them. I was new to radio broadcasting at the time. I took the tapes and over the course of time, I noticed on one of the boxes the Koufax no-hitter. It piqued my curiosity, but I took my time with it. I didn't rush right into the studio to listen to it. It wasn't until I was working in broadcasting and had access to some digital components where I could digitize the tape. This would then have been the late 1990s when I loaded it into the computer to digitize it. What I heard come out of the speakers, when I slowed it down, was pretty remarkable to me—Vin Scully's voice. I remember thinking, "Wow! This is real historical stuff here." I wasn't thinking that it was a one-of-a-kind tape. I figured they probably had something in the archives somewhere. But at the same time, I thought that it could be something special that the Dodgers or Vin Scully doesn't have.

It amounted to about 40 minutes in length, and I saved it and burned it onto a CD for myself. I sat on the recording for seven or so years. I wanted to get it into the right hands. I knew in my heart it belonged to the Dodgers and to Vin Scully. Being a long-time Dodger fan, I wanted to get it into their hands, but at the same time, I didn't want to make a misstep and get it into someone's hands it shouldn't be in.

> "Wow! This is real historical stuff here."

Part of me was also thinking, "Well, gee, maybe I can make a few dollars off of this." I was going over all the different possibilities.

Finally, in the fall of '06, I was put in touch with Mark Langill, the team historian for the L.A. Dodgers. We connected at first by email. I gave him a little tease of what I had. I had an audio clip of the tape that I sent to him in an MP3 file via email. He just about jumped through the computer. He was really, really interested in hearing what I had.

What ended up happening then was that I went down to the stadium and met up with Mark one day. He had a little boom box. We sat down, put the CD in there and began to listen to it. Of course, I'd already heard it several times, but just seeing his reaction the first time he listened to it really put a charge into me. I thought, "Wow, this really is pretty special!"

I had an official copy made that Mark was going to send to Vin Scully. It was the off-season so he was planning to mail it to Vin's home. I was pretty excited to think that Mr. Scully is going to hear this recording of something I was able to preserve. That really excited me.

Sure enough, after several weeks went by, I got a letter in the mail, hand-signed by Vin Scully, thanking me for the tape. He expressed how he was thrilled to hear the voice of his good friend Jerry Doggett on the recording, who has passed on.

> I've got a pretty significant recording over the radio of the first game played at Dodger Stadium.

Willie Stargell's autobiography makes a comment about Vin Scully, "Vinnie is by far the best play-by-play guy in baseball." He said one of the reasons he liked Vinnie so much, and his mother enjoyed listening to Vinnie, is Vinnie was the only play-by-play guy to call him by his real given name, Wilver Stargell. Here's this book, written by a ball player 25 years ago, who is now deceased, and it praises Vin Scully. Pretty amazing.

I have another tape I haven't revealed to the public yet. My dad, who is 69 years old, clued me in on a tape he made. I've got a pretty significant recording over the radio of the first game played at Dodger Stadium. The Dodgers do not have it. In fact, nobody to my knowledge has it. I've got the recording of the first home run hit at Dodger Stadium, over the air. Wally Post hit it. Jerry Doggett is doing most of the play-by-play calling. I've got that, and I'm sitting on it for now.

JIM MURRAY STRUCK OIL
AT THE ALTAR WITH THIS GAL!

LINDA MURRAY

*Linda McCoy-Murray began her career in India-napolis as administrative assistant to the president of the **INDIANA PACERS***. She has contributed articles to Golf News Magazine. McCoy-Murray was married to Pulitzer Prize winning writer, Jim Murray. She is the President/Founder of the Jim Murray Memorial Foundation. She has risen to remarkable heights in her own right as a veteran marketer, promotion specialist, fundraiser, public speaker and awards presenter. She resides in La Quinta, CA.*

Jim would go to the Dodger games and would eat with the people in the press box and would walk through the club-house. Oftentimes, when we would go to a game, Jim would pop into the announcers' booth and say "Hi" to Vinnie. Jim's eyesight was very bad, and he didn't drive at night so I would drive him to games. He would go down on the field and do his interviews. While he was spending time doing his thing and being with Vin, I would sit up in the loge area where we always had a couple of seats. After a couple of hours, he'd come up and sit with me during the rest of the game. For the World Series games, he would always go to the press box, and I would sit elsewhere. He would be in the dining area with the guys and would see Vinnie there.

He and Vinnie were close to being brothers, I would say. Jim didn't have a brother. I think he and Vinnie were very, very close in that respect.

*When Steve Alford was a senior in high school in 1983 in New Castle, Indiana, his high school team averaged more people in attendance per game than the INDIANA PACERS.

Jim did not like to go to all the *rubber* chicken dinners-banquets, as he used to call them. He would only go if he had to. He didn't want to depend on other people to drive him—because of his eyesight—so I would go with him when he went. He did a lot of Lakers' games in the wintertime.

We saw Vinnie around often. They would play golf together on occasion. We were members of Bel Air Country Club; although, Jim and Vinnie liked Riviera because it was Hogan's Alley...and he revered Ben Hogan. He and Vinnie golfed there. They both love Jim Garner, who is a member at Bel Air, and they would golf with him. They were getting up games all the time and didn't make a big deal out of who else would be going. They were all just "the guys."

Drugs and alcohol led to the death of Jim's son so Jim quit drinking after that. As an Irishman and a writer, you can imagine giving up booze! He quit cold turkey in 1982. If the guys stayed around after the game to have a drink, Jim might stay with them and have a Coca Cola. If it was in the wintertime, he had to make sure he left in time to be home before sunset.

Vin Scully would never say anything negative about anyone. He's a very unique man. The way he comes off on the air is exactly the way he is in person. I was at the unveiling of Walter O'Malley's bronze plaque at the Coliseum a few weeks ago. Vinnie spoke. When I first went in, Vinnie was talking with three or four other men. They were laughing and visiting. Vin saw me out of the corner of his eye. He immediately turned to me and put his arms around me and asked, "How are you doing, Linda?" It's never about Vinnie. He has this incredible innate ability to transfer all the energy to somebody else. It's never about him.

Everybody who knows him loves him so much. Jim had that humility, that integrity that everybody covets. Vin Scully is a remarkable man. He's a saint—that's the only way I can think of describing him—in every sense of the world.

Several years ago, Jim did an article about broadcasters which I sent to Charley Steiner recently. It's just a hoot. It's so typical of

Jim to point out that there are so few good ones left. Vinnie certainly *is the best.* He just has that melodious voice.

I would guess that the first time Jim and Vin met would be when the Dodgers came out to L.A. In January of '44, Jim came to L.A. and went to work for Jim Richardson at the old *Herald-Examiner* and later worked for Time and Life as their Hollywood correspondent. Then when Henry Luce decided he wanted to start up another magazine, it narrowed down to a sport magazine, and he thought of this guy, Murray, out on the West Coast. So, Jim went back to New York in '53 and helped establish *Sports Illustrated,* which didn't even have a name until the second dummy copy. The first copy was published on August 16, 1954, and Jim passed away on August 16, 1998.

Jim didn't want to stay in the East so he came back to L.A. and stayed in the Time bureau. The *L.A. Times* came knocking at his door in February of '61 and hired him, and he was there for 37 years. He covered Walter O'Malley when he first came to L.A. He wrote the piece for *Sports Illustrated.* There was a lot of breaking news—the Lakers were coming in from Minnesota. Jim was right at the infancy of both of these clubs. He and Chick Hearn and Vin Scully were very, very close friends. Vin and Chick Hearn were friends because of their love for broadcasting. I don't know how much their social life intertwined, but I do know they were friends and had a lot of respect for each other.

I love Sandy Scully as much as I love Vinnie. Jim died, on a Sunday night, after he had been down to Del Mar and wrote a column on the Pacific Classic. He got home afterward and three hours later, he died from a heart attack. The next day, Sandy and Vinnie came to the house. There were a lot of people there. She took me aside to the corner and said, "I know how difficult this is. I want you to know that if you need anything, we're here for you. The media will be all over you, and the cameras will be on you, and the funeral will be huge." She went down a list of things that I should be aware of. It made me feel like she was my guardian angel. I'll never forget her for that.

FANECDOTES

Vin Scully makes such a difference in the broadcasting of the game. I love the little personal facts that he gives about the Dodger players. It makes them real people instead of just a name. I like to know where they grew up...where they went to school...and if his wife just had a baby. Those are fun things. I just admire his performance and his delivery and how he gives all the details.

I'm a little bit hearing-impaired, and Vin's enunciation is just terrific. I think he is absolutely the best. I remember when my daddy took me to the baseball games. I've always been in love with baseball. I fell in love with Tony Moore, the shortstop for the Dallas Steers, when I was about 10 years old in about 1933.

Vin Scully enunciates—he says each word clearly rather than running things together. Other announcers talk faster and sometimes my hearing aid can't pick them up. So the way Vin talks is a big help for me. Vin's delivery and enunciation make it more enjoyable for me. I can understand everything he says.

—FRAN JONES, 85, Simi Valley

When the Dodgers moved out here to Los Angeles in '58, I was just a kid and was happier than anything. I started listening to Vin do the broadcasts.

I was listening to Vin do a game one year—can't remember the year or who they were playing, but seems like it was the Giants—when Jerry Doggett was working with Vin. A bean-ball brawl broke out on the field. Doggett was calling the action at the time. He was stumbling and having the hardest time trying to describe the action. I'll never forget how he just, all of a sudden, said, "Hey, Vinnie, you take over and you describe it." Vinnie came right in out of the blue and took over the mic and, with a smooth transition, proceeded to continue telling what was going on out on the field—like he was calling an Ali-Frazier fight almost. He was describing everything that was going on. I thought it showed Vin's professionalism.

I was watching TV and Stu Nahan was doing an interview with Vin between innings. They were sitting there talking and Vin has his back to the action. Then, just like perfect timing...the

INNING STARTED*, and Vin turns away from Nahan and goes smoothly right into the calling of the game. I'm always amazed at how smooth and professional he is. He's always prepared.

To me, Vin is Dodger baseball. The players are like mercenaries traveling through the organization, but Scully is the constant. He's always there. I'm sure Vin has as much to do with attendance as a lot of the ballplayers over the years.

> ...Scully is the constant. He's always there.

   —JOHN GRUSH, Newport Beach

In San Francisco, years ago, I got in an elevator and Vin was in there. I said, "Oh, Vinnie, would you say hi to my dad on the radio?" He said, "Hi to your dad on the radio."

That's my big story.

I grew up a Dodger fan, and I'm a transplanted Angel fan. I grew up in Torrance and was a Dodger fan. Now I live about 10 minutes from Angel Stadium so we go to more Angel games.

   —KIM WIBBEN, Anaheim, CA

Growing up as a kid, it always seemed like summer had arrived when I heard Vin's voice on the radio. We always had the Dodger games playing.

I loved the story he told about how Mike Scioscia met his wife. She came to a game with her girlfriend, and she "noticed" Mike— she liked what she saw so the next day, she baked a batch of cookies and brought them to the game. She then "worked" her way down to the field and gave the whole plate to Mike. He, in turn, "noticed" her and left her tickets for a future game, and the rest is history. "I wish I would have baked cookies for Eric Karros...."

   —CHRIS GOETHALS, school teacher, Pasadena

For anyone who doesn't know this, anyone can watch a baseball game on mlb.tv as soon as it is over. You go to www.sports.yahoo.com/mlb and then go to the sides where the

---

*TIME of advertising breaks: 2 minutes and five seconds in the regular season, except on nationally televised games when you add 20 seconds; post season=2:55.Starting times are influenced by the fact that half of the U.S. population lives in the Eastern Time zone.

scores are listed and instead of clicking on box score, click on "mlb.tv" archive. The whole game is broadcast with the home team announcers.

Vin never finds it necessary to use cutesy phrases or scream and shout or get hysterical. He's just smooth, tells a great story and makes the whole game even better.

I remember when Vin Scully used to do national broadcasts. Why on earth Fox wouldn't pay the moon for someone like him instead of the guys they have now? I don't get it. I suppose that Fox isn't interested in excellence.

—LISA GRAY, Houston Texas

I went to a Dodger game in the early 80s, and it was souvenir baseball radio night. The first 20,000 fans got baseball-shaped transistor radios. All the fans were holding the radios up to their ears watching the game with their eyes and listening to Vin describe it with his words. It seemed like every radio was on. The stadium was like your living room. It's Vin who unites us. Culture, class and race notwithstanding.

Another tidbit was from Phil Simms, NFL broadcaster. He was answering a question about how the networks could improve their telecasts. He said, "Maybe we could shut up a little more. It gets hard for me, since I want to talk about everything. I heard a replay on the radio one day of Vin Scully doing a Dodger game. I also heard a broadcaster of the other team. When you listened to the other announcer, he used a hundred words. When you listened to Vin, he made the same call in about 20 words. I went, "Wow!" It's how quick you get your point across, how few words do you need. Quarterbacks are trying to complete passes, I'm trying to get my thoughts cleaner and more concise. That is what I think about now."

> ...other team. When you listened to the other announcer, he used a hundred words. When you listened to Vin, he made the same call in about 20 words.

I also have a story from my youth in Brooklyn. My brother was selected to be on a show with two other kids from our Little League. They had the three kids, and one of the Dodger players would "tryout" the three kids by tossing balls to them and would select the one he thought was the best player. The show was hosted by Happy Felton. It took place along the right field line. The best one would then have the opportunity to go back to a subsequent game and sit in the dugout the entire game. He also would get to interview the player of his choice on television at second base. He would stand at second base with the player and would ask him questions.

I recall this very well because the game when my brother was on the show was the first game I ever attended. The game was a doubleheader against the Phillies. It was on a Sunday in September, 1955. I remember that Don Hoak was the third baseman for the Dodgers at that time. He tried them out. My brother dropped a ball. He actually muffed a play, but his form and balance and agility were so striking that Don Hoak selected him as the winner.

I recall seeing him on TV at a neighbor's house. He chose Jackie Robinson for the interview. As far as I know, he was the first winner to choose an interview with Jackie Robinson. He remembers **JACKIE ROBINSON*** being very friendly and very nice.

Happy Felton did the show in a Dodger uniform. I think he had a show business background. I read somewhere that Happy and Vin Scully were co-emcees at the Pee Wee Reese night in Brooklyn in 1955.

—GARY ISON, Brooklyn native, L.A. casino host

I was excited when I heard there was going to be a pre-season game in the Coliseum to kick off the Dodgers 50th Anniversary season. The mood was festive for the game. There must have a dozen ceremonial first pitches. Some of the names—Sandy Koufax, Fernando Valenzuela, Duke Snider, Wally Moon and even Kareem Abdul Jabbar.

But the moment I'll never forget is when Vin Scully stood at the lectern to address the crowd...the fans rose and gave the

---

*What major league player has a street named after him in Cairo, Georgia, JACKIE ROBINSON's hometown? Willie Harris, currently of the Washington Nationals. Harris scored the winning run in the 2005 World Series and in 2007 had six hits in one game for the Braves.

---

man, who has been with the Dodgers for every day of their 50 years in Los Angeles, a standing ovation.

When Vin, who would eventually say he is simply "an ordinary man who was given an extraordinary opportunity," tried to quiet the crowd, the masses refused to listen and cheered all the louder with gratitude, admiration and love. The games may not have mattered, but for 115,000 souls the gathering was nothing less than everything. During the game, try to imagine 115,000 people lining up to buy everything from beer to funnel cakes, and listening to them screaming, "Here we go Dodgers!"

Also, imagine traffic-jammed freeways in every direction and paying $60 for premium parking...but when Vin came to the mic, he stole the show.

I wish I could meet Vin Scully sometime. I'd love to be able to shake his hand. Before I thanked him for being the announcer for the team I've come to love over all these years now, I would first thank him for his service—being a Navy veteran. I'm always struck with the astonishing humility he shows when dealing with that whole period of his service in the Navy.

> —JIM RULAND, blogger ("Vermin on the Mount") and author
> (*Big Lonesome*)

I was at a fund-raiser dinner a few years ago at a temple. They had a question-and-answer period with Vin Scully. Somebody asked Vin about the very first game he announced. He might not have been an official announcer yet. He talked about a ball that was hit over the outfield. Being that Cal Abrams was Jewish, he decided to talk about this story and about the very first game he ever announced. He said it was a 1950 spring training game in Vero Beach. He talked about how the ball had gotten hit over Cal Abrams' head. Abrams ran into a ditch. Came out without the ball—the reason being that the ball had landed in the coils of a snake.

I was never a good ballplayer growing up in L.A. I was not a good athlete...I wanted to be Vin Scully. I would be in my room with my baseball cards announcing the game like Vinnie did, with the players on the field—of course, they were baseball cards and weren't really players...and I wasn't Vin Scully.

> —MATT FEDERGREEN, Owner of the oldest baseball card
> shop in L.A....since 1982

I don't know Vin personally but I've been a fan of his for years. The first time I can remember hearing him was when he was doing a World Series—I think it was the '65 World Series. Not long ago, I heard a recording of the ninth inning of the Koufax game—the perfect game. That's the one that often gets published...usually under the chapter, "29,000 People and a Million Butterflies."

Some of my favorite Scully moments have nothing to do with the Dodgers. My classic was the way he can pull a punch line without even realizing it.

Remember Game 7 of the 1986 World Series. The Mets have just taken a two-run lead. Strawberry leads off the inning with this monstrous home run. A few hitters later, there's a runner on second and the relief pitcher, Jesse Orosco was up. Vin and Joe Garagiola are doing their usual side-by-side and are talking about a possible bunt situation and watching the Red Sox put this rotation play on to try to choke the bunt. They muse about whether he might take the bunt sign off and let him take a swing. Garagiola says, "I'd have to bet the house he's going to bunt." Two pitches later, the Red Sox put the play on—that's where the third baseman and first baseman come down toward the plate and the middle infielders go toward the baseline bases. Here comes the pitch. Orosco pulls the bunt back...and this is Scully's word-for-word call. "Swinging, and a ground ball into left center field. In comes Knight. It is 8-5 Mets, and Joe, you just lost your house." That, to me, was definitive for the man.

> "Swinging, and a ground ball into left center field. In comes Knight. It is 8-5 Mets, and Joe, you just lost your house."

He pulls on all these years of experience, all this knowledge he has, and yet every time you turn on a Dodger game, or anything else he does, it's like you're hearing him for the first time... and this is a guy who's eighty years old. He doesn't sound it. He doesn't act it. Every time he gets in front of that mic, it's something brand new. It's not that he makes you forget what he's done before, it's that he is fresh every day—and it really is something brand new for him…and he calls himself *just a guy who got lucky and goes to work every day.*

Sandy Koufax once said, "It may sound corny, but I enjoyed listening to Vin Scully call a game almost as much as I enjoyed playing in the game." I believe it. We will never hear his like again.

—JEFF KALLMAN, A native New Yorker, now living outside
Las Vegas

I was in the stands one night listening to the radio—it was the second game of a Dodgers/Diamondbacks series—and Vin Scully decided to latch onto the compelling story of that night's opposing pitcher, Livan Hernandez, and how Hernandez dramatically defected to the U. S. from Cuba. "This'd make a great movie," Vinnie exclaimed, and then went on to explain how the pitcher, whose desire to leave his homeland was apparently widely known, was throwing in a game in Monterey, Mexico, when he was approached by an apple-cheeked young lady with an autograph book. She extended it and Livan opened it, ready to sign. What he discovered inside, instead of a blank page, was an open-faced note which said somewhat ominously, "*El gordo quiere verte* (The fat man wants to meet you)." In the story, El Gordo turned out to be the man who facilitated Hernandez's escape from Cuba via life raft. You could hear Vinnie getting kind of starry-eyed as he thought about the possibilities, as well as getting a trifle annoyed that the game kept interrupting his reverie. But he kept on and began to speculate as to who could be cast in the movie. His first and only suggestion for the role of Livan Hernandez—the far-too-old and dashing Antonio Banderas—betrayed strikingly little imagination. Luis Guzman would be more convincing, for crying out loud.

But when he began to think of who would make a great El Gordo, Vinnie took older listeners on a real trip down memory lane. He left the rest of us scratching our heads. "The first fella I think of is, of course, Sydney Greenstreet," clearly assuming the young punks in the audience would be culturally literate enough to know *Casablanca* or *The Big Sleep* without mentioning them by name. "But if you really wanna go back…." And my ears perked up, anticipating something great—"You have to think of one of the great characters of all time, who was always filling out the card when it came to rotund scurvy villainy....Akim Tamiroff!"

Then Casting Director Vinnie, likely jostled out of his *Cinema Paradiso* daydream by one of two spectacular defensive plays made in left field that night by Diamondback Eric Byrnes, chuckled with satisfaction and went back to his day/night job, undoubtedly adrift throughout the game on further unspoken memories of Turhan Bey or Lionel Atwill or J. Carroll Naish, leaving it for the Great Unwashed to go to their Internets, Google away and get their Tamiroff on. As if we needed it, this is just one more reason why Vin Scully is the absolute best—he's never more than a pitch away from another expansive story about Takashi Saito or Rich Aurilia...or Peter Lorre.

I've never talked to Vin before, but I've had one of his signature moments on the TV side. About eight years ago, my first daughter was born and I took her out to the ball park in late September when she was six months old. I got a field seat. I was excited to take her because I'd never taken her before. Just as a lark, I set up a VHS tape and taped the game. I really don't know why I did it.

> As if we needed it, this is just one more reason why Vin Scully is the absolute best...

I was sitting there during the beginning of the game. I was holding her. I saw one of the stadium cameramen walking up through the crowd. I cornered him and said, "Hey, wouldn't it be fun if you could get a picture of this little girl and put it on Diamondvision?" They caught me in the third inning and came over and took her picture. She was up on the screen, and we were very excited.

When I left the game, I gave my parents-in-law a call and said, "Hey, you'll never guess what happened to us. We got on Diamondvision, and my daughter was on there." She said, "Yeah, I know. I saw you." I said, "What do you mean you saw me?" "Yeah, we saw you on TV holding the baby." I raced home thinking, "My God, I've got this on tape. I can't believe it. I can go home and check this out for myself." I went back over it and during the seventh inning, because they had been clued in to the Diamondvision thing, the TV crew got a picture of me holding my daughter, who by then was asleep on my shoulder. Sure enough, Vinnie stopped everything in the middle of the broadcast and does one of his things where he starts getting excited about the baby. "Oh, isn't that wonderful?" He said, "Oh, there she is...asleep on dad's chest...best pillow in the world."

I got home and I saw that, and I couldn't believe that not only had it actually happened but that I got it on tape so I could see it. A couple of years before that, my wife and I had lost a baby boy. I'd had all these thoughts about someday taking him to Dodger Stadium and maybe meeting Vin Scully or somebody else like that. To have that happen and to be able to see it and show it off and save it for my daughter's scrapbook was just overwhelming to me. I was part of one of Vin's signature moments. I was part of that with my daughter. I'll just never forget that. I wrote to him afterwards telling him how excited I was about it. I feel like there was that one moment there that will never be repeated and yet I can see it any time I want. For him to say that.... It would have been neat if it was any announcer on any game had done that. But the fact that it was Vin Scully who said it.... That's what going to Dodger games is all about for me. Whether or not they're good or bad, Vinnie's always been there. Year after year, he's there for all of us.

—DENNIS COZZALIO, accountant, Glendale, CA

One time, several years ago, during a World Series game, it was very cold. The snow was falling, and Vin noticed that the lineups hadn't been posted. He said, "They must be looking for volunteers." Then he went on to say, "Some may say it's tough for these players to play in these conditions, but have you seen their salaries?"

A few years back, during a game, there was a runner on base and he was half-way on a long fly, and it was too late to go back and tag up. Vin said, "If you're thirsty, it's too late to dig a well."

One day, Vin was talking about players and what they do off the field. He said he remembered hearing a story about a player who got back to the hotel after a night on the town. He told the front desk he wanted a 7 A.M. wake-up call. They told him, "Sir, you just missed it."

Someone was talking about momentum one day, and Vin said, "I remember talking to some manager years ago. The manager said, 'I'll tell you about momentum. Momentum is tomorrow's starting pitcher.'"

Vin had talked with George Culver, a pitcher for **CINCINNATI*** years ago, and George was saying that out in the bullpen they listen to him on the radio. Once during a game, there was a pitcher warming up in the Reds bullpen, and Vin couldn't see who it was because someone was standing in the way. So on the radio, Vin says, "Hey George, if that's Wayne Granger warming up, give me a wave." I'll be a son-of-a-gun, but here comes the wave. It was Granger warming up.

Another time, Vin was making a confession. For a well-needed dose of reality, Vin put a twist on his words. He said, "Friends, confession is good for the soul. I'm going to confess something to you tonight. We're broadcasting with the window closed because it is so cold."

Back in the black-and-white television days in the late 50s and early 60s, Vin was doing a telecast of a game from San Francisco, which was delayed because of fog. There was no back-up programming while everyone waited for things to clear up. Vinnie had to keep talking. When it seemed he had run out of things to say about the game and the players, he gave the viewers a tour of the broadcast booth and even demonstrated the "cough" button that would mute the microphone.

> "…he wanted a 7 A.M. wake-up call. They told him, "Sir, you just missed it."

Now Vin is in his 80s, and his mellow voice hasn't changed. I don't believe there are any Dodger employees working there today who were there when the Dodgers came West from Brooklyn in

*In 1998 the **CINCINNATI** Reds started an outfield trio of Chris Stynes, Dimitri Young, and Mike Frank. You might know them better as Young, Frank, and Stynes. (The author couldn't resist. He'll show himself to the principal's office now.)

1958. He's outlasted the players...the coaches...and even the owners! If I could have lunch with Vin Scully, I'm not sure I'd even talk or ask any questions at all. I think I'd be happy just sitting with *an old friend.*

I remember listening to somebody interviewing Vin Scully on the radio. He said, "People would ask me if I would write a book—no. I'll never write a book. I don't have the drive or the ego or the desire to write a book. But if I did, I have the title, and the title would be *My Life in Dentistry.*"

One final thing: Does anyone but me think that John Wooden looks like Connie Mack, David Beckham looks like Brett Favre, Nomar Garciaparra looks like Frank Deford, Mike Scioscia looks like Bobby Knight and Jeff Kent looks like a jerk?

—BOB ADAMS, 68, Retired stockbroker, originally from Glencoe, Illinois

I met Vin Scully through Peter O'Malley and Danny Kaye. Danny Kaye used to call Vin Scully the Jascha Heifetz of commentators. Heifetz was perhaps the greatest violinist ever. Danny Kaye was always a Dodgers fan, always, since the Brooklyn days.

Whenever I hear one sentence on the radio, I recognize it is Vin speaking. Vin has an elephantine memory and when commenting on any player, he can tell you his average from 15 years ago, where he was educated, his weight and his height. Vin is a statistical monster.

Vin's sentence starts from the first inning...and ends with the ninth inning. He has one long sentence that goes right through the game, which is quite unbelievable.

Vin loves classical music. He comes to concerts. He came to the opera in Munich when I was conducting. He has come to my house for meals.

—ZUBIN MEHTA, World-famous musical conductor, conducted for Three Tenors concert at Dodger Stadium in 1994

I'm 63 years old. I went to Ebbets Field as a kid. I was 12 years old when the Dodgers moved to the 'left' coast. I always tell people they never moved—they're on an extended road trip.

Yeah, Vin looks great. He looks good, and he sounds the same. I can almost hear his voice now. It's a very unique sound. I used to see him on TV in black and white. We didn't have a color TV until 1963. One interesting story about Ebbets Field. My father took me to my first game there in 1952 when I was seven years old. We had box seats behind home plate, behind the netting. I'm holding his hand to go walking up the ramp. As soon as I caught a glimpse of the field for the first time, I stopped short. My father said, "What's the matter?" I pointed to the field and said, "The grass is green." He said, "What are you talking about?" I said, "On television, it's black and white."

I remember listening to Vin Scully when we would go to the beach and on picnics. There's a big shopping street here called Kings Highway. The public school I went to I had to walk about seven blocks to get there. A lot of the games back then were played in the afternoons. At school, not during the regular season, but during the World Series some of the teachers would allow students to bring a radio to class and we could listen to the World Series game in the classroom. As we walked home after school, at three o'clock, all the stores on Kings Highway would have the score in the windows of their stores. Every half inning, they would go out and fill in the score so that people who were shopping on the street would know exactly what the score was.

At a card show a number of years ago, I picked up—for $15—a little pamphlet. It's more than a pamphlet, maybe 20-25 pages, published in 1958 by the radio station that broadcast the Los Angeles Dodger games, the first year the Dodgers were out there. The pamphlet is called, "The Housewives' Guide to Baseball." It was so the wives could know all the terminology of what's going on out on the field. Everything you can think of that the announcer would announce is in this booklet so the housewives could learn baseball lingo. There are pictures in it of all the announcers at that radio station. At the beginning of it is the history of the Dodgers, starting from Brooklyn, and how the Dodgers got their name—from the fans who had to dodge the trolley cars and who became known as the Brooklyn Trolley Dodgers. There's a picture, an artist's rendering, of a trolley with the word 'Flatbush' on the top 'cause Ebbets Field, where the Dodgers played was located right on the border of Flatbush and Crown

Heights, two Brooklyn neighborhoods. I have that book in my basement with all my Dodger memorabilia.

—RON SCHWEIGER, Historian, Brooklyn Chamber of Commerce

Vin was doing a ball game when Joe Torre was catching with the Atlanta Braves. Torre got hit by a ball and was nursing an injury. Vin said on the air that if he didn't come back the next day, Joe Torre would always be known as "chicken catcher Torre." The day Torre was named manager, Vin got up in front of everybody, on the dais with Torre and everybody, and related the story again. Torre laughed at the time, but I don't know if he'd heard it before.

—RANDY KERDOON, KNX 1070 News Radio

I went to college in Chicago and am a huge Cubs fan. I tried to go to the first night game on 8-8-88, but I couldn't get tickets...I did get tickets for the second night. The first night, the game was rained out. The next night was a game NBC was televising. Vin Scully and Joe Garagiola were the broadcasters. Back in those days, before they had the new press box in Wrigley, they would set up a temporary press box in the front row of the upper deck right behind home plate.

We were sitting about three rows behind them as they were doing the game. We were just out of college and we were enjoying some Old Style beer. We gained enough courage so that after the game, we thought, "They have to come out past us so we're going to say Hi." The game ends...Vin and Joe are coming out and people are pestering them for autographs. A couple of my friends and I go up to them and say, "We don't want your autographs, guys, we just want to shake your hands." Scully figured that was better than signing an autograph, so he shook our hands and kept right on going.

I might have been the one millionth inebriated fan who wanted to meet Vin Scully. With the exception of the Gibson homer, I think Vin's most memorable moment of '88 was meeting us.

—KEVIN CUSICK, sportswriter of "The Loop" column for the *St. Paul Pioneer Press*

Chapter 5

Scullypalooza

Too Much Ain't Enough

IF YOU SAY KAREEM'S NAME REALLY FAST, IT SOUNDS LIKE A FAT LADY TAKING OFF A GIRDLE

GARY OWENS

When you think of Gary Owens, the legendary Los Angeles radio personality, you might remember him as the wacky announcer on the 60s & 70s TV variety comedy show, "Laugh In." Owens is best remembered for coining the phrase "Beautiful Downtown Burbank." He appeared in every episode for six seasons on NBC from 1968-1973 and became a household fixture.

Owens was born in Mitchell, South Dakota and began his "announcing" career in the Midwest in the late '50s. He came to KFWB in Los Angeles in 1961. From there, Owens moved to KMPC in 1962 where he remained for the next two decades. During this period, he hosted the first season of "The Gong Show" in 1976. Owens was inducted into the Radio Hall of Fame in 1994.

I got a big thrill playing with Mickey Mantle at Dedeaux Field when they dedicated it with a celebrity game. Coach Rod Dedeaux was a great guy. I batted right after Mickey Mantle and Mickey and Rod told me to choke up on the bat. I was trying to swing for the fences. After I choked up, I got a hit almost immediately. Thanks to Mickey Mantle and Rod Dedeaux. Some years ago, Al Stump, a sports writer for the *Herald Examiner* and the *Herald Express*, took me to lunch with Ty Cobb. That was a big thrill for me. Ty Cobb, of course, owned a lot of stock in Coca Cola. When I was a sportscaster, I just loved that I would be sitting across from Joe Louis and people like that.

To me, Vin always was the best baseball announcer ever. He is sort of the Hans Christian Andersen of baseball. In other words, he could not only get the excitement of the play-by-play, but put it into some anecdotal way that was like somebody telling a fable...but it was true. Everything he said was true. But he had such a wonderful reportage to him.

When you're involved in sports and you love sports, you have your favorites. Vin Scully, is the best baseball announcer in the history of the game. He has a panache about him that is so good that he keeps your interest at all times. He never talked about any scandals off the field, which a lot of sportscasters do. If there was any argument among players, that would never be mentioned during the game.

The beauty of the whole thing with Vin is that he wants to give you the game—the excitement of the game. Anything surrounding the game was not necessarily part of his broadcast. It might have been for others, but not for him. That is why he is unique in the business. We had Vin on "Laugh In" and he did a marvelous job. He's just a great, great sportscaster all the way around, always a gentleman.

For 30 years, I was the play-by-play announcer for the Hollywood Celebrity Game at Dodger Stadium. I worked with everybody— Frank Sinatra, Dean Martin, Sammy Davis, Jr., Lou Rawls, Harvey Korman, Ed McMahon, Tim Conway, Telly Savalas. Kareem Abdul Jabbar and Billy Barty—we would always do shtick. Billy would come over and argue about a call against Kareem Abdul Jabbar's knee. We had everybody from Carl Reiner to Rob Reiner to Mark Harmon—who was a great athlete when he went to UCLA. Jack Lemmon, Walter Matthau, Robin Williams, and Greg Morris also played. Jill St. John, Stephanie Powers, Pamela Anderson, Heather Locklear—they would all be batgirls.

I started it in **1966*** and stopped doing it in 1998. I would do the play-by-play for the first three innings, and then I would go out in

Sports Illustrated rated New York City circa 1966 as the worst time and place to be a sports fan. The Yankees, Knicks and Rangers finished last, the Mets escaped last place for the first time and the Giants were 1–12–1. The best time and place to be a sports fan?: Philadelphia, 1980.

right-field or center-field and play. It was quite a thrill to be playing before 56,000 people out there.

He is sort of the Hans Christian Andersen of baseball.

When any guest star came on "Laugh In", they would do about 20 different things so you could insert them into different shows. We might have six things happen in one minute or less. There had never been pacing like that on television ever before. When Vin or any celebrity would come in, they might do as many as 30 jokes...some facing one direction and some another direction. Whether they were looking at us in the cast or whether they were looking at Rowan and Martin, it looked like it was a different show each time. We had 40,000,000 people watching each week. I believe Vin was on twice—1971 and 1972—he was a great guest—very professional.

Vin is on a pedestal. As he should be.

UMPIRES:
A HARD WAY TO MAKE AN EASY LIVING

PAUL RUNGE

Paul Runge graduated from Arizona State University. A former Major League umpire, 1973-1997, Runge is the middle of three generations of Major League umpires. His father, Ed Runge, was an American League umpire from 1954-1970. His son, Brian, has been an umpire since 1999.

He was the first son of a Major League umpire to reach the majors. After retiring, he became the National League's Director of Umpires in 1998-1999.

Vin always stopped in our dressing room because he's always interested to find out what's going on or to say hello, or if there is anything that would bring him closer to the field.

The other thing I liked about Vin is he always gave the opinion, as far as officiating, that when we made a mistake he'd say, "Well, he's down there, and he's closer. He must have seen it this way." He threw the human element into it. He always gave us a chance. He's in the box, and he's got the replay, and he gets plenty of time. He knows we had a split second, and we made a decision. He never jumped on the bandwagon like a lot of announcers do of beating up officials because it seems like the "in" thing to do. It's a home-town, excite-the-people type deal.

There are only a couple of announcers who understand—or even care to understand—what we do. I can count the announcers on one hand who have been in our dressing room. I don't know that I ever went to Dodger Stadium when Vin didn't come by our dressing room...not every day, but once during every series.

He did that with all the umpires. He had a relationship. If he had a question, we were tickled to death to give him an answer. He would say, "What about this rule? What about that? How are you guys doing?" His visit would be just a "stick your head in the door" type thing. He always had a relationship with us, in my opinion, above and beyond what he had to do or needed to do.

To me, that just made him that much better. He knew who we were. He threw a little personality into the relationship.

> There are only a couple of announcers who understand...

When we were wrong, he said it was his opinion we were wrong, but he would always put in the caveat of saying, "But he's down there, and I'm up here," or something to that effect. Or he would say, "They're only human. Just like players, they make mistakes." He would always say something like that instead of boom-boom-boom! I always respected him for that...plus, I always loved listening to him.

Vin was, in my era, the best. He was the best because he didn't feel like he needed to beat up on anybody, and he could give a fair accounting of what was going on, and he didn't have to be a homer. If Garvey or Cey or somebody made a mistake, he'd say, "Look at that. He did that wrong. He threw to the wrong base." He wasn't afraid to be factual.

It's not like Vin "gets away" with something. We all know they have a job to do. You've got to report things the way you see them. If we make a mistake, or a player makes a mistake, you're supposed to report it. We all understand that. But...don't beat it to death! If you look at our percentages of all the calls we make and all the things we do, our percentage is higher than any fielding percentages. We make fewer mistakes than anybody on the field.

When I make a mistake...I'm entitled to make a mistake...I'm human! There's no way I'm not going to make a mistake. I make as few as I possibly can. There's no worse feeling than making a mistake. Umpires may say it doesn't bother you—but it does bother you. Sometimes it bothers you for two or three days. You hate making mistakes. If you didn't make a mistake, you'd be a lot happier. It's not like we want to make a mistake.

In my opinion, Jack Buck is the only guy who came close to Vin Scully. He'd stop by our dressing room. Once in a while, he'd interview an umpire, just to get a little different slant on things—just to see what happened. Jack would throw a little human element into the umpire instead of him just being a number down on the field, or somebody in uniform.

The umpire job has gotten better. It's better financially and medically. My dad, in his era, said, "At its best, the job's not that good." In my era, the job got better. We got unionized and got some better things going. In my son's era, it's way better than it was for me. My son once said he'd never want to be an umpire, but the job got better. My son learned more at the breakfast table than a minor league umpire could learn in a year. That's why we now have umpires whose fathers were also umpires. My son will still call me in situations, "What do you think about this?" It's a great avenue to learn. If anything though, my son had to work harder to get to the big leagues than anybody else, because I got better after I retired. I hardly miss any plays now! My son misses some plays, but I never missed any. He gets that comparison with me and they say, "Oh, well, Paul Runge was a great this or that." It's funny how that happens. I was never as good as my dad. My son will never be as good as me...till he retires.

It's a great life. If I had to do it all over again, I'd do the same thing. It was a great time—a great era. Scully went through that great era, in my opinion—when you could talk to the players. There was church and state. You could talk to them off the field and on the field. You had a job to do, and they understood that. The ones who didn't understand it, you just didn't talk to them.

They've taken the personality out of the game with TV. They have a deal now that they're negotiating for where they've got balls and strikes on the computers. I don't care what you say, you can't take that human element out of that plate game.

I was always a pitcher's umpire. I had the same strike zone in the first inning as I did in the ninth. Yeah, I'm going to miss some pitches, but percentage-wise, I'm going to be right up in the high 90s. The better pitchers—do they get better calls? Yeah, because they're more consistent. The catchers are sitting there nice and calm and you see everything. Catchers are a key part of umpiring. If they're jumping all over the place, and doing a bad job of catching the ball, it's very difficult to call balls and strikes.

> They've taken the personality out of the game with TV.

Nowadays catchers will sit way outside and then the ball is outside. They jerk it in. Young catchers will do that. I say to them, "Thanks a lot." He goes, "What?" I say, "Well, every time you pull a pitch, if there's any doubt in my mind, it must be a ball because why would you pull it if it was a strike?" I think to myself, "What sense does that make?" Somebody teaches them to do that. They pull it...and hold it. You didn't have to pull it if it was a strike!

Vin Scully will go down in history as the greatest. He is respected by everybody. No one dislikes Vin Scully. No one. Even when he says things that make you look bad, you still like him because you know he's telling the truth.

I've never gone out to dinner with Vin, or sat down and had a cocktail with him, but I just like to listen to him. And I seldom listen to anybody. Vin is a very talented, generous, gregarious man. He loves what he's doing and it shows. He's not afraid to speak the facts. He doesn't speak them with any anger or any hurtful intent. As a matter of fact, if he does have to say something that's tough, he always gives the possibility of their being another side to it. People don't do that nowadays.

Vin is an easy guy to say good things about.

MILLIONS OF ORGAN DONORS BUT NO PIANO DONORS

GARY PRESSY

Garry Pressy has been the Chicago Cubs organist since 1986. He has played at 1,776 games. From 1977 until 1984 Gary wrote letters to the Cub organization expressing his interest to play at Wrigley Field. After seven years of persistence and disappointment, he finally landed an actual interview. It still took two years after the interview before he got the job. He first took his seat behind the organ on opening day, 1987, and has not missed a game since. In 1990, during a rain delay, against the Atlanta Braves, Pressy played the organ from 1:20 till the game was finally called off at 3:00. Don Sutton, the Braves broadcaster, said Pressy was the player of the game, and they would send him a watch. Six weeks later he received a watch—engraved, saying "Star of the Game."

After Harry Caray died, the Cubs decided to have different people serenade the crowd with "Take Me Out to the Ball Game." It was apropos for Vin to do it because he is one of the great announcers.

He was excellent. He said he would do it only the first year because that was a tribute to Harry. He is the "Picasso" of baseball announcers, believe me. You could visualize listening to him all those years, and he still is as great as always. He was the best we've had over all these years, and I know he did it with all his heart. That's the key, too.

Vin's call on the perfect game of **SANDY KOUFAX*** against the Cubs was just picture-perfect. What other announcer would tell you what time it was when the pitcher was ready to pitch. Then Gibson's home run is another good one. I remember watching that on TV.

*In **SANDY KOUFAX**'s first year in the big leagues he struck out every at-bat: 12 at-bats, 12 Ks.

When Vin would do the game of the week—he was obviously a Dodger announcer—but you couldn't tell 'cause he would cherish the game so much that he wouldn't cheerlead for the Dodgers. He would cheerlead for a good play by anybody.

The Cubs marketing department determines who sings "Take Me Out to the Ball Game" at the Cubs games. If I picked, I'd have Vin sing every day. His rendition was the best we have had in the 11 years we have been doing it. The organ started at Wrigley Field in 1967, but they did have the organ for one game on April 24, 1941 as a special treat from owner P. K. Wrigley for the fans.

These are the recording artists, bands and musical acts that have sung "Take Me out to the Ball Game" at Wrigley Field since 1998. Vin was ranked the best by the Cubs.

Trace Adkins '03
Frankie Avalon '98
Lance Bass 'N Sync '01
Chuck Berry '01
Michael Bolton '00
Kix Brooks-Brooks&Dunn '01
Meredith Brooks '02
Jimmy Buffett '98, '99, '03
Peter Cetera '03, '07
Kenny Chesney '08
Chicago '06
Deborah Cox '99
Kevin Cronin-REO Speedwagon '07
Charlie Daniels '00
Dennis DeYoung-Styx '00
Joey Fatone- 'N SYNC '01
John Fogerty '06
Peter Frampton '02
Debbie Gibson '05
Andy Griggs '02
Buddy Guy '98, '99
Mickey Hart-The Grateful Dead '00
Julianne Hough '08
Cyndi Lauper '99
Simon Lebon-Duran Duran '08
Richard Marx '99, '03
Martina McBride '98

Tom Morello '08
Jor Nicholas '05
Kellie Pickler '07
Oak Ridge Boys '03
Tony Orlando '00, '02, '04
Ozzy Osbourne '03
Kenny Rogers '99
Frank Sinatra Jr. '03
Koko Taylor '98
George Thorogood '07
Joe Trohman Fall Out Boys '08
Shania Twain '03
SheDaisy '04
Eddie Vedder-Pearl Jam '98, '03, '06, '07
Mary Wilson-The Supremes '01
The B-52's '00
The Buckinghams '00
Cheap Trick '98
The Fray '07
The Grand Ole Opry '00
Hootie and the Blow Fish '99
Journey '04
KC& The Sunshine Band '00
NY Radio City Rockettes '00
Styx '04, '08
Lee Ann Womack '06

MORE STARS THAN THE BETTY FORD CLINIC

JOE SIEGMAN

Joe Siegman is a TV producer and writer. He founded the International Jewish Sports Hall of Fame and wrote Jewish Sports Legends. *Siegman has earned the Directors Guild of America Bud Greenspan Lifetime Achievement Award. He lives in Beverly Hills*

We did the Hollywood Stars game. Some of the people who appeared in the game would go up to the broadcast booth and call a couple of at-bats and schmooze with Vinnie. Billy Crystal was one who did that. Vinnie always stayed upstairs. I don't remember him ever being down on the field.

Gary Owens called it on the **P.A. SYSTEM*** for over 30 years. He would be down on the field where we had a riser. He did all the commentary having to do with the Hollywood Star games. Originally when Jack Gilardi and I started, I don't remember who did it at first, but the first person I remember was Ed McMahon. Then came Gary...and Gary did it forever.

When the game started, Jack and I were each managing a team with Jack on the third-base side and I was on the first-base side. We always worked with Gary ahead of time with the lineups. I used to stick in my own little jokes if he wanted to use them or not. Gary always had jokes...some were spontaneous, of course, but he always had lines that were written. The way he presented them always sounded like they were spontaneous.

---

*The public address announcer for the Houston Colt '45s (later the Astros) in their 1962 inaugural season was Dan Rather...the P.A. announcer for the Brooklyn Dodgers in 1936 and 1937 was John Forsythe, later a TV and movie star.

After the Stars Game, Jack and I would go up to the press box. Before there were skyboxes and all these elaborate luxury boxes like they have now, there used to be at the opposite corner of the owner's box, down the first-base line, there was a visitors' auxiliary broadcast booth. It was also used as a VIP room when necessary. The amazing thing for that time was that they served us dinner there. Jack and I would have our small family entourage watch the game from there. Quite often, we would have some of the celebrities who had played in the game in that booth with us for dinner. They would then walk to the other side to do a half-inning or have a conversation with Vinnie.

> This celebrity/ Dodgers game was a unique promotion the Dodgers did.

We had some contact with Vinnie in the sense we would walk over to his booth with one or two of the celebrities. He was not as interested in us, but we would walk over with the celebrities and say hi to him while he was taking a break. We'd shake hands and say "hi" and he would tell us what a wonderful game it was. It was *always* a wonderful game! Then he'd kid around with the celebrity. Sometimes the celebrity stayed for a little banter. I would always go back to my booth.

This celebrity/Dodgers game was a unique promotion the Dodgers did. Other teams tried to do celebrity games…in fact, Jack and I used to take celebrities to other cities to do these games, but it didn't have the same flavor. For some reason, it wasn't the same as in Los Angeles where we would have 30 celebrities—major stars in movies and television. Nobody sent a limo for them. They drove their own car there. It was a terrific evening for the players themselves as well as for the fans. We would have the celebrities go in two-three weeks ahead of time and do little conversations with Vinnie or Jerry Doggett and whoever had the pre-game shows. They would do an interview talking about some of the things they did in previous years at the Hollywood Stars Game or how they were looking forward to playing in the game.

From what I heard from the players, the people who have been at these recent softball games—it *ain't* the same.

The Hollywood Stars Game, the celebrities, no matter how big they were, were thrilled about being on the Major League field, and they wanted to hit the ball and they wanted to run and they wanted to make a good play. They wanted to play *a game!* They wanted to lose themselves for an hour and a half to two hours. The players liked doing it, and their own children would sit along the foul lines or in the dugout to meet the celebrities. It was a gathering of famous people who all had respect for each other and for what each one did.

About 10 years ago, we had Joe Piscopo. He arrived at the same time I did. He was with his girlfriend. We walked through the stadium and it was empty. I told him to follow me, and we wended our way down to the field. I had booked him but, at that time, I did not know him. We got to the dugout and I pointed out the dressing room to him. At that time, he disappeared. He walked out to the field and stood at home plate and he said, "I can't believe it. I'm standing at home plate in Dodger Stadium." I hated to tell him he had to go get dressed because he was in such awe of where he was. He wasn't the biggest star, but he was hot at that time. It was a feeling that was shared by Jack Lemmon, Will Smith...when **KEVIN COSTNER*** came out, it was the year he won two Oscars for Dances with Wolves. The guy was at the top of his game at that particular time as a filmmaker. Still he couldn't wait to get into the game and play ball.

***KEVIN COSTNER** has appeared in four baseball movies: *For Love of the Game, Bull Durham, The Upside of Anger,* and *Field of Dreams.* In *Bull Durham,* Costner's character, Crash Davis, said: "Don't think, just throw." In *For Love of the Game,* Costner's character, Billy Chapel, said: "Think, Billy, don't just throw."

WE'RE READY FOR YOUR CLOSE-UP, MR. SCULLY

SAM RAIMI

Sam Raimi has directed more than a dozen movies. He has been in the business since 1980. He directed the movie, For Love of the Game, *starring Kevin Costner, Kelly Preston, John C. Reilly, and J. K. Simmons in 1999. The movie was based on a script by Dana Stevens, from a book by Michael Shaara.*

Vin Scully is so recognized as the voice of the Dodgers that people in New York felt it was wrong to use Vin Scully because of his recognizable voice and his relationship with the Dodgers. They felt the New York fans wouldn't like that. I felt there was so much heart in the guy, so much soul and goodness, and so much poetry in his speech and how he sees things. We couldn't make the picture without him.

> People in New York felt it was wrong to use Vin Scully...

Vin wanted to do his part of the movie unscripted. I asked him how he wanted to do it, and he said, "Here's how. I want the biographies on all these players, their stats, their averages, where they're born. I'm going to wing it like I do on all my shows." He worked with his statistician in preparing for it. We gave him the information and the way the characters names were spelled and pronounced. These were two fictitious teams so we gave him as much real back-story as we had on as many as we could. Vin just went in there like such a professional. He really lent so much credibility to the baseball players and to the story.

I showed him footage I had of Kevin Costner pitching the innings. It's the story of a perfect game. Costner is the aging Detroit pitcher pitching his final game—the last game of his life. Vin would take his stats on the players and he'd watch the footage and he'd call the game. He added so much poetry and so much beauty to the film. The action had been filmed and Vin could see a rough version of it, but he called it the way he saw it. What we had filmed was very, very dry, but he made it sound beautiful.

He wrote all of his lines, and I didn't have to change a one of them. It's my favorite part of the film. His part was there on the set in Los Angeles, where we had built a little sportscast booth for him. Vin did everything he had to do in one day—and he was really great in the film. This was filmed in the winter so it was not during regular baseball season. We had to wait until after the Yankees were done playing before we could shoot in Yankee Stadium.

> I showed him footage I had of Kevin Costner pitching the innings.

The script that Dana Stevens wrote took place as the season was winding down. The Tigers were out of contention, but they were going to play the Yankees tough because they wanted to be fair to the Boston Red Sox, who were also in contention. It was a really important game for the Yankees. They think the Tigers are going to be a pushover. But the Tigers give them a run for their money and beat them with this perfect game.

I only met with Vin one day and shot with him one day. He was wonderful. All I can tell you is that he was the ultimate professional. He's an incredible gentleman, and the sweetest man I ever met. He's so poetic and is so beautiful in all the options he gives the director. I never had to direct him. He did his own thing. I would ask him how things would work, and he would explain it to me. We wanted him to be accurate and real. There's a line in the movie he wrote for himself about our main character, Billy Chapel, how Chapel had turned the cathedral that is Yankee Stadium into a holy place with his perfect game—something like that. He uses words in such great ways. Also he mentions in the picture that he had previously called a perfect game.

This was the only baseball picture I did. Everyone was great to work with. Kevin Costner was the producer in the picture, and he chose me. He was the guy who hired the director. He knew how to do it. He had the physicality and the skill to really sell a professional baseball player. Kelly Preston, John Travolta's wife, was the female lead. During the game, he announces his retirement—while the game is in progress. He learns that the Tigers have been sold and there are new owners. He's had a great career. The new owners are going to trade him away to the Giants. He'd spent his life with the Tigers. I'm from Detroit, and they're my favorite team. I got lucky that the screenwriter decided the Tigers were the team. We got a college baseball coach who took a lot of college players and guys from Double-A for the game. It was very important to Kevin and me that the baseball looked very real. The scriptwriter gave the players their names.

When we were in pre-production, we had to cast our broadcaster. I remember talking with our producer, Amy Robinson, about who we should work with... Vin was the guy. He came up with a lot of the players personal attributes with the help of the statistician. Dana Stevens, the screenwriter, also participated. She knows baseball very, very well and is a huge fan so it was very authentic.

SO SAY YOU ONE, SO SAY YOU ALL

I think Vin Scully is one of the greatest guys around for the average fan. I come from the state of South Dakota, and we don't have a Major League team, but we have a lot of fans who go to Minneapolis or St. Louis or Chicago or Denver. I've had a lot of conversations with Vin Scully. He's a man for the average fan. It's hard to find anything that's "not perfect" about Vin Scully, and that's why I like him.

A lot of times when I, as a Senator, would talk to some people, they would talk about the anti-trust contention or the owners or all this big-time stuff that has come into professional sports. But Vin Scully, in my conversations with him, always seemed more interested in the average fan than in these things. I felt that was unusual.

When I was in Congress and would be in the Los Angeles area, I would play golf with friends and go to dinners and would sometimes come in contact with Vin then. I was very honored that Vin contributed to my campaigns and was as proud of getting a contribution from Vin as from anybody.

> —LARRY PRESSLER, Three-term U.S. Senator from South Dakota

I was the announcer on a show called "It Takes Two." I think it was the only game show Vin ever did. Vin was the host. My job was to be out in the audience to pick people to participate in the game. I would pick people and Vinnie would run the game up on the stage. It was a game where there were three couples, usually celebrity couples. He would present them a problem. He would separate the couples, and both would vote about the problem. For example, "What does a carburetor do on a car?" The men always knew...the women came up with funny answers usually. That was where the title came from. We hoped to pick people who would come up with humorous answers.

I had only met Vin one time at a social affair before we did the show. He was selected for the program by the producers. Vinnie had very little to do with the actual show. He'd come in and do the show, and then he was off to do other things, and I had other obligations too, so we never became close friends.

We did five shows in a day to broadcast for a week. The show ran for 26 weeks. Ralph Andrews was the producer for the show.

It was a great experience working with Vinnie because he was so professional and so easy to work with. We didn't have to rehearse the show. Vin would come in and we'd do the show. It was a set show and the same things happened every day—just the contestants and the results were different. There was a writing staff who came up with the questions for Vin.

> I was the announcer on a show called "It Takes Two." I think it was the only game show Vin ever did.

On these types of shows, sometimes people would try to do something to the emcee. There was once when Vin had to get the answer to the question out of the trunk of a car that was onstage. When the trunk opened, it was not visible to the audience, but there was a scantily-clad woman in there who handed Vin the answer. Of course, this was never seen by the audience or on camera. Vin had to maintain his composure for the TV audience and for the audience there. I would have been out in the audience when it happened so didn't get the benefit of seeing inside the trunk.

Other than that, Vin was never ill-at-ease and he ran the show very well. Our relationship was strictly professional. He would come in, do the show and then leave. I never even talked baseball with him.

—JOHN HARLAN, considered the "Prince of Announcers" for his work on Bob Hope Specials, "Name That Tune," and others

While teaching freshman composition at Loyola Marymount, I assigned university students the task of writing a description essay about a place for which they have strong feelings. One student came to see me in my office. He had chosen Dodger Stadium in his home city of Los Angeles as his topic because he loves baseball and thought he could write about it. He had associated many images with the topic, including the voice of Vin Scully, the announcer he had listened to for years on TV, when he watched games at home with his father. "But where do I start?" he said, "I have so many memories and thoughts about baseball."

As we talked, my student told me that he had recently gone to Dodger Stadium for the first time after listening to the games at home. At the ballpark, he searched for a glimpse of Vin Scully and could almost make out where he was sitting. He suddenly realized, though, that he wouldn't be able to hear Scully like his father would be at home because Scully's voice was being broadcast over radio and TV, not over the P. A. system. He experienced a moment of shock when he realized that this game, the first live one he had ever attended, would not be narrated for him by Scully's familiar voice.

I asked him to describe the moment when he went to Dodger Stadium and looked for Scully and saw him. What did he think at that very moment? He said he wondered about his dad, listening at home, who had turned his son onto baseball, but had never gone to the stadium himself and now refused to go. And yet, unlike his father, the son wants to see the game live. So the occasion of the essay is going to Dodger Stadium for the first time and realizing he would not hear Scully's familiar voice.

—SHEILA BENDER, English teacher, **WASHINGTON STATE***
    University

We are not a typical college radio station—it's 50,000 watts. We have a budget of over three million dollars. We have 70 students who work for us, half of whom are on the air. They all are paid a salary under the University's work study program. Many of these students pursue radio as their career.

When Vin Scully worked at the station in '47, it was a humongous three-watt station. Charles Osgood and Vin Scully are probably our two most famous students, in fields of sports and news.

On April 29, we raised $700,000 at our first Spring Gala held at Sotheby's Auction House. The station honored recording artist

*Pullman, home of **WASHINGTON STATE** University, has a population of twenty-five thousand. Martin Stadium, the home stadium for the Washington State Cougars holds thirty-eight thousand...In the late 1950s, the Cougars had a home game during a blizzard. The paid attendance was 1. The Athletic Department gave that paying fan a lifetime pass to Washington State football games.

Emmylou Harris, as well as CBS journalist Charles Osgood and Vin Scully. At the press conference before the ceremony, Vin said that his award was even more meaningful than the honorary degree he received from Fordham in 2000. In his acceptance speech, Scully recounted a trip to the Vatican with Ralph Branca, in which Pope Pius XII granted them an audience. "The Pope turned to Ralph and he said, 'Where are you from, my son?' Ralph said, 'Mt. Vernon, New York, your Holiness.' He said, 'Oh, yes, I remember,'" because he had been to Fordham a couple of years before.

> When Vin Scully worked at the station in '47, it was a humongous three-watt station.

"And, I'm standing there, 'cause my moment's coming, and I'm going to remember everything. Now the Pope turns and there I am. My throat is dry, my knees are shaking, my palms are sweaty, and he looked at me and he said, 'Are you with them?' I answered, 'Yes, your holi....' And he left. So all my life, whether it was doing Major League baseball, NFL football or PGA golf, I have always felt, "I'm with them." When WFUV is ever mentioned to me, or I read about it, believe me, I say, "I'm with them."

The second gala will probably be sometime next April. At this particular point, we have not released the procedure to anyone. We are in the process of formulating plans. We're going through with it. I've talked to Vin about it because he did want to be kept abreast of what we did because his name is on the award. It's being given for professional broadcasters with a minimum of 25 years of professional broadcast experience. The award with Vin's name is given for sports broadcasting and the award with Charles' name on it will be given for news broadcasting. There is a student play-by-play award, which is named after Marty Glickman, who taught here.

> —BOB AHRENS, executive sports producer at WFUV, Fordham University's radio station...home of New York's longest-running sports call-in show.

I was president of Fordham University so I invited Vin to do our 2000 commencement address and receive an honorary degree. It was a rainy day, and we had to have the commencement indoors, and Vin gave a fine address in our McGinley Center.

I used to see Vin whenever we would visit alumni on the West Coast. We made those trips every year, and frequently I would meet with Vin. Typically, as the president, we would try to visit with the Alumni Clubs regularly. When we would visit the Fordham Alumni in Los Angeles, Vin would be at some of those gatherings.

Fordham played Yale in baseball in 1949, and Vin played center field for Fordham, and George H. W. Bush played first base for Yale. I saw the program from that game.

—FATHER JOSEPH O'HARE, Former president of Fordham University

I played baseball at Fordham with Vin and Johnny Bach. I pitched and played shortstop. Vin was a pretty good outfielder, but one day at practice, Vin was practicing his broadcasting. We all said, "What is Vin doing—he should be down here taking batting practice!" He was already looking ahead. He was just so interested in broadcasting.

We couldn't understand Vin's love for broadcasting. I guess he knew what he going to become. Even during the season, Vin spent most of his time at WFUV, our student radio station. It was a great training ground for him. We also had a lot of fun. We did a Saturday Night Disc Jockey show—we had the Queen Mary docking on Fordham Road. It shocked everyone.

—NICK BALDINO, retired banker

I remember one incident. Vin would do his TV show "It Takes Two" on NBC. He had celebrities and their spouses. He had Frankie Avalon and his wife, Kitty; Jimmy Darren and his wife; and I was married to Annette Funicello. It was a baseball panel show where Vin would ask questions. He asked the question, "What's a perfect game? How many outs in a perfect game?" Annette said "81." Vin said, "What?" Koufax came out and said to Annette, "You go to the games with your husband and to the All-Star games and all that, and you said 81?" She said, "Well, I thought 9 x 9." Vinnie just broke up. He couldn't stop laughing.

> ...I was married to Annette Funicello.... "How many outs in a perfect game?" Annette said "81."

Annette and I were doing the Hollywood Stars game. Jimmy played and Frankie played and Vinnie was always there for us. Vin was on the field with us. He helped us with the celebrities.

In all the years I've known Vin, he's never changed. He's never one to upstage anybody. He's always a gentleman. Just recently I saw him at the John Wooden presentation. He was awesome, just as charming and warm and wonderful as anybody could be.

I remember the day Jackie Gleason, a client of ours, played in the game, and Vin was kidding Jackie because we had to make a special uniform for him—he couldn't fit into ours. Vin said, "Are you ever going to get down to size?" He said, "I will never get down to size because I'm a big man."

Vinnie was always a class act. Vinnie can get up before five people or 50,000 people. He was comfortable and always neatly dressed, nattily dressed to perfection. He was very much at ease. He could talk to a group of kids or to a group of retired people. He could charm the honey out of a bee. Working in the different sports was a challenge to Vinnie. He wanted to work. Working was nourishment for him.

> —JACK GILARDI, Hollywood agent, was married to Annette
> Funicello

Vinnie and I played baseball together at Fordham. Our coach was Jack Coffey. Vin played outfield, and I was a catcher. Coach Coffey had the distinction of being the only big-league player to play with Ty Cobb and **BABE RUTH*** in the same season—1918. He coached at Fordham for 33 years.

I remember Vin had a huge tape recorder that he used to practice broadcasting— Fordham had started a radio station and a broadcasting curriculum. Vin got great training at Fordham and was innately good as well. Vin was like the rest of us in college—mediocre if you're talking professional baseball. He loved the game. Jack Coffey was a great teacher of baseball. Red Barber was a great teacher for Vin at sportscasting.

We didn't get a great deal of batting practice because Coffey taught situational baseball. Boy, did his teams know how to

*In **BABE RUTH**'s first major league game in 1914, he was removed in the seventh inning for a pinch hitter.

throw through and throw to the right base. You knew how to run the bases. He taught all his life. I know that Vin picked up so much from him, and is still using it on his broadcasting. He was an apt pupil.

Even as a kid, Vin had a really good voice. It was a sonorous voice—wonderfully salving, deeper than you expected. If you saw him, he was a skinny, red-haired kid, but he had a beautiful voice. Apparently the training and his love for the game benefited him. I recognize that voice now when checking through those broadcast stations on satellite.

> Even as a kid, Vin had a really good voice.

I wish I had known when Vin was being honored by WFUV. Some of my favorite people were there. Emmylou Harris was there and got an award. I've gone to 25 of her concerts and have met her and invited her to come sing the National Anthem before a Bulls game. She was so accommodating it's unbelievable.

My voice now, at 84, is getting raspy, but Vin's seems to be well taken care of, as it should be. Vin had a wonderful disposition. He liked baseball. He wasn't pompous about the work he was doing. Let's face it—I don't know how many people they had in that course at Fordham, but it must have been 20, and he clearly was the best. WFUV taught it and Vin took advantage of it. It was one of the first of its kind.

Recently, I was asked to come up to Fordham to a reception. I'm standing there with a drink in my hand...and there's the Cardinal. John Foster Dulles' son, Avery, was there. He was in black and didn't wear the Cardinal red so I didn't recognize him. Avery Dulles is one of the few Jesuit Cardinals in their history. I had walked over to him earlier. The president asked me if I had recognized him. He had been there as a student Jesuit with us. He said, "Johnny, go over there and apologize to him. He's the Cardinal of the church." I went over and he said, "Oh, no problem, John." He would have to be close to 80 now and has not been gifted with good health. He was walking with a cane.

As an old catcher, I'm doing pretty good. I haven't had a day's trouble with my legs.

—JOHN BACH, 84, long-time basketball coach at Fordham, Penn State and in the NBA

Thanks to XM Radio, anybody in the country or the world can hear Vin Scully from Dodger Stadium. That was a gift that came along far too late, but it's a gift that was given to baseball fans everywhere. You can hear that voice late at night here in Florida. It's the sound of baseball.

I wrote a book that came out a couple of years ago called, *How to be Like Jackie Robinson.* I spent almost four years immersed in the project, did about 1200 interviews. I absolutely immersed myself in the life of Jackie Robinson. It was part of a series. I've done nine of those "How to be Like...." books. *How to be Like Walt Disney, How to be Like Coach Wooden, How to be Like Michael Jordan.* Enormous research projects and labors of love, but the Robinson book was an absolutely riveting experience for me.

I told the publishers I'd really like to do the Jackie book if Rachel Robinson would give me her blessing, which she did. I was able to pour myself into the whole Dodger world through that. I talked to every one of his living ex-teammates. It was a great experience. Health Communications in Deerfield Beach, Florida, published the book. They're the *Chicken Soup for the Soul* publishers. The book took different qualities of his life that set him apart. I did a chapter on each of those unique qualities of his. What life lessons can we learn from Jackie Robinson was really the thrust of the book. I did a chapter on Jackie Robinson as a leader. A chapter on character. A chapter on courage. A chapter on perseverance.

> —PAT WILLIAMS, founder of the Orlando Magic and perhaps the most enthusiastic and accomplished individual in all of sports...world-famous as an author, motivational speaker and sports executive.

When Vin Scully was an undergraduate, he would sit in the balcony during basketball practices. He would sit there and broadcast the practices...to himself. All the players on the team thought he was crazy. This guy would show up every day at practice and go sit up in the balcony and talk to himself. I don't know if he had a recorder with him, but he was talking.

He spoke here recently at a WFUV dinner. It's a 50,000 watt station and is very popular. They are a National Public Radio station, and they do a lot of our athletic events. Vin and Charles Osgood were the honorees. Tickets were sold for the event, and we had a great crowd. It's hard to get Vin to come to New York—he very rarely does it. He came back for this dinner, and his talk was phenomenal.

—FRANK MCLAUGHLIN, former Fordham star basketball player

I remember when I was behind home plate with the Jugs radar gun, before we put the velocity on the scoreboard. I'd give Vin the reading by fingers—if it was 90, I'd give him a 5 and 4. For 92, I'd put 5-4-2.

Now I sit in the press box to use the radar gun and sometimes I sit in the scouting section. I don't have to be by Vinnie because I don't have to give him the numbers anymore. They go directly to the scoreboard. They've been doing that for the last 10 years. Now, when the World Baseball Classic comes, I'm going to be right behind home plate with the Jugs gun.

A lot of people think I'm from Mexico, but I'm from Cuba. I left Cuba to come to the United States before Castro. Castro played baseball as a pitcher with Havana University. If he would have been a good pitcher, he would have left the country to play baseball. Unfortunately he was a lousy pitcher. I never played in the Majors—the highest I played was AA.

When I go out of the country to talk to baseball players, everybody knows Vinnie. They know Vinnie everywhere. Every place where they speak English, they know who Vin Scully is.

—MIKE "THE HAT" BRITO, Long-time Dodger Scout

The times we've asked Vin for assistance in projects, he's never said no, which shows that, despite his legend status, he's never lost his humility. One time, he narrated a short piece we have on Ebbets Field. It is a re-creation of Ebbets Field that was done and then enhanced through computers. It's huge. When visitors go into our ballparks exhibit, you can actually navigate your way in and outside the stadium. Vin was very good in narrating that piece for us. He recorded it for us at a studio in L.A. When we've asked him for scorecards from different events, he's always obliged. He served as a voting member, since he won the award, on the Frick Committee for many, many years.

These honorees are honored by the Hall of Fame, but are not actually in the Hall of Fame. There's no plaque for them here, but there is a calligraphied award and a presentation with a photograph and biography for each honoree which is displayed on the wall the year of their induction. This would be in our Scribes and Mike Men Exhibit.

The award for writers started in 1962, and for broadcasters started in '78. Mel Allen and Red Barber were honored in '78, Lindsay Nelson in '79, Russ Hodges in '80, Ernie Harwell in '81 and Vin Scully in '82.

For Vin Scully, we have his "pearls-on-a-string" call for the consecutive scoreless innings for Don Drysdale. We have the Kirk Gibson home run call. We have the Koufax perfect game call. We get these from the local radio stations or from the teams. Today we get them from Major League Baseball. We have about 12,000 hours of recorded media.

Every year, we honor one person in these fields. It is voted on by all of the living awardees, plus five journalists, who cover the radio-TV industry. Unlike the players, these honorees can be active. This is done by paper ballot.

—JEFF IDLESON, President of the Baseball Hall of Fame.

When I was named to my first athletic director job at Cal State-Fullerton, lo and behold, within a couple of days, there's a cassette tape in my mail with a note from the director of broadcasting saying, "Vinnie wanted you to have this." It was Vinnie saying, "Long-time Dodger executive, good friend of the Dodger family, Bill Shumard, congratulations and good luck." I've still got that tape. Those kinds of things mean a ton.

One of the things that fell under my purview for many years there was the **OLD-TIMERS*** game. I would write the introductions for each of the old-timers. To fill up those rosters, we'd have a few Hall of Famers, but we'd also have a lot of guys who were

*In July 2007 Yankee starting pitcher Roger Clemens was older than five of the retired Yankees who played in that day's OLD-TIMERS game.

just guys. On typical old-timers day, guys can't play more than a few innings. Introductions usually lasted about 45 minutes, and the game itself lasted half an hour. Vinnie would introduce each guy and they would come up out of the dugout and go to the line. Vinnie would build them up so much, guys would come back into the dugout and say to me, "Wow! I didn't think I was nearly that good." What a great moment for an old-timer who was mainly 'just a guy.' Here they got their moment in the sun, and Vinnie builds them up in front of a capacity house...what a great, great touch!

Gordy Verrell, a well respected sportswriter covered the Dodgers for the Long Beach Press Telegram for two decades. Back in the day sportswriters served as official scorers. One game, Gordy was faced with an either/or call—hit or error. He called it a hit. Vinnie took Gordy to task on the radio, "I can't believe it. That ball was clearly an error." That got Gordy a little steamed—to get second-guessed by 40,000 people because Vinnie called him into question. Gordy said, "To add insult to injury, my mother called me the next day and chewed me out." "How could you make a call like that?" "Mom, how do you know it wasn't a hit?" *"Because Vinnie said it wasn't!"*

—BILL SHUMARD, Dodger Executive, 1975-1988

Late in the '70s or early '80s, Vin's son was a batboy with the Dodgers for a couple of years. When I was working at Dodger Stadium, he would bring me balls or bring me a glass of water or a towel and would try to get his dad's attention. Vin would look down and would have a little wave for him.

At the end of my career, the last two years, when I took the crew to home plate for the ground rules for a Dodger game, we would take off our hats and put them across our hearts and then we would bow to him. It was a tribute to him for all his years of service and what he meant to the game, what he meant to me personally as a guy with class who treated me well all the years I knew him.

I'd put Vin in the class with another fellow who passed on a few years back, Jack Buck, who was my very good friend. These are two guys who stand tall in the baseball business in what they do.

Vin occasionally would come by the umpire's room. When I made my last trip to L.A. last year, the Dodgers gave me a gift of a Dodger shirt in a beautiful frame that he, Lasorda and Jaime

Jarrin signed—all Hall-of-Famers. It was a very, very nice gift from the Dodgers. I was called to receive it, and I was really happy that Scully had taken the time to personally sign it for me, as I was with the other two guys who signed it.

I had an experience with Scully in the early '80s. We came into Houston and the ballplayers and the umpires were all staying at the Shamrock Hilton, a terrific hotel near the **ASTRODOME***. They gave us rooms there that have never been matched. The umpires got suites. If you wanted to stay by the pool, you could, but the suites inside the hotel were fantastic. We had come in on a Sunday night. The Dodgers were coming in as the Phillies were leaving. The Dodgers had come into town, and we were in the bar. I struck up a conversation with Scully sitting in there. I asked him about his reputation of never bothering umpires. He said it was a practice he had learned early on. He wanted to be a reporter and not get into opinions. He said that one of the only things that bothered him was umpires who didn't hustle and umpires who gave him a delayed strike call because "I'm on the radio, and my pace is geared by what the plate umpire does on balls and strikes." He said a delayed strike made it tough for him. There were a couple of guys at that time who had delayed strikes in the National League. He said that other than that, he never went out of his way to berate an umpire because of his opinion on a safe or an out. He reported what it was and would tell about the argument, but said it was his practice not to beat up on umpires. He held to that for all the years I've known him.

Vin is a man with a lot of class, and I consider him my friend... and a friend of the game...and of umpires. This is almost unheard of...but, I have NEVER heard a bad word about Vin Scully.

—BRUCE FROEMMING, Major-league umpire since 1971

*On June 15, 1978, the Pirates were "rained in" at the Houston ASTRODOME. Ten inches of rain flooded the Astrodome parking lots and access roads. The teams made it to the park, but the umpires, fans, and stadium personnel did not.

In all the years I worked there with Vinnie, I can only recall one player criticizing what might have been said or what Vinnie said on the radio. There's probably only one other person besides me who knows about it. It was the relief pitcher, Mike Marshall. He came up to me on the Dodger jet to complain. He didn't say Vinnie by name. He was complaining about the "cigar store indians" comment and how the announcers were treating it. Marshall had said something about the Dodger infield was being bunch of "cigar-store indians." We had Cey, Russell, Lopes and Garvey. I couldn't believe what I was hearing. He was saying it loud enough where Vinnie could hear him. Vinnie was just sitting there—reading his book. He's as professional as they come. I think Vinnie probably rapped him on the radio and Marshall heard about it. That's what happened. The  Jeff Kent thing has just come up so that brought memories of the other one time in 18 years where one guy complained. Two complaints in two decades. Most announcers get that many every game.

In addition to what Vin has done for the Dodgers, think of what that voice has done for Farmer John and for Union 76. We didn't have that many sponsors in those days. I think we only had the Union 76 and Farmer John. We were not on TV often in those early days. It was the radio. We had the nine TV games in Candlestick Park because of the Giants being arch rivals. We had nine games a year. Now with the advent of cable, look at how far we have come. Vinnie only did the nine games on TV, otherwise, you had the transistor radio turned to KFI, a 50,000 watt station.

    —STEVE BRENER, Dodgers P.R. Director, '70-'87

I got more thank-you notes from Vin Scully, by far, than any other broadcaster. It seems like anytime I wrote about him, and, obviously I wrote a lot of positive things about him, he sent notes. My guess would be somewhere between a dozen and two dozen in the 34½ years. And, the one time he was upset, he didn't send a note he was upset, I heard second-hand about it.

For my final TV column, the *Times* said I could do a farewell column, which appeared Friday, September 14, 2007. Here's what I quoted Scully as saying, "I'd say the biggest change I've seen is the technology. I think the equipment that allows producers and directors to do so many different things has helped revitalize baseball telecasts." Scully spent 20 years on network television, first in football and golf with CBS and baseball for NBC. He left NBC in 1989 after CBS acquired baseball's television rights. Through it all, he continued to work for the Dodgers. He said he enjoyed many years at the network but not once did he ever have a yearning to go back.

In digging through boxes and scrapbooks of clippings I found one of the many notes Scully sent me through the mail over the years. This one was dated January 26, 1978. Scully's words were in response to something I had written, and he concluded with, "Some big deal I am. I read your column but I still have to put out the garbage!" He wrote his notes to me on his own personal stationery. When I called him, and this was important to me, he said, "Well, my biggest concern is that you are happy." He's more concerned about if this was a good thing for me and was I okay with the switch from the TV beat to horse-races.

—LARRY STEWART, retired, famous critic

Most people grew up wanting to be Willie Mays or whomever. I didn't. I grew up wanting to be Marv Albert or Vin Scully. At some point, I realized that producing was more for me than on-air. Meeting them and working with them was, and is, still tremendous. I don't take them for granted any day. To me, it's almost second nature, at this point, but when people find out who I work with, it's, "Oh my God—you know *him!*" I don't think you ever outgrow that.

I did a game with Ernie Harwell in Yankee Stadium. Wayne Gretzky, at the time, was playing for the Rangers. Wayne is hovering in the back of the booth...like a shy kid—*Wayne Gretzky*. I said, "Hi Wayne." He goes, "Hi. I'm sorry to bother you." I said, "You're not bothering me. Come on in." He said, "No, I don't want to intrude." I said, "What's the matter?" He goes, "Is that Ernie

Harwell?" I was like, "Yeah, it is. Why? Do you want to talk to him?" He goes, "Oh no, no, no. I've never met him in person, and I grew up listening to him. Do you mind if I just listen for a little bit?" He was just like a kid—*Wayne Gretzky!*—the greatest hockey player of all time. He was like a five or ten year old kid. During the break, I say to Ernie, "There's somebody here to see you." He turns around... and he introduces himself to Ernie Harwell, "Hi, I'm Wayne Gretzky." Like Ernie doesn't know who he is. Ernie said, "I know who you are." Wayne was literally so nervous his voice was quivering. He was like a kid meeting his boyhood idol. This is a guy he grew up listening to. He was so respectful and so genuine. Gretzky told him, "I grew up in Brantford, Ontario. I used to fall asleep listening to you every night." Harwell said, "I used to put a lot of people to sleep." It's not a Vin story, but the point is it's the same way when you work with Vin.

I don't care who you are...I don't care how long you've been doing this, when you work with Vin, you work with Ernie, and you work with Jack Buck—if you had any sense of the history of broadcasting, you'd have to look around and say, "Wow!" It's like your first at-bat in the Major Leagues, while you're in Yankee Stadium or in Dodger Stadium, the crowd's going crazy...you still have to hit. At some point, you feel like, "Oh, my God. I've made it." While working with all those guys, I can tell you that when Vin said my name for the first time, when giving the credits for a game, I was like, "Vin said *my name* on a World Series game—I've made it." In baseball, when Vin said it—and no offense or disrespect to any of the other guys—it was special because I was a New York guy. I'm sure if you asked Vin about me, he wouldn't remember me from a hole in the wall.

My memory of Vin Scully is after Game 1 of a World Series, my job was to get them out of the Yankees parking lot. Normally, we have a car service, but because I knew the city—having gone to high school in the Bronx—I knew a back way out of there so I would just take them out. They pile in my car. I'm going

> I felt awful... that Vin got the finger from a nun.

down the up-ramp of the parking structure. No one is going up at that time...the game is over! We get to the exit. There are three or

four cars angling for the exit. I come out of the side, out of nowhere. As I'm angling out, I guess I cut off two nuns. One of the nuns gives us the finger! Vin, in the car, goes, "Now, I've seen everything...getting flipped the bird by a Sister with a habit." Vin was on the passenger side, so Vin's the one who bore the brunt of 'the finger' from a nun. I felt awful...not for cutting them off, but that Vin got the finger from a nun.

—HOWARD DENEROFF, 40, long-time CBS producer, now with Westwood One

CLONES ARE PEOPLE TWO

JON MILLER

Jon Miller is ESPN's lead voice for it's telecasts of Major League Baseball. He is also the lead play-by-play announcer for the San Francisco Giants, his home town. He has received numerous awards for his work, including a cable ACE award and several Emmy nominations.

I was born eight days after Bobby Thompson's home run...so Vin has been in the booth longer than I've been alive.

For me, Vin Scully is the best in the business...and the best there has *ever* been in the business. He was an inspiration to a lot of young baseball broadcasters. When I was a kid, growing up a Giants fan, I thought Vin was terrible and that Russ Hodges and the Giants broadcasters were as good as anybody could possibly be. Russ would say, "Bye-bye baby" whenever the Giants would hit a home run, and Lon Simmons would say, "Tell it goodbye." Vinnie would just say, "She's gone," or "Awaaay back, and she's gone." I remember thinking, as a ten-year-old, "Oh, my gosh, that's terrible. No wonder he's working in a jerkwater town." As a Giants fan—a ten-year-old Giants fan—you hear, "Bye-bye baby," and you get goose-bumps. As a ten-year-old, I hated Maury Wills, and hated Don Drysdale—it was impossible to hate Sandy Koufax, but I hated it when he pitched against the Giants.

Later on, when I grew up, I realized how good Vinnie is. Sometimes when the Dodgers would play, and they were on a powerful station, KFI, I'd have the Giants game on the radio, and I'd get another radio and put Vinnie on. I wanted to hear both broadcasts. I was already having aspirations to be a broadcaster.

I've spent time chatting with Vin and picking his brain because he grew up a Giants fan, and **MEL OTT*** was his favorite player. He calls him, "Ottie." He talked about being at the Polo Grounds, and he would like to get up in the stands right behind "Ottie." He told me Ott would play in a certain spot. It was very short down the right field line at the Polo Grounds. Ott wouldn't have a whole lot of shifting from one hitter to another. He always played way off the line, trying to guard that huge gap. Vin said he'd watch Ott and see him wear a hole in the grass—there'd be like a little patch of dirt out there and he knew that was where Ott had been playing all day.

I once said to Vin a few years ago, "Why don't you just leave the Dodgers and come work with me doing Giant games. You would have come full circle. It would be incredible!" I don't remember the specifics—maybe it was the last time the Giants got sold. Vinnie laughed. I said, "You grew up a Giants fan and you would come back and finish your career with the Giants. That would be a big story." He looked at me and said, "Oh, that would be a big story. I don't think that's going to happen."

All announcers *could* work like Vinnie—in the booth alone. The beauty of when Vin was doing the radio with Jerry Doggett, if you tuned in and you heard Jerry—who was an excellent professional announcer—you'd be disappointed it wasn't Vinnie. "Where's Vinnie? Oh, must be Jerry's inning." There's sort of a phenomenon involved in that, which was that you turn it on...you realize Vinnie's not there, and you realize that you miss him. Then, he's back on, and you're happy that he's back on.

When I was a kid, nine or ten years old, I would play the Strat-O-Matic baseball game. I would broadcast the games and do the crowd noise and do the public announcements. If it was a Dodger game in L. A., I'd be doing Vinnie doing the game. I'd be doing John Ramsey announcing the batters.

> *The first big-league home runs by **MEL OTT** and Duke Snider were inside-the-park....Sandy Koufax once gave up an inside-the-park homer to *Mr. Ed* on a TV show of the same name.

A lot of people tell me my imitation of Vinnie is good. When I got to Boston in 1980 to do the Red Sox games with Ken Coleman, we had to fill the rain delays. It rained often...stopping the game, and we had to stay on the air. After we'd been driving all over Florida all spring, telling each other stories and having laughs, we get into this rain delay on Opening Day at Fenway Park. Ken starts it off by saying, "Jon, you did this impression while we were driving across Florida, and I really loved it. Will you do Vin Scully?" So, what was I to do? We were on an 88-station network. I had never done it on the air. It was just a joke between me and other announcers. I did all my Vinnie material. By that night, I was on a local TV station where they had asked me to come on and do the Vin Scully imitation on the 11:00 news...in Boston. Then, Jack Craig, the media critic at the *Boston Globe*, a couple of days after that, interviewed me for a story about the new broadcaster. The headline said, "Red Sox New Voice(s)."

A couple of years after that, Vin started doing the NBC Game of the Week. It was amazing that even before he was at NBC, you could do his voice and everybody already knew who it was. He had done World Series games.

I figured I'd better get a tape of Vin and study him if I'm going to be known for that. I wanted to get him right. I don't think my style is anything at all like his. A lot of young broadcasters who grew up with Vinnie sound like him. You can always tell where these young guys grew up by the veteran broadcaster they sound like. You get a tape from a guy, and he sounds like Jack Buck, and you get another guy and he sounds like Harry Caray. Most of them were sounding like Vinnie. But, the ones who sounded like Vinnie weren't just from one geographic part of the country. He, by that time, was on NBC so everybody knew him.

Al Michaels did the '72 Series. I remember when the Series moved to Oakland, I was working for a small-town TV station. I went to the game but I had to leave early so I could get back to my station in the North Bay. I left the Coliseum and put the game on the radio. I remember thinking, "Well, Vinnie's doing the radio. Why is that? I thought they just used guys from the host teams." And, that's what they did in those days. Come to find out, the broadcaster was Al Michaels. He sounded dead-on like Vinnie in those days. I was astonished. Then, Al came to the Giants in '74, which was also the first year I got into baseball. I was doing the A's games that same year. I remember occasionally I would have a chance to hear him and he sounded so much like Vinnie.

It's fun to be working in San Francisco. Everything that happens to the Dodgers is of interest to Giants fans. A lot of people who live in the Bay area grew up in L. A., and vice-versa. We have a broadcasters' roundtable on the radio during the post-game show, where the two TV guys come over with the two radio guys, and we talk about the game and have a few laughs...depending on how the game went. The Dodgers were going to be coming in next, and we're talking about that. That's always of great interest to Giants fans. Then, in the background, I just started doing John Ramsey announcing Maury Wills or Willie Davis. Mike Krukow grew up in L. A. Whenever he hears this John Ramsey impression, he just goes nuts. Bruce Jenkins, who is a columnist and sportswriter with the *Chronicle* called me the next day. He and his wife had been driving home from the ballpark, and they heard this John Ramsey in the background, and he said they almost drove off the road. I don't know how many people actually knew what was going on, but the ones who did know loved it.

Vinnie knew that I did an imitation of him. One time, when I was doing the Baltimore games Vin was there for the Game of the Week telecast. My partner on the Baltimore broadcast went to Vinnie and said, "Jon does this great Vin Scully." He says, "I think it would be funny if you did a tape doing Jon." Vinnie basically just did himself...but used my name. It was something like, "This is Jon Miller. The Orioles are playing here in Boston today. When that series is over, they come home, and they'll be taking on Kansas City starting Monday night. You can tell that to your mom. You can tell it to dad. You can tell it to the Marines." He was just saying all those things—I'm sure he had never even heard me do a broadcast.

We did a thing on ESPN one time and Vin was at a studio in New York for Game of the Week, and I was at a studio in Seattle where I was with the Orioles. A guy at ESPN in Connecticut was interviewing the two of us. He brought up my Vin Scully impression, and he asked me to do it. I did Vinnie. I did him as being so famous that when I was in **JAPAN***, I had a chance to hear the legendary voice of the Tokyo Giants, and I was amazed that Vinnie's fame had spread so far that when I turned it on, this guy was doing Vinnie. So, I did Vinnie in Japanese, as that guy. Vinnie laughed, and the host laughed. Then, Vinnie did a little Japanese himself.

I had a bizarre experience. Roy Firestone used to have a show. I went on that show periodically and did Vin in Japanese. I used the name of the Tokyo announcer. The next day, I rejoined the Orioles in Oakland. I go out on the field during batting practice and head to the batting cage. Standing there is the Japanese announcer—the voice of the Tokyo Giants. I was astounded and thought I was seeing things. He walks over to me 'cause we know each other. We say hello, and I said, "This is such an amazing coincidence. Yesterday, I did a television show on ESPN and did a little comedy bit, and I used your name." He said, "Ahhh. Yes. Yes. I saw the show. Vin Scawee. Velly funny." He actually saw me on the show as him doing Vin Scully. I don't know if he even had the slightest idea of what I was doing. He told me he thought it was very funny.

I have a thing about the Polo Grounds. I don't know why because I didn't grow up in New York. I grew up with the *San Francisco* Giants. Russ Hodges used to talk about the Polo Grounds. Every

*The Yomiuri Giants are sometimes called "The New York Yankees of JAPAN." They have won the most pennants and have the deepest fan base in Yakyu (Japanese Baseball)....The Nippon Ham Fighters give free tickets to foreigners on "Yankees Day."

year he played a tape of Bobby Thompson's home run at some point in the middle of the season. He described the scene, and he described the Polo Grounds. I remember when I was 10 years old, the Giants Yearbook they put out every year had pictures of all the ballparks in the National League. That was the year the **METS WERE BORN*** so they had a picture of the Polo Grounds because that's where the Mets were playing. I remember looking at that and thinking, "That is so bizarre." I'd heard Russ describe it as 483 feet to center field. It was 279 to left and 257 to right. It was crazy. I was fascinated with it. To this day, I've collected several photographs of it, and I have them on the wall in my office.

Vin paid me this great compliment at a big banquet one night. He said, "Jon Miller, over here, is the best baseball broadcaster in America *in his price range!"*

---

*After the Mets had played their first nine games in their <u>INAUGURAL 1962 SEASON</u>, they were 9½ games out of first place.

THE SON ALSO RISES

RYAN LEFEBVRE

Ryan Lefebvre is a native Los Angeleno—having graduated from L. A. Loyola High School in 1989. He played baseball at the University of Minnesota...and was named team MVP in 1993. He made All Big Ten as an outfielder in 1991 and 1993. He is the son of former Dodger player Jim Lefebvre. He was named 2006 Boys and Girls Club of Greater Kansas City's Role Model of the Year. He is in his 10th season as a Kansas City Royals broadcaster and 14th season in the majors. In 2008, he moved into the television booth full-time. Lefebvre was hired by the Minnesota Twins at age 24. He lives with his wife, Sarah, in Lake Winnebago, MO.

When my dad was coaching in 1978, I first saw Vin. We didn't live that far from each other, and my mom was friendly with him so sometimes when we would pass by his house, we'd stop and say hello. I just knew Vin as the "Voice of the Dodgers," as a kid growing up in Southern California. I never really studied him as an announcer until after college and I realized this is what I wanted to do.

When I first got the job with Minnesota in 1995, my mom—she was a huge fan of Vin—said I should try to get in touch with Vin, "I'm sure he'd love to know what you're doing." I thought, "Well, I don't want to bother him." At this point, he was larger than life to me—just listening to him and studying him and realizing how good he was—not just because he was *my guy* growing up. I hemmed and hawed and my mom kept on, "I think he'd like to know that you're doing the same thing he's doing." I remember saying to my mom, "Yeah, and while I'm at it, I'll call Tiger Woods and tell him I play a little golf too."

To put that into perspective that I was doing the same thing he was doing—I may have been in the same profession, but I never thought I was doing *what Vin was doing* for a living!

When I was with the **ROYALS*** in 2003, we went to Los Angeles for Interleague play. At that point, Vin wasn't traveling. I was really looking forward to going back to Dodger Stadium because I hadn't been there since I was a little kid. More than anything, I was excited about getting a chance to talk to Vin. At this point, I'd been doing broadcasting for nine years. I was looking forward to getting to spend some time with him and telling him how much I admired him and maybe picking his brain. I hadn't even seen him since I was about nine or ten years old.

> There was that unmistakable voice echoing in the hallways. I knew it was him.

I was all excited for the big moment...the first game we played at Dodger Stadium, I got to the ball park early. Our booth was about two booths down from where Vin was. There was that unmistakable voice echoing in the hallways. I knew it was him.

Having grown up in this environment, I'm not awed by many things. I respect people I have been around—growing up in Major League baseball my whole life. I've never been awed by people. But I was really nervous about walking into the booth. I wasn't even sure if Vin would remember me. I finally pulled enough courage together to walk down to the booth and go in.

As I walked in, he looked at me. I approached him and started to stick my right hand out to say, "Hi Vin. I'm Ryan Lefebvre." I knew he hadn't seen me in forever. As I started to stick my hand out...before I could open my mouth...he goes, "Well, Ryan. After all these years. Look at you." That's one of the greatest thrills I've

*In the 1979 baseball draft, the Kansas City <u>ROYALS</u> selected Dan Marino in the fourth round and John Elway in the eighteenth round. That same year the Royals hired Rush Limbaugh for their group sales department. Limbaugh left in 1984 for a radio opportunity in California.

ever had in my life—that Vin remembered who I was. We had a great chat, and he treated me like a peer, as he was giving me information on the Dodgers, and I was giving him information on the Royals. We sat and talked...like I do with every other broadcaster in the Major Leagues when our teams get together. But with Vin, it was a little bit different for him to treat me in that way.

The next day I got to interview him on our radio pre-game show. I probably spent more time preparing for that interview than I have for any other in my life because he's such a master at the language, that I was afraid I was going to mis-speak or use a word in the wrong tense or anything. I had a wonderful interview with him. I saved it and burned off a bunch of DVDs and sent copies to all my family and friends. Just doing that whole series...thinking, "Wow, I'm calling the same game Vin is calling."

> That's one of the greatest thrills I've ever had in my life—that Vin remembered who I was.

I remember asking Vin, "How has broadcasting changed since 1950?" He said, "First of all, I want to say that it's great to be on here with you." He mentioned my dad by name and my mom by name. He remembered me as a little kid. That was really neat for him to say that on the air, and for me to be able to pass that along to our audience and my friends and family. He answered that there were a lot of subtle ways broadcasting has changed, but most of the change is in statistics, and how often we use statistics. He said, "Some of us," of course, including himself, which I thought was very humble, "use statistics like a drunk uses a lamp post—for support, not illumination." I thought that was such a great line. That's what makes Vin so good. What separates him, and I think of how he was a pioneer of broadcasting, is that he doesn't talk down or over the heads to listeners who maybe like baseball, but they don't know a lot about baseball. They love the Dodgers, but they're not hard-core baseball fans. Vin has a way of using these analogies to make sense to people who are just trying to learn about the game. That was a perfect example. I'd never heard that line before. I thought it was a classic example of Vin Scully's play on words.

Denny Matthews, who I do the radio games with, and I did a little round-table discussion with Vin. It was a long interview. We both had questions we asked Vin. I asked him questions about his career. He didn't tell many stories about my dad but I come to find out later that during the broadcast, he got a picture of my dad and they put it on and he talked about my dad's career and talked about my career. That was really neat for all my friends and family who still live in Southern California.

Whenever I have a spare moment, I'll dial Vin up on the Internet, just to listen to Vin talk. I just love the way he presents the game.

In the interview, Vin talked about when he was a young boy growing up in Brooklyn, how his parents had this large console radio in the living room. He said he would sit underneath this radio and listen to the games. The way he put it, "the roar of the crowd, like water coming out of a showerhead, would come over me, and I would be carried away."

I asked Vin about doing his simulcast where he's doing a radio broadcast for three innings, and then he kicks into television only. He talked about how in radio you've got your empty canvas and you have your different size brushes and your paints. You mix your paints and you create your word description of the game for the listeners. He said, "But on television, the picture is already there for you." He just has these great examples. Whether or not you love baseball, he presents it in a way where it makes sense. It's not "baseball vernacular" where if you're not following the game, it goes right over your head, "What's he talking about?" That's the genius in his work.

> He said, "Bob Gibson pitches like he's double-parked somewhere."

Vin is the only guy who can really pull off doing every out of the ball game all by himself. I've heard games with him in the playoffs where he has had a color analyst, and he works great with a color analyst, but he's at his best when he's all by himself. I don't know if you could really have the Vin Scully experience if he was sharing the booth with someone else.

Vin did a **BOB GIBSON*** line I've used on the air in reference to how fast Bob Gibson pitched, and I always give Vin credit for it. He said, "Bob Gibson pitches like he's double-parked somewhere."

When I hear Vin come out with one of his priceless lines, I laugh out loud and shake my head, like I usually do when I'm listening to him, thinking, "Man! How come I didn't think of that one? That's a good one."

Earlier this year, Larry Bowa was thrown out of the game because he got too far out of the third-base coach's box. There was a big controversy. Vin said something like, "You could hang the nets from the Coliseum on the veins of Larry Bowa's neck—that's how mad he is!"

Then there's the way Vin did Sandy Koufax's **PERFECT GAME*** in '65. I've heard that English professors from all over the country read the written transcript and they couldn't find one single grammatical or English error in the entire presentation of those nine innings. So not only does Vin capture the moment, but he does it with perfect English.

***BOB GIBSON** played basketball with the Harlem Globetrotters several off-seasons....In 1972, Bill Cosby signed a lifetime contract with the Globetrotters for one dollar per year. In 1986, the Globetrotters gave him a nickel raise. Cosby made several appearances with the team and is an honorary member of the Basketball Hall of Fame.

*In 1995 while pitching for the Expos, Pedro Martinez pitched nine perfect innings versus the Padres. In the 10th inning Bip Roberts, of San Diego, doubled. Martinez was the winning pitcher, but did not get credit for the **PERFECT GAME** or the no-hitter.

Every year, when I get the Dodger media guide in spring training, I read it to look for one phrase in Vin's bio. I look every year, and it was always there, "a master of the English language." For some reason, the last couple of years it has not been in there. I was in L.A. with our PR director and we tried to call the Dodgers PR office to ask why it wasn't in there anymore. I thought, "Man, how many guys could have that in their bio—a master of the English language?" But that's what we're doing—we're communicating, and trying to do it as best as possible. He has such a command of it that the Dodgers obviously were confident to put that next to him.

When I left Dodger Stadium after our series, I wrote him a letter and I left it with his producer to give to Vin. I wanted to express to him how much he has meant to me as an announcer, and now as an adult reconnecting with him. I haven't seen him since, and that was five years ago. I was so impressed with what a good man he was and what a kind person he was, and the time he took with me and just watching him interact with the people around the booth. He knew everybody's name and greeted them warmly. That's how I think of him now, in addition to how great he is as an announcer.

I hope he never, never retires!

TO BE CONTINUED!

We hope you have enjoyed *Vin Scully—I Saw It On the Radio*. You can be in the author's next book, *For Dodger Fans Only*, if you have a neat story. You can e-mail it to printed page@cox.net (please put DODGER FANS in the subject line and include a phone number where you can be reached), or call the author directly at (602) 738-5889. The author can't type, has never turned on a computer and has never seen the Internet, so if you need an immediate response, use the phone rather than email.

In addition, we'll be putting together *For Brooklyn Dodgers Fans Only*, so if you are a Brooklyn Dodgers fan and have a great story, e-mail that as well to printed page@cox.net (please put BROOKLYN DODGERS in the subject line and include a phone number where you can be reached),

Note: There were no actual Giants fans harmed during the making of this book.

Other Books by Rich Wolfe

Da Coach (Mike Ditka)
I Remember Harry Caray
There's No Expiration Date on Dreams (Tom Brady)
He Graduated Life with Honors and No Regrets (Pat Tillman)
Take This Job and Love It (Jon Gruden)
Been There, Shoulda Done That (John Daly)
Oh, What a Knight (Bob Knight)
And the Last Shall Be First (Kurt Warner)
Remembering Jack Buck
Sports Fans Who Made Headlines
Fandemonium
Remembering Dale Earnhardt
For Yankees Fans Only
For Cubs Fans Only
For Red Sox Fans Only
For Cardinals Fans Only
For Packers Fans Only
For Hawkeyes Fans Only
For Browns Fans Only
For Mets Fans Only
For Notre Dame Fans Only—The New Saturday Bible
For Bronco Fans Only
For Nebraska Fans Only
For Buckeye Fans Only
For Georgia Bulldog Fans Only
For South Carolina Fans Only
For Clemson Fans Only
For Cubs Fans Only—Volume II
For Oklahoma Fans Only
For Yankees Fans Only—Volume II
Tim Russert, We Heartily Knew Ye

All books are the same size, format and price.
Questions? Contact the author directly at 602-738-5889.